We Can't Eat Prestige

In the series

Labor and Social Change

edited by Paula Rayman
and Carmen Sirianni

We Can't Eat Prestige

The Women Who Organized Harvard

JOHN HOERR

Temple University Press
Philadelphia

Temple University Press, Philadelphia 19122

Copyright ©1997 by John Hoerr

Published 1997

Printed in the United States of America

∞ The paper used in this publication meets the requirements of the American National Standard for Information Sciences—Permanence of Paper for Printed Library Materials, ANSI Z39.48-1984

Text design by Nancy Johnston

Library of Congress Cataloging-in-Publication Data

Hoerr, John P., 1930–
    We can't eat prestige : the women who organized Harvard / John Hoerr.
        p.   cm.—(Labor and social change)
    Includes bibliographical references.
    ISBN 1-56639-535-6 (alk. paper)
    1. Harvard University—Employees.   2. Harvard Union of Clerical and Technical Workers.   3. Women clerks—Massachusetts—Cambridge.
I. Title.   II. Series.
LD2120.H64   1997
331.88′113781′12—dc21   97–1722

For Peter and David

C O N T E N T S

Acknowledgments   ix

Chapter One   1

Chapter Two   16

Chapter Three   29

Chapter Four   45

Chapter Five   63

Chapter Six   76

Chapter Seven   87

Chapter Eight   105

Chapter Nine   121

Chapter Ten   136

Chapter Eleven   152

Chapter Twelve   170

Chapter Thirteen   186

Chapter Fourteen   209

Contents

Chapter Fifteen   235

Epilogue   268

Index   271

Photographs follow pp. 205, 231, and 265

A C K N O W L E D G M E N T S

*T*his book is a true story of an extraordinary group of women (with a few men) who waged a very long fight to form a union of office and laboratory workers at Harvard University. Along the way, they developed innovative methods of organizing and representing workers based on their own values as working women. The story is told largely from their perspective, supplemented by versions of the same events told by people on opposing sides. It is in this sense a contemporary history, which describes in part how the women's movement of the early 1970s began to seep into Boston workplaces, giving birth not only to unions led by women but also 9to5, The National Association of Working Women. But this is not a scholarly study of the women's movement, or of women and unions. For the most part it focuses on one group of women who fought enormous odds to establish the Harvard Union of Clerical and Technical Workers (HUCTW).

I owe special thanks to the members, staff, and leaders of HUCTW and especially to Kris Rondeau, Bill Jaeger, Marie Manna, Martha Robb, Donene Williams, and a former leader, Leslie Sullivan. Although I undertook this book independently with full control over its contents, the union gave me unrestricted access to internal files and proceedings. Over a four-year period, I sat in on dozens of private meetings of staff, executive board, and other union groups. I also wish to thank Harvard University administrators and union representatives who allowed me to attend meetings of Joint Councils in various parts of the university.

Many former Harvard officials and managers willingly talked to me about the part they played in labor relations in the past. With a few exceptions confined to 1992 and early 1993, current Harvard officials refused to be interviewed. The old belief among employers that a union plays only an adversary role in the institution, and that journalists and writers of labor history have no object but to dramatize conflict, is still current in the Harvard administration. I am grateful to a few individuals who spoke without official sanction.

Thanks also are due to leaders and staff members of HUCTW's current and former parent unions, the American Federation of State, County and Municipal Employees, and the United Auto Workers. Many former organizers and officials of now-defunct District 65 talked with me at length about internal politics and especially about the role of women organizers during this union's pioneering efforts to organize white-collar workers in the 1970s and 1980s.

I use the narrative form for this story because of its inherent drama. But the book contains no invented scenes or fictional dialogue. All quotes come from interviews and published material. In the relatively few places where small snatches of dialogue are used, they are reconstructed from the memories of the talkers. The interviews were conducted from 1992 to 1996, in Cambridge, Boston, New York, and Washington, and most were recorded on audio tape. The unprocessed archives of HUCTW were used to supplement interviews about the early days of the union. These files contain minutes of organizing committee meetings from 1973 to 1977, newsletters published off and on from 1974 to 1983, internal union memos, and antiunion campaign literature used by Harvard in three separate campaigns. The *Harvard Crimson* and the *Harvard Gazette* were good sources of day-by-day happenings at Harvard. Statistics on gender and racial breakdown of faculty and students were drawn from university documents.

Information relating to the many National Labor Relations Board (NLRB) cases involving Harvard and the union is contained in NLRB files in Washington. David Parker of the NLRB was particularly helpful in obtaining material. Historical documents of 9to5, The National Association of Working Women, are archived at the Schlesinger Library, Radcliffe College. Organizing and bargaining at Yale University is described in *On Strike for Respect* by Toni Gilpin, Gary Isaac, Dan Letwin, and Jack McKivigan.

Several books consulted for historical background are named in the text. The following list contains other books and articles used as primary sources and is not meant to be an exhaustive bibliography.

History of Harvard University

Samuel Eliot Morison, ed., *The Development of Harvard University: Since the Inauguration of President Eliot, 1869–1929*

Morison's *Three Centuries of Harvard, 1636–1936* and *The Founding of Harvard College*

Richard Norton Smith, *The Harvard Century: The Making of a University to a Nation*

Moral and Psychological Development of Women

Carol Gilligan, *In a Different Voice: Psychological Theory and Women's Development*

James Q. Wilson, *The Moral Sense*

Judith V. Jordan, Alexandra G. Kaplan, Jean Baker Miller, Irene P. Stiver, and Janet L. Surrey, *Women's Growth in Connection: Writings from the Stone Center*

Women and the Labor Movement

Philip S. Foner, *Women and the American Labor Movement: From World War I to the Present*

James J. Kenneally, *Women and American Trade Unions*

Diane Balser, *Sisterhood & Solidarity: Feminism and Labor in Modern Times*

Nancy F. Gabin, *Feminism in the Labor Movement: Women and the United Auto Workers, 1935–1975*

Ruth Milkman, ed., *Women, Work & Protest: A Century of U.S. Women's Labor History*

Dorothy Sue Cobble, ed., *Women and Unions: Forging a Partnership*

Marion Crain, "Feminism, Labor, and Power," *Southern California Law Review* (May 1992), and "Gender and Union Organizing," *Industrial and Labor Relations Review* (January 1994)

Women Workers in New England Mills

Thomas Dublin, *Women at Work: The Transformation of Work and Community in Lowell, Massachusetts, 1826–1860* and *Transforming Women's Work: New England Lives in the Industrial Revolution*

History of Whitinsville: Thomas R. Navin, *The Whitin Machine Works Since 1831: A Textile Machinery Company in an Industrial Village*

Acknowledgments

A number of people provided miscellaneous documents, background information, and photographs. These include Richard Balzer, Joseph Chabot, Ellen DeGenova, John T. Dunlop, Susan Eaton, Fred K. Foulkes, Marlene Goldman, Charles Heckscher, Dr. Mary Howell, David Kuechle, Karen Nussbaum, Mary Rowe, and Rick Stafford. Michael Ames, editor-in-chief of Temple University Press, contributed ideas and encouragement. An early version of the HUCTW story appeared in the summer 1993 issue of *The American Prospect*.

I owe much to those who read and commented on portions of the manuscript, including my wife Joanne, Peter Hoerr, Jamie Leighton, Tina and John Lillig, and James J. Healy. My largest debt is to the many organizers and members of the Harvard union, too numerous to mention individually, who received me graciously in their meetings, always responded when I called, and answered my questions freely and without restraint.

We Can't Eat Prestige

CHAPTER ONE

*T*hey called it "ballooning." Starting before dawn on that day in 1988, dozens of volunteers set off on foot with clusters of balloons trailing aloft. Others bound for distant places piled into vans carrying helium tanks and boxes of rubber balloons, inflating them as they went. At designated places they jumped out of the van and tied strings of balloons, two or three in a group, to any object to which a string could be tied. They tied them to railings, door handles, lamp posts, and shrubs; to metal stakes that held ropes strung around plots of newly planted grass; to the wrought iron bars on gates leading into Harvard Yard; even to the granite book lying open on John Harvard's granite knee on the pedestal in front of University Hall.

Harvard University awoke that day to a startling sight. Hundreds of gaily colored balloons were bobbing on their tethers along city sidewalks and everywhere on campus. Harvard Yard, a fenced-in area of twenty-two acres, might have been rigged for lighter-than-air flight—or decorated for a party. Either way, the effect was to lift spirits if not buildings, to lend a sense of ease and fun, perhaps even liberation, to an event of overwhelming importance, not for students (for this was not a student stunt), but for university workers who served the students. It was to be a festive occasion, as the women leaders saw it, not a grim ritual capping a conflict. If the balloons also seemed to mock the stuffy solemnity of the men who laid down all the rules and made all the important decisions, and who knew themselves to be at the center of the universe—so be it. A little light-hearted mockery can be a civilizing force.

In springtime, dawn usually breaks hard and brilliant over Massachusetts Bay. In one great leap across the water, it is suddenly in Boston, splintering against skyscrapers and church spires, forming airy, interstitial shadows. It strikes sparks off the glistening Charles River, running between Boston and Cambridge. Two miles up the Charles, in the university area, racing shells slice through shreds of mist, the crews bending and pulling, bending and pulling. Joggers already are plying the paths on both sides of the river. Cyclists wearing crash helmets and backpacks whiz by, dark-goggled and tight-lipped. The pathways skirt the river, interrupted only by bridges and a few boathouses with wharfs slanting into the water. These are the recreation grounds of America's intellectual elite: students, teachers, researchers, poets, scientists, musicians, lawyers, medical experts, economic luminaries, Presidential advisers, and academics who know all there is to know about organizing human energies (most efficiently, most equitably) in the workplace—and earn huge fees by advising others how to do it.

This section of the Charles runs through one of the world's premier centers of learning and research. Boston University, with more than 25,000 students, stretches along city streets a few blocks south of the river. On the Cambridge side, the Massachusetts Institute of Technology (MIT), the nation's leading scientific and engineering school, sits in a clump of massive academic halls just beyond the Charles. Farther upstream and around a ninety-degree bend to the north, Harvard University straddles the Charles. Harvard Business School, the fountainhead of strategic studies for corporate management (and, consequently, the recipient of massive corporate beneficence), sits on the left bank. A bridge spanning the river here feeds directly into Cambridge's oldest street. Once a path into the wilderness north of Boston, it is now JFK St., named after an illustrious Harvard graduate. The university's academic buildings and residence halls occupy huge swatches of property extending more than a mile north of the river.

At the approximate center of this urban campus is Harvard Yard and the adjacent Harvard Square, both of which are historic landmarks of breathtaking age. Puritan farmers were pasturing cows here within a decade after the Mayflower landed at Plymouth. In 1636 the leaders of Massachusetts Colony chose a "cow yard" just north of the present-day Square as the site of a college which would become the first institution of higher learning in North America. Indeed, one historian calls it "North America's oldest non-governmental institution." The first class of thirty-one young ministerial students entered Harvard College in 1638.

Three hundred fifty years later, in 1988, Harvard University had about 16,900 undergraduate and graduate students and 1,700 faculty members. The old Harvard College, combined with the formerly all-women Radcliffe College, still formed the core of the university. There also were eleven professional and graduate schools, including the Schools of Medicine, Public Health, Law, and Business. An institution of immense prestige, wealth, and influence, Harvard University was ranked among the very finest private research universities in the world. It had played a major role in all great events in U.S. history, by supplying research and leaders in every field of public affairs and scholarship. Six presidents of the United States had graduated from Harvard, as well as thirty-three Nobel Laureates and innumerable diplomats, war heroes, and distinguished men (and, only recently, women) of letters. Wall Street and the upper echelons of corporate America swarmed with people armed with MBAs from Harvard Business School. A very short list of Harvard's alumni includes Ralph Waldo Emerson, Oliver Wendell Holmes, Henry Thoreau, Henry and William James, Henry Adams, and Franklin D. Roosevelt.

Over the decades and centuries, Harvard had faced many adversities and challenges, ranging from financial crises and religious schisms to disputes over fundamental questions of curriculum and student discipline. Dishonest administrators and a variety of scandals occasionally had blackened its reputation. There had been student revolts, even riots on occasion. In modern times, charges of racial and sexual discrimination had forced Harvard to reform its admission and hiring policies. It had been criticized for engaging in government-funded research on military weaponry, for maintaining investments in racially segregated South Africa, for tearing down poor neighborhoods to build dormitories for its elite students.

Despite this buffeting about, Harvard not only had survived and prospered but also had served the nation and society with distinction. It had done so in large part by balancing the often competing demands and interests of students, faculty, administrators, governing boards, and alumni. Each of these constituent bodies had a formal voice in governing the university proportionate to its role. Even students had forced their way into the governance process as a result of the campus revolts of the sixties. But one group remained on the outside, a group that performed vital services yet had no voice, or standing, or recognition of any sort. This group consisted of about 3,500 employees comprising the university's "support staff," nonteaching assistants and technicians of all sorts.

On May 17, 1988, these forgotten workers—originally known as "servants" of the university—would finally find a voice: they would vote on whether they wanted to be represented by a union. For fourteen years the Harvard administration had vigorously opposed organizing efforts by this union. Twice before, in 1977 and 1981, the administration view had prevailed when workers in one section of the university voted against unionization. This time, however, the election would be university-wide, covering all support staff. Even in the long eventful history of Harvard this would be a dramatic occasion, the day when "servants" would give their collective opinion of the management of one of the world's most prestigious universities.

It would be a secret ballot election ordered and conducted by the National Labor Relations Board (NLRB). Thousands of such elections are run every year, but this one was different in several respects from most. In size it dwarfed all NLRB elections of recent years in the United States and for this reason had attracted national attention. But a much deeper significance lay in other areas.

The union seeking recognition had been formed by women who worked or had worked at the university. It was not a union sent in by a segment of the impersonal, dreaded, male-dominated force known as "organized labor"—which, according to popular belief, had plundered industrial America. Rather, it was a union that would control its own destiny, respecting Harvard as a great research and learning institution while not being blind to its weaknesses; a union made up mostly of women who demanded equality of treatment, the traditional feminist goal, without promoting hostility toward men in general; a union that did not denigrate management as a class but simply wanted to participate in managerial decisions that affected its members; a union that promised to be very different from typical American unions; a union that employed innovative techniques based on women's ways of establishing relationships and getting things done. It was that rarest of creatures in a society of self-serving interest groups—an organization of people banding together to improve and reform the institution that employed them.

They called themselves the Harvard Union of Clerical and Technical Workers (HUCTW). They worked as faculty secretaries, library and research assistants, laboratory technicians, financial and data entry clerks, alumni recordkeepers, telephone operators, general all-around "staff assistants," animal keepers at research centers, and morgue attendants at Harvard Medical School. HUCTW had existed for nearly two years as an independent union, a wandering stray, happy but poor. By 1988 it had acquired a union parent, the American Federation of State, County and Municipal Employees (AFSCME), a huge national organization with about

1.3 million members in state and local governments, hospitals, and similar institutions. But the Harvard union had grown to young adulthood in her own peculiar way, developing her own values and principles out of her own experience in a rough and sometimes harsh world. AFSCME, wisely, had not tried to lay down any laws of deportment for its adopted child, or try to change its values, or impose any standards. HUCTW was an unusual creature in the world of American labor: it had invented itself.

Kristine Rondeau, the lead organizer, had met with her staff until late on the night of May 16, 1988. For days and weeks they had devoted every waking hour to preparing for the election—phoning workers, holding information meetings, drawing up lists of employees and pruning them down to only the names of those expected to vote for the union. It was too late now to convert the unconverted.

Rondeau and her husband lived in a third-floor condominium just off Inman Square in Cambridge. She awoke at 4:30 A.M. on May 17. Instead of the usual faded jeans, she dressed in a blue skirt and a black, long-sleeved jersey with the slogan "It's Not Anti-Harvard to Be Pro-Union" in white letters across the front. In the evening she would have to appear before many people, either celebrating one of the best days in her life, or lamenting one of the worst. Either way a certain formality was called for. She was of average height, five-foot-three to five-foot-four, and had flaxen-colored hair which fell straight to her shoulders. She wore little makeup, but there was no need to accent her quarry-blue eyes. She had a rather wide mouth with lines rippling out from the corners to support a dramatic, flaring smile. She smiled much of the time as she talked. On May 17 Rondeau was a few weeks short of thirty-six.

At 5:30 A.M. Rondeau and her husband left home and drove toward Harvard Square. Like many working women who came of age during the seventies, she had kept her maiden name when she married James Braude. Even in the car he towered over her, being every bit of six-foot-five, with black hair and brown eyes. A lawyer and former union official, Braude now headed a political action group in Boston. Rondeau usually referred to him in the third person as "Jim Braude (Brow-dee)", grinning wryly as she said it, not letting him forget that when they met he was a rising star in a union that treated its women in a patronizing way.

It was a short drive. Within minutes they rounded a sharp curve which brought the Square and Harvard Yard into view. The Square was awash in balloons floating gaily above a news kiosk and subway entrance. Early daylight brought out the normal contrasting colors in the Yard: the deep red of Harvard brick with daubs of white window trim set against the green of old beech trees. Today, nips of yellow, pink, red, green, and blue intruded on the traditional Harvard tableau. The sight of the balloons, Braude later recalled, created a "joyous mood, a wonderful feeling, that entered your head and soul."

This was precisely what Rondeau and her friends intended. When an employer strenuously opposes a union, as Harvard had, the resulting tension and fear will stalk a worker's consciousness even as she marks her secret ballot. A festive atmosphere would help reduce this tension. As Rondeau would later put it, "The balloons said that Harvard's antiunion campaign hasn't worked, and we are not slinking off to the polls scared and nervous." For her, however, the possibility of losing a third time at Harvard was "scary." Usually, the "scarier" the event, the more resolute she became.

They left the car in a parking garage and walked to Rondeau's office. It occupied the basement of an old brick building on Winthrop St. about two blocks from Harvard Square. Braude stayed outside. The office was his wife's domain. He was there merely as a volunteer directing other volunteers. More than a hundred unionists from around Boston had offered whatever help they could give. They were men for the most part, local officials of building trades and government unions, who regarded the HUCTW women and their balloons as an aberration of sorts. But somehow these women had forced Harvard University, one of the largest and most powerful employers in the Boston area, to submit to an election. It was one of the few signs that the "labor movement" still deserved to be called a movement.

At 6:00 A.M. Rondeau called her staff together for a final briefing. During three years of furious activity and little time for cleaning, their office had deteriorated from shabby to seedy, cluttered with donated desks and partly broken chairs, overflowing wastebaskets, piles of newspapers and assorted scraps of paper, old pizza boxes and empty soda cans. There was no large meeting room, simply an open space known as "The Area Between Kris's Office and Ralph's Desk."

Staff members jammed against one another, sitting and standing in a rough circle. There were twenty-five full- and part-time staff organizers (eighteen women and seven men) and a few employee activists. Most were under thirty, had college degrees, and had quit their jobs at Harvard to work for the union.

Standing on the edge of the circle, Rondeau went over election day strategy for the last time. The staff referred to it as "GO-TV," the pronounceable form of GOTV, which stood for Get Out the Vote Campaign. More accurately it was a Get Out *Our* Vote Campaign, for nobody wanted to bring out the "no union" vote. The organizers would go to their assigned areas on Harvard's several campuses and report back to headquarters the names of prounion workers who actually voted. Rondeau and her small group at "Command Central," working with a master list of potential prounion workers, could determine who needed to be reminded to cast their ballot.

It was an extraordinary staff, unknown to other unions or even in the parent AFSCME. They didn't fit the image of hard-shelled, out-of-the-factory labor organizers. But among these young people were some of the best organizers anywhere, not in a traditional sense of persuading workers to vote "yes" because they hate the boss and want more money. To organize for HUCTW had a deeper meaning. It meant to teach people to have confidence in themselves, to take responsibility for changing their situation in life, to form a community so strong that nobody on the outside could chip away at individual self-confidence and frighten members into submission.

In the two previous elections, Rondeau had experienced the power of the university-as-employer when it set out to defeat the union. The first time, in 1977, she herself had been a Harvard employee. By the second election, in 1981, she had become a full-time union organizer. In both cases the union lost the election and both times she had seen first-hand the devastating results of an employer's ability to undermine workers' faith in themselves.

As she looked around the room, Rondeau realized that only three other staff members, all former Harvard employees who had been involved in previous elections, understood how difficult this day would be. They were Marie Manna, Rondeau's second-in-command, a thirtyish woman of impressive calmness who had taken a Harvard job just so she could help organize the union; Martha Robb, restless and forgetful, but a superb organizer; and Jeanne Lafferty, a flamboyant redhead with political roots in the antiwar movement of the Vietnam era. The three had worked with Rondeau for years and all had become close friends.

When she ended her short talk, a student activist passed out beepers, walkie-talkies, and a few cellular phones and explained how to use them.

The organizers frowned. They would be going into battle loaded down with equipment. But the success of GOTV depended on good communications between Command Central and organizers in the field. So they tucked the walkie-talkies and beepers in their bags and wished each other good luck and drifted out to their posts. Voting would begin at 7:15 A.M.

Rondeau retreated to her tiny office with a sliding glass door. Deep within herself, unacknowledged to anybody except Jim Braude, she had grave doubts about the union's chances. "The closer we got to the election, the more I thought it couldn't be done," Rondeau recalled. "After the 1981 defeat, I had become convinced that some things are unwinnable. I thought maybe Harvard was one of them."

The officers and deans of Harvard had entrusted the antiunion campaign to university lawyers and personnel managers. They, in turn, had done everything they could think of, legally, to encourage a "no union" vote by employees. But they had not thought to do this one final thing: to float opposing balloons on election day. When they arrived at their offices on the various campuses that morning, they were not amused. In Harvard Yard, the presence of those novelty-store playthings hovering about the statue of John Harvard—the obscure seventeenth century minister who gained immortality as the school's first donor—seemed demeaning, even irreverent. From a distance his sitting statue looked like a balloon vendor at a zoo. It was an unverifiable likeness of a man who died in 1636, leaving behind no portrait or death mask or other likeness, but a bequest of four hundred English pounds and a library of books to establish a college.

A university lawyer named Anne Taylor, who had been put in charge of antiunion strategy, was convinced that the campus decorations had poisoned the atmosphere. In a study later written by Harvard Professor David Kuechle, she described the scene on JFK St. outside the Kennedy School of Government: "Every single telephone pole, mailbox, parking meter, anything that didn't move, had a poster on it." The overwhelming presence of posters and balloons, it seemed to Taylor, sullied the "laboratory conditions" under which, the U.S. Supreme Court had said, a representation election must be conducted. She took the union behavior almost as a personal affront, for she had tried very hard to conduct a scrupulously correct campaign. She was no union-hating troglodyte but one who truly believed that workers would harm themselves by voting in the union.

Harvard President Derek Bok took a more benign view. He had been around Harvard, as president, dean of the Law School, and professor for nearly thirty years and had seen many a student demonstration. The presence of a few balloons was nothing compared to the angry protest marches and building takeovers of the late sixties. A university that taught reverence for the Bill of Rights could hardly condemn freedom of speech on its own campus, much less order its police force to go around deflating balloons. The battle with the union, however, had put him in an agonizing personal quandary, posing a conflict between his beliefs and what he regarded as his duty.

Bok believed in the right of workers to form unions and engage in collective bargaining. He had taught labor law and had written approvingly of unions "in theory." As a scholar, he believed that it was "a good thing for America and for working people that employees have the opportunity to vote for a union." As a university president, Bok contended that the clerical and technical workers of Harvard should not *have* a union. A union would inhibit individual initiative and flexibility, which are "at the heart of the academic enterprise," he had said in a letter to employees. Bok had authorized the antiunion campaign but insisted that it not employ intimidating tactics. The question was, from the union's point of view, can a powerful employer not be intimidating when it calls employees into meetings and urges them to vote one way or another on an issue profoundly affecting their jobs? Administration officials, on the other hand, raised a question about union behavior on election day. How could employees not feel threatened by having to walk a gantlet of balloons on their way to polling places?

Except for the posters and balloons it was a typical spring day at the university. Endless streams of people flowed into Harvard Square, self-segregating there into three tributaries: Cantabridgians descending into the T station bound for work in Boston; shoppers headed for the array of stores and coffee shops; and students, professors, and Harvard employees filtering through the many gates into Harvard Yard. In addition to thousands of students, the university attracted individuals of all descriptions—people on research grants, spending the day in one of thirteen libraries; people ensconced in various Harvard-related institutes, thinking for a living; and of course all the spouses and dependents of students and professors, pushing perambulators and sitting on benches in scattered small parks. There were always parents around at this time of year, strolling through the Yard, or standing transfixed in front of shop windows, as if to say, "No wonder she kept writing for spending money."

In the Yard, a large white banner with the words "STANDING WITH THE UNION, MAY 17 AND BEYOND" was draped across two or three windows on the third floor of Hollis Hall, a freshman dormitory. Most students were aware of the election, though only a minority took a real interest in it. *The Harvard Crimson*, an independent student newspaper, had supported the union consistently over many years, but then student newspapers, as everybody knew, were notoriously, foolishly liberal.

Harvard University was a huge place. In Cambridge alone there were six separate campus areas, each big enough to hold a small college. At two major sites in Boston and scattered outposts elsewhere, university employees worked in some four hundred buildings. To accommodate all the workers eligible to vote in these locations, the NLRB had set up nine polling places. Board agents would conduct the balloting in the presence of management and union observers. Under NLRB rules, there could be no campaigning in the vicinity of voting areas. To avoid any appearance of misconduct, the union had ordered staff members to stay out of these buildings. They could ask workers if they had voted but not how they had voted.

Shortly after the polls opened, Joanna (Joie) Gelband had one of the nicest experiences of her life. A 1985 graduate of Vassar, she had worked as a faculty assistant at Harvard before joining the union drive in 1986. Since then she had organized scores of workers, chatting with them in their offices, or at lunch, or over a beer at the end of the day. But she had never met Margaret, who worked the night shift as a Harvard phone operator. For two years the two had chatted regularly on the phone, and Margaret had long since committed herself to the union. On election day, the two met for the first time when Margaret got off work.

"It was an enormously touching moment," Gelband said. "We were so delighted to see each other. I walked Margaret into the Yard and pointed her to her polling place in Boylston Hall. The Yard was full of balloons. She liked that."

At about the same time, Ellen DeGenova went to the offices of University Health Services (UHS) where she herself worked part-time and had organized several employees. The daughter of working-class parents, DeGenova wrote poetry and sang jazz, occasionally performing in public. She felt particularly close to an older woman named Gerry at UHS.

"She was so sweet," DeGenova said. "Her son had been killed while jogging, by a drunk driver. She had every reason not to bother with this thing. But she and another older woman listened to what I had to say and signed [membership] cards. I was so proud, I wanted to vote with Gerry."

As DeGenova left the UHS office with Gerry, two younger antiunion women watched suspiciously. DeGenova thought nothing of it. She and Gerry walked through the Yard to Boylston Hall and cast their ballots. "That made the day meaningful for me," she said. "Those younger women later claimed that I coerced Gerry on the way over. What a crock! Actually, I was telling her that I'd love to own a piano."

Throughout the university hundreds of prounion employees worked from the inside to get out the vote. One was Donene Williams, a twenty-five-year-old graduate of California State University who had come east in 1987 to take a staff assistant job at Harvard Law School. Cheeky and irreverent, Williams quickly became a union activist and was not afraid to speak out. When Law School administrators held employee meetings to argue against the union, Williams and other activists wore their union buttons to show where they stood. The bosses glowered at them but didn't dare say anything, not in a university.

On May 17, Williams took a personal day off. Her assignment was to get out the vote on the third floor of Pound Hall on the law campus. Early that morning she and a co-worker drove to a hospital where her best friend, Kim Neeb, was recuperating from surgery. Her doctor had agreed to allow her out for an hour. The three went to the polling place in Pound Hall, accompanied by three other workers from their office.

"One of these women asked to come, and we knew she was anti-union," Williams said. "But we weren't going to say, 'No, Mary [a fictitious name], you can't go with us.' It was such a celebratory mood that day there was no reason to leave her out. I think my other friend Sharon [fictitious name] also voted 'no' but told us she voted 'yes' because she thought that's what we wanted to hear. She didn't have enough life experience to know that working women will not get a fair deal by working hard. We were twenty-four, twenty-five, our first or second job out of college. What did we know about anything? I thought I would get out of college and make $37,000 a year. At Harvard I was making less than $17,000." Williams took Kim Neeb, feeling "very weak and tired, but happy," back to her hospital room.

Back at Command Central, voting reports were beginning to pour in by mid-morning. Three or four staff members were constantly on the phone, taking calls from organizers and relaying voters' names to people at tote boards. These were large plywood panels holding computer lists of nearly two thousand Harvard employees thought to be prounion. Three markers checked off the names of those who had voted and kept a count.

One of the markers, Tom Canel, was a transplanted British subject who had graduated from Harvard with a bachelor's degree in philosophy and worked for the university as an accounting assistant. Near-sighted, a bit portly, and humorous, Canel had never paid much attention to sartorial matters. He wore items of clothing appallingly unsuited to each other or to the weather. A few days before the election, Jeanne Lafferty and Martha Robb decided to do a Canel make-over. They "frog-marched" him to a number of clothing stores and made him buy new duds, including a good-looking shirt with white stripes on green. He wore that shirt on May 17.

Canel had a good grip on philosophy and mathematics but little control over the red, green, and black Magic Markers used to check off names. "I had more than one in my hand at all times," Canel recalled, "and by the end of the day, I was a particularly attractive color combination." His new green and white shirt had metamorphosed into a black and red sack with arms sticking out. People stopped by the tote boards just to get a glimpse of him.

Rondeau, meanwhile, paced back and forth between the tote boards and her office along the north wall. "Give me a count, please!" she would call to Canel. She would take the number to her office and try to reconcile it with other calculations. As the morning wore on, her concern mounted. The number of people recorded as voting was increasing at a much too slow pace. What more could be done?

"Get those people to call in," she would say to the phone handlers, and they would work through their lists of beeper numbers. A few times she went outside to do TV interviews or give a pep talk to the volunteers stationed in the Lutheran Church on Winthrop St. across from the union office. The union had rented the church basement for the day, and dozens of people were busily engaged there. Some inflated balloons from eight helium tanks, others set out and replenished a buffet lunch for all the staff and volunteers, and still others worked on more phones.

Jim Braude never stopped moving. In normal times, he talked fast and walked fast, but today he stirred up cyclonic whirls of dust as coordinator of the GOTV drive. He and two other union spouses, Martha Robb's husband Bob Metcalf and Marie Manna's husband Mac McCreight—all paid-up members of the HUCTW Ladies' Auxiliary—had taken the day off from their own jobs. McCreight worked on phones in the church basement, and Metcalf stood in the middle of Winthrop St. using a walkie-talkie to keep in touch with volunteers driving cars and vans. They had rented for the day two blocks of parking spaces on nearby JFK St. and, with the permission of friendly police, had sealed off Winthrop St. to other traffic. The quick response motor pool provided transport for prounion workers who lived or worked far from the polling places, or who needed a ride from doctors' offices or bus stations. Two or three vacationing workers flew in from far places, one even from the Bahamas, to vote on May 17. Braude arranged for them to be picked up at Logan Airport, driven to the polls, and deposited back at the airport in time for a flight out. He had a physician on hand in case of illness and even a midwife. Two or three prounion workers were known to be pregnant and approaching term, though they would not give birth this day.

When Rondeau went outside and saw the frenetic activity, she had to laugh with delight. Back in the office, she grinned at the sight of multicolored Tom Canel. But her smile faded when he gave her the latest count. She kept thinking, "Could it really happen again?" They had learned so much from the first two defeats. But the chances of victory seemed again to be slipping away. It came down to this: The NLRB had certified about 3,400 workers as eligible to vote. More than 60 percent had signed cards saying they wanted an election. A 60 percent prounion vote would be quite comfortable, but Rondeau knew there had been slippage in the three months since she had filed the election petition. A good many prounion workers would have left Harvard for one reason or another (the university had a high turnover rate). Some would have changed their minds during the antiunion campaign; the weaker ones would have been "turned" just by hard looks from bosses.

In the week preceding the election, Rondeau had told her organizers to be ruthless in purging the prounion list of uncertain votes. By election day, 1,700 names remained on the list, slightly more than half of eligible voters. If all 1,700 actually voted as expected—more precisely, as *hoped*—HUCTW would win, but by the thinnest of margins.

Out in the field, staff members were getting worried by what they saw and heard. One of these was Bill Jaeger, a twenty-six-year-old Yale graduate who had joined the staff in 1985, even though the union, then independent, could pay no salary. Now he was making his rounds in the Divinity School area, reminding people to vote. He came across a young engaged couple who worked together in one office. They seemed upset and wanted to talk. "The man in particular had gone through a number of cycles of doubt and confidence," Jaeger said. "I could recognize by his expression that he was in the doubt cycle. They had heard a rumor that if you form a union, you have to go on strike. I talked it over calmly with them." The couple went to vote, but he never asked—and never knew—how they voted.

It was disturbing, but not surprising, that workers could be influenced by such rumors so late in the game. Jaeger, in fact, discovered that a number of employees on his list of prounion votes had not even come to work that day. "My gut feeling was, they stayed home because they were afraid," he said. "The big thing that freaked people out was why the university was against the union. Even when they discovered the employer was being deceptive, that raised a new contradiction: 'My God, Harvard cares so much about this, they'll do anything.' That makes people not want to get out of bed."

Organizer Stephanie Tournas also had quit a Harvard job to join the union staff, without pay, in 1986. She had noticed in the week before the election that Harvard's campaign was having an effect on undecided workers. When she approached them, "the look was, 'Here she comes again!' I could see they were exhausted by contacts from the university and the union. Our job was to keep it happy and positive and dispel tension. But it was getting very tense. That was exactly what the antiunion campaign was designed to do."

The tensions of election day exacted a toll on most of the staff organizers. "The atmosphere was incredibly charged," recalled Jana Hollingsworth. "We knew it was going to be really, really, really close, and we had to keep going back to people and asking if they'd voted. If you pushed them too much, they'd get angry." Bob Rush had been seeing faces in his sleep for nights on end, the faces of people he had organized. "It was like a slide show with a projector, just faces looking at me, one face at a time." Jeanne Lafferty, who worked with Tom Canel on the tote boards, had been through the two previous Harvard elections and was "reluctant to invest myself emotionally in the possibility of winning this time. I thought we were going to lose."

In late afternoon Rondeau saw that the prounion count was falling short, not by a few votes, but by a few hundred. The question was whether people were not voting, or whether the reporting system had missed them.

Rondeau recalled, "I looked at the numbers and said, 'It's not there, do anything, get other people in to help with calls.' We pulled out all the stops. It was very high energy those last few hours."

Sue Dynarski, working on the phones, remembered those last minutes. "Only fifteen minutes left, and Kris got this desperate edge to her. She went into the hole [where the tote boards were] and started yelling out names from the lists. People would run to the phones and try to call the person."

A constant ringing of phones, people shouting, curses, cries of dismay. Field organizers, their work done, were trickling in, craning their necks into the tote-board area. There stood Tom Canel, a bedraggled mess of red and black Magic Marker.

Ralph Vetters, a Harvard graduate who joined the staff in 1986, returned to the office feeling ill. He was sure that three or four of "his people," older women, had turned against the union. They hadn't wanted to talk to him. Standing in an alleyway outside the office, he burst into tears. "I cried openly," Vetters said. "I felt I could count on those women, but they must have thought, 'I can't put so much of my life on the line for this young man. I am twenty years older than he is. He's young enough to go some place, I'm going to be here.'" Vetters asked himself, "'Did I give them enough sense of security to allow them to take a leap in the dark?' Maybe I didn't."

Suddenly, it seemed, time was up. The polls closed at 5:30 P.M. "A hush came over the room," Lafferty said. "It was like hitting a brick wall. We had been running as fast as we could and we hit that wall, and it was dead still. You want to do more, but you can't cross the line back into time."

She and Martha Robb pushed through the crowd and out into the alleyway to smoke cigarettes. They came upon Vetters. Robb hugged him, but neither of the women said, "Don't cry, Ralph." Both knew he had to cry.

A few minutes later, Rondeau called the staff together. They jammed into The Area Between Kris's Office and Ralph's Desk. Some found a chair, some flopped exhausted on the floor. Rondeau told them they had done a "wonderful" job. But her face was grim. She held a piece of paper but didn't bother looking at it. Many staff members would recall her next words. "We don't have it," she said. Backing off slightly, she added, "It's too close to tell. But it's very likely we didn't win." She reminded them that the ballots would be counted that evening in Memorial Hall. Hundreds of people would be there, including workers, reporters, TV crews, and Harvard managers. "Whatever you do," she said, "don't cry in front of management and don't cry in front of the cameras." She tried to look at all their faces. "Whatever happens, we're going to be okay. We'll be together. We're going to keep working on this because it's the right thing to do."

The meeting broke up with a feeling of dread. People wandered off in small groups, some to eat, some to have a drink, some to break the news to their most loyal activists, before going to Memorial Hall.

Jim Braude and Manna's husband, Mac McCreight, joined their wives and walked in a foursome across the Yard. Rondeau kept thinking, "'What am I going to say if we lose? What are we going to do tomorrow? Should we try again?' I cared a huge amount about the life we had built together, and I wondered, 'Is this really impossible? How did I get into this?'"

Losing was such a wearisome business. She might have been better off if she had followed her initial impulse when a man named Ross came to see her twelve years ago.

*B*oston and Cambridge celebrated the bicentennial year 1976 with parades, historical reenactments, musical programs, art exhibits, fireworks. Tall-masted sailing vessels suddenly appeared in Massachusetts Bay, and the 44-gun frigate *USS Constitution*, Old Ironsides, freshly hulled and rigged after a 150-year dockside slumber, sailed out of Charlestown Navy Yard on a sentimental cruise.

Kris Rondeau had a personal reason to celebrate in the spring and summer of 1976. In May, a month shy of her twenty-fourth birthday, she landed a job as laboratory research assistant at Harvard Medical School. She was happy but unsure of herself. She still bore the stamp (or so she imagined) of a small-town hick pretending that she had just taken the first step in a long-planned "career" in medicine. She had grown up in Whitinsville, Massachusetts, only forty miles west of Boston geographically but generations distant in worldliness and function in society. Born of America's Industrial Revolution, Whitinsville was one of the earliest of New England "mill villages," a community so small (and shrinking further as the mills moved out) that it never gained the status of town. Once a major producer of machinery for the New England textile industry, Whitinsville had emerged from a state of industrial feudalism only at the end of World War II. People born into the Whitinsville working-class did not plan careers as doctors, lawyers, or scientists. It was considered a marvel of luck and planning merely to avoid working in the Whitin Machine Shop for the rest of your life. Rondeau had gotten out of Whitinsville and had graduated from a small college in Vermont. And now she dared to think about a professional future in medicine. She felt privileged to be at

Harvard, doing important work, associating with eminent scientists. "I thought I had died and gone to heaven," she recalled.

Harvard Medical School was impressive in every way. Located in the Mission Hill section of Boston, three miles from the main university campus in Cambridge, it looked like a plot of great marble temples transplanted from ancient Greece. This was the intent of the men who designed and built the school in 1903–06. At the beginning of the twentieth century, with the work of Darwin, Pasteur, and Curie, the world was thought to be on the brink of a marvelous scientific revolution. Institutions devoted to science were housed in splendid structures reflecting the brilliance of both the subject and its practitioners. The new school consisted of five massive buildings enclosing three sides of a central lawn flanked by paved walks. Constructed of white Vermont marble, the entire area gave off such a dazzling whiteness that people called it "the great white quadrangle." At the head of the quadrangle on a high terrace, stood Building A ("A" for administration) commanding the group, fronted with six Ionic columns rising more than fifty feet. Buildings B through E, housing laboratories and teaching amphitheaters, sat in a flanking position on the lower level, facing each other across the central court.

By 1976 nearly a dozen more buildings had risen behind and adjacent to the original quadrangle group. There were two additional schools, the Harvard School of Public Health and School of Dental Medicine, as well as four large hospitals affiliated with the Medical School. Known as the Harvard Medical Area, this complex had become one of the world's great centers of medical research and teaching.

Rondeau and other research assistants, mostly young women, worked at benches in well-lighted but somewhat cramped lab rooms, stocked with glassware and equipment like microscopes, centrifuge machines, and heat shields. In the first months, she learned a lot about lab procedures, and also about Harvard Medical School itself. For about a century after its founding in 1783, it was noted chiefly for supplying the medical profession with mediocre physicians and hewers of limbs. In the late 1800s, a more enlightened administration began to encourage faculty members to conduct research if for no other reason than to keep abreast of advances in the field. In 1871 the school established laboratories of physiology and microscopic anatomy. By the 1970s, laboratory research at the Medical School ranked practically on the same level as teaching, particularly in the areas of biochemistry, physiology, and microbiology. The school and its affiliated hospitals did pioneering work in organ transplants and neurobiology, resulting in Nobel prizes for Harvard-connected physicians and researchers. Research projects were headed by faculty members known as "principal investigators" (PI), each of whom was a recognized authority in some field of research. The PI ran his or her own laboratory on funds contributed by foundations and government agencies, a portion of which went directly to HMS to pay for central administration. The daily work of the labs, setting up and performing experiments under the PI's direction, was done by research assistants. Though hired by principal investigators to work on specific projects, the assistants were employees of Harvard Medical School.

Rondeau split her time working for two principal investigators, one in physiology and one in biochemistry, who were cooperating in a long-term study of brain activity during sleep. Her job involved surgery on lab animals. She would slit open the skulls of anesthetized rabbits and rats and implant electrodes in the brain to monitor brain waves as the animals slept. Rondeau quickly became proficient at this work and, meanwhile, came to know other lab assistants whom she liked very much. There was one thing about the job, however, that vaguely troubled her from the beginning.

She barely had found her way around the lab on the first day when a middle-aged man with a friendly face entered the room and approached her. She remembered his words. "Hey," he said, smiling broadly, "you're the new person, aren't you? We're forming a union and you can be part of it." He introduced himself as Ross, an electronics technician.

Startled, Rondeau thought, "Oh, my God, get me out of here!" A union! What did that have to do with her? She was wearing a clean, white lab coat. Didn't he recognize the status it conferred on her? She smiled vaguely, wanting to be polite if not friendly. Ross didn't press the issue. He said he'd be back. She wished the whole thing would go away because the idea of a union seemed so out of keeping with everything she had assumed about her job. A union? At Harvard?

Growing up in Whitinsville, from the time she became aware of anything outside her family and home, Rondeau knew that two large shadowy entities existed just outside the front door, the company and the union. The company was the Whitin Machine Shop, known by everybody as "The Shop," and the union was simply "the Union." Everybody worked at

The Shop and got paid by the company and yet they also belonged to the Union, and the distinction between them was baffling. They didn't teach it in the Whitinsville schools. It was one of those things you grew up pretending to understand. She had a sense that relations between the two groups were always being stretched to the breaking point—without breaking. As she got older, she learned that the Union was a local of the United Steelworkers of America and that there was such a thing as a strike and that every three years, when the "contract came up," everybody worried that the union would go on strike. But aside from the year she was born, no strike occurred as long as she lived in Whitinsville.

A much easier distinction could be made between the two principal divisions in Whitinsville, the bosses and the workers. You came from one side or the other, and Rondeau came from the worker side. Her father, Joseph Rondeau, a descendant of French-Canadians (one of the largest ethnic groups in Whitinsville), worked in The Shop as a skilled machinist. Her mother, also a native Whitinsvillian of French-Canadian and Dutch extraction, was a secretary in a factory office. They lived in a company house.

Whitinsville was only one of scores of mill towns that blossomed and withered in the springtime of America's Industrial Revolution, but it was perhaps the most unusual. In 1809, Paul Whitin, a blacksmith, invested in an early cotton mill built on the banks of the fast-flowing Mumford River south of Worcester. By the time he died in 1831 his sons were running two profitable mills that employed practically all able-bodied men in the area. Village fathers thus named the place Whitinsville, the largest of four communities that made up the "town" of Northbridge. The Whitin firm branched into the machinery-building business and by the middle of the nineteenth century the Whitin Machine Works had become one of the nation's largest suppliers of textile machines.

The company and the Whitin family owned much of the village and "took care of" their villagers in every conceivable way. Most workers lived in company-owned housing, bought milk from a company-owned farm, and used water piped in free of charge from company-owned reservoirs. The Shop never laid off workers during bad times but put them to work on the company farm or elsewhere. The Whitins tried to create "a workers' village . . . with a close-knit community of interest and a social stability such as had once been known in the feudal manors of medieval times," says a business history of the company written in the late 1940s by Thomas R. Navin, a Harvard Business School professor. This policy insulated The Shop against labor "trouble," until 1945, when workers voted in the Steelworkers union. Aside from a 13-week strike in 1946 and another in 1952, Whitin and the USW had a peaceful relationship. But the coming of the union ended the company's lordly power over plant and village alike, and the family's heart went out of the business. Inevitably, as textile manufacturing shifted to the South and then abroad, Whitin saw its best markets wither away. The Whitins sold the firm in 1965. The Shop turned to nontextile products for a while but closed down in 1983.

In the fifties and sixties, Whitinsville remained uniquely isolated in space and time. Situated in a narrow valley, surrounded by rocky hills and highlands, it was bypassed by highway and turnpike builders. People stopped going to Whitinsville. The village contracted and folded into itself.

People who grow up in small factory towns tend to develop a powerful sense of physical place. Noise and smoke and workers filing in and out of the factory gates; the noon whistle that brought workers home for a quick lunch; the four o'clock traffic snarl when the production and maintenance workers quit; and the five o'clock mess when the white-collar employees finished up. In Rondeau's world view, all height was measured against the weather vane on a brick bell tower perched atop the offices of Whitin Machine Works.

Whitinsville also gave her a strong sense of social place. Rondeau remembered the tremor that would pass through the Presbyterian congregation on Sundays when a certain top-level manager of Whitin Machine Works walked down the aisle. "People just quaked when they saw this man. They were very afraid of him." As in many mill towns, the owners and senior managers lived in manor houses on various hills. The ordinary people lived below in the feudal village, subsisting on low-wage jobs in low-rent tenements. Everyone was glued to a web of industrial circumstance that quivered to the rhythms of work and cooperation (or strife) in The Shop. All sights, sounds, odors, and events flowed out from the center or in from the periphery, pulsating through the web and brushing each person in passing. If everyone didn't *know* everyone else, everyone *knew about* everyone else. Close at hand were pettiness, cruelty, and misery as well as friendship, selflessness, and love. Most people had to struggle. Even after the union came to town, poverty was never further away than a few months' unemployment. In this small world, young Kris Rondeau knew where she was and who she was and to which group she belonged.

When people spoke to Rondeau of her father, they described him as "a strong union man." He served for years as a steward in the local union, representing skilled workers. Even so, Rondeau said, "I didn't grow up with a sense of loyalty to unions, because my father wasn't a big part of my life." Joseph Rondeau and her mother separated when Kris was three years old. He stayed in Whitinsville and continued working at The Shop, but his daughter rarely saw him. For the next five years, she and her mother lived with her maternal grandparents. Her grandfather had an office job in The Shop, and her grandmother worked at the ticket window of the community swimming pool, owned by The Shop.

"Those were the happiest years of my life," Rondeau said. "My grandmother was a loving, flexible person who taught me openness and tolerance. She had room for lots of people, lots of things. She and my mother were very generous people."

When Rondeau was eight, her mother married a local physician. Young Kris understood that this entailed a significant change in status, or income, or both. She remembered people telling her, "This means you'll go to college." She had two stepsisters and a half-brother, and they all lived in a house on Main St. where her stepfather also had his office. As a teenager, Rondeau worked in his office, doing paperwork, making appointments, cleaning up.

But she disliked her stepfather and didn't get along with him. Family life deteriorated. Young Kris sank into a depression that verged on the suicidal. She had been a cheerleader and vice-president of her high school class, but quit all activities midway through her senior year. She felt that she was barely clinging to life but managed to apply for and enter college. While there she suffered a severe emotional breakdown and enrolled in psychological therapy.

When she started the Harvard job, Rondeau was still in therapy and still trying to overcome, or at least live with, the emotional scarring from the early years. She desperately wanted to make good. The more solid her view of herself, the tighter her grip became. And so she concentrated on learning everything she could about lab work. The idea of union was not part of the picture.

"I wished I didn't have to deal with it," she said. "It was inconvenient. I asked myself how was it that my father, a blue-collar worker, was in the union, but I was a white-collar worker and why should I have to join a union?" What could a union offer women lab workers at a university?

Ross, the friendly technician, kept coming back. Nearly every day he stopped in her lab to say hello or to work on the equipment. When you work in a lab dependent on sensitive machinery, you can't very well make an enemy of the repairman. And Ross was a very nice guy. He kept talking about the union and asking her to sign a union card. But he never became aggressive or demanding. Rondeau couldn't send him away or refuse to talk. She put him off in a kindly way.

Years later she knew enough to analyze her reactions back in 1976. "I didn't say, 'No, I'm not interested,' because in part I perceived myself as being an open person. I was aware at the time that I wanted to have a reason to say 'no' to him. I was afraid. I thought that unions were just filled with conflict, and the idea of being in one filled me with conflict. But I didn't want to say 'no' just because I was afraid. I wanted to have a reason. So I listened and I asked questions."

In the very act of resisting Ross's appeals, she became aware of certain things. She learned that a union organizing campaign had been under way for a couple of years in the Harvard Medical Area. Some workers wanted the union and some did not, and the administration vigorously opposed the idea. Legal complications had arisen. Everybody was waiting for "the labor board" to decide whether an election would be held. And Ross spoke of a woman named Leslie. "Leslie says . . . " or "Leslie thinks . . . " or "You should meet Leslie . . . "

Leslie Sullivan could not say precisely when it began. In her first few years out of college, she kept getting fuzzy snapshots of the world from the internal photographer that records and analyzes all experiences. Later, sometime in 1972, the images began to emerge clean and crisp, presenting her rather suddenly with an absolutely clear, sharp picture of the world—or at least one part of it, the working part. She had become familiar with the rhythms of worklife and the ways of large organizations, and she had developed her own sense of what work should be—and not be. And, late one afternoon in 1972, she ran out of patience.

Sullivan was twenty-five at the time, dark-haired and buoyant, with the kind of wide-eyed Irish face that can break to either side, toward laughter or scorn. She had an orderly, practical mind and tended to push herself in unwavering pursuit of one goal at a time, like a cross-country skier driving for the finish line. A woman of the sixties, graduating from college in 1968, she dabbled in political activity as an antiwar liberal and felt no guilt whatsoever about putting off marriage until she had done some useful work in medical research.

That afternoon she was standing on a sink top, sponge in hand, washing down walls in a laboratory room at the Harvard School of Public Health. Her anger had been growing since morning. The faculty men in charge had brought in buckets, mops, and boxes of Spic and Span and ordered a general cleanup. All lab work would be suspended for two days while the research assistants (RAs)—Sullivan and about twenty other women—scrubbed down floors, walls, cabinets, windows, equipment—everything on the two floors occupied by the microbiology department. The RAs also should resterilize thousands of already sterile bottles, tubes, beakers, and other glassware. The lab had to be made sterile and spotless for a site visit by a funding agency.

The RAs were furious. They had been hired to perform lab experiments, not to scrub floors. It would have been a different story if everybody, including the lead researchers and postdoctoral assistants (all men), pitched in for the good of the department. But the men had disappeared. The RAs knew, of course, why they had been given the job. The men had thought, "Why hire outside scrub women when there were plenty of women right here in the building?"

Sullivan worked with seven other women in the same lab room. All day they had been talking as they scrubbed, calling to one another from cubicle to cubicle, cursing the work, ridiculing the absent bosses. Toward the end of the afternoon, Sullivan was standing on a sink counter and staring at a sponge in her hand. Suddenly she said aloud, "I refuse to do this any more." She threw down the sponge. "I'm going to have coffee," she announced, climbing down from the sink.

One by one, the other women dropped brushes and sponges and followed Sullivan to the coffee room. It was like a nineteenth century journalist's description of a strike: "The workmen lay down their tools and absented the work premises." Rarely was mention made then of "factory girls" quitting work on impulse. That would have been impudence beyond public contemplation.

Spontaneous work stoppages occur all the time in the American workplace. If Sullivan and her friends had ended their rebellion at the coffee machine, nothing remarkable would have happened. But they quickly realized that their protest might come to nothing because there had been no witnesses. The bosses would return to the lab tomorrow, and the women would be back on the ladders, sponges in hand, and nothing would have changed.

"No!" they said. They had had enough of this foolish cleaning up, and the way to put an end to it was to threaten the vital interests of the principal investigators. The PIs wanted, most of all, to impress foundation officials on the site visit so that they would renew funding of the projects. But gleaming sinks and glassware alone would not cause the visitors to open their checkbooks. They would want to see experiments in progress. "What we decided to do was, when we came in the next day, to go very, very slow on the cleaning job," Sullivan said. "If we didn't set up experiments, they couldn't show the lab."

The next morning, Sullivan's supervisor, the highest ranking faculty member in the department, saw that the cleanup had barely progressed from yesterday. This made him nervous. "Why aren't you done yet?" he asked. The lab women shrugged, Sullivan said, and replied, "Well, you know, it's pretty hard work . . . "

The professor hurried off. He returned ten minutes later, presumably having conferred with other men. "Don't bother, forget it," he said. "Don't do any more. Get ready for the site visit."

The assistants stored the glassware, put away the cleaning materials, and began setting up their experiments. They had won the battle. "We were feeling pretty good about sticking together," Sullivan said. But it had been an isolated episode. On that one day, she and her friends possessed an unusual degree of leverage. Within a week the microbiology labs had returned to business as normal, the men just as patronizing and authoritarian as before. Sullivan's picture of the world, however, had moved into sharper focus.

Leslie Sullivan spent a happy girlhood in the snowy, gnarled hills surrounding North Adams in the northwest corner of Massachusetts. An old factory town, North Adams sits in a crook of the Hoosic River near the Vermont line—mills, whistles, and smoke at the foot of a mountain, hemmed in by forests and state parks and tumbling water that once provided power for the mills. By the age of ten, Sullivan had become an adept skier on downhill trails over in Vermont. In summer she was constantly out in the woods, hiking and fishing on the slopes of Savoy Mt., a few miles from home. She enjoyed the outdoors life because that was what there was for a girl growing up in North Adams and because she threw herself into it.

Sullivan's mother taught grade school, and her father was the high school principal. Encouraged to read at home, she did well in school. Her parents sent her to Elmira College, an all-women's school in upstate New York. In 1968, when Kris Rondeau was a high school sophomore in Whitinsville, Sullivan graduated from Elmira with a B.S. in biology. She immediately went to Boston. North Adams with its ski trails and abandoned shoe factories fell behind in the snowy mists of girlhood.

She intended to work for a while, apply for graduate school, and enjoy life in the big city. In those days, many young women were going to Boston seeking work. When Americans think about patterns of worker migration, they typically trace the paths of single men, or families led by a male breadwinner, from region to region. To the degree that single women pick up roots, conventional belief has it that they are searching for a man, marriage, family—not a job. Men move looking for a job, and women move looking for a man. This is one of the many manifestations of the old view that whatever women do in the workplace—the skills they develop, the pay they receive, the influence they may have on the way work is organized and carried out—carries far less significance than if they were men.

Yet the first farm-to-factory migration in U.S. history involved young, unmarried women who provided labor power for America's Industrial Revolution. Starting in the 1810s, the nation's earliest factories sprang up along swift-running rivers in New England. The owners imported girls from impoverished farms to perform unskilled labor at spinning and weaving machines. Generation after generation of women came in from the farms, including great aunts of Leslie Sullivan's father who settled in North Adams. For many the opportunity provided a welcome source of income. But for many also the jobs entailed vicious exploitation, or at the least patronizing treatment, by mill owners. In some cases the women joined militant communities of workers to strike for their rights (as in the great strike in Lawrence in 1912). Gradual mechanization of the mills in the era of electricity shrank the openings for women, who were denied skilled jobs. When their working years were over, some women returned to the farms, but many stayed in the mill towns and formed families.

The flow of women off the farms and into the factory towns had slowed to a trickle by World War II. New England's textile, shoe, and clothing industries had been losing ground to low-wage producers in the South for decades. During the war, as in other industries, women temporarily returned to fill jobs vacated by men. But immediately after the war the decline of New England manufacturing accelerated. By the late sixties, Massachusetts was already in a severe slump, though the dimensions did not become clear until the recession of 1970. In a five-year period ending in 1972, the state lost more than 112,000 manufacturing jobs.

Leslie Sullivan was one of thousands of young women and men who left behind the old factory towns of New England in the 1960s and 1970s. For women in particular it was a sequel to the mill-town migration of the nineteenth century. Women seeking office work (as clerks, typists, secretaries) had always moved to big cities. But in the sixties and seventies there were many more of them. They were much better educated and primed by an emerging women's movement to expect and demand more from society, and especially employers, than ever before.

As the social and intellectual hub of New England, Boston offered an open, liberal-minded environment that appealed to young women college graduates. There also existed an insatiable demand for female workers in old and new service industries which were expanding even as New England manufacturing continued to deteriorate. Dozens of universities and colleges in the Boston metropolitan area employed many thousands of nonteaching workers, largely women. Boston also was headquarters for insurance companies, publishing houses, medical research institutions. It had many large hospitals, banks, libraries, government offices, temporary help agencies. The white-collar positions advertised by these employers promised interesting, clean, even challenging work for women who wanted more than a job that would tide them over to marriage. But even by the early seventies it was apparent that the reality would not match the promise, which is why a national movement of female office workers would get under way in Boston.

The seeds were sown in the late, apocalyptic years of the sixties. Sullivan arrived in Boston in the summer of 1968 and took a job as research assistant at Massachusetts General Hospital. Society was in turmoil. Martin Luther King and Robert Kennedy had been struck down by assassins' bullets. The civil rights movement was in full swing, and protests against the war in Vietnam were expanding. Sullivan and her friends marched and demonstrated against the war. Bobby Kennedy was her political idol. She believed in reform, not revolution. "We grew up expecting things to have a rhyme and reason and a moral," she said. "We were shocked to find they didn't, and we were willing to try to make the world better."

Her first exposure to work-a-day America would not be a happy one. At Massachusetts General, she worked alone for a prominent neurosurgeon, Dr. X, who conducted research as well as performed surgery. She acquired useful technical skills in Dr. X's lab. But when he asked her to take on his office work, she found that he was a man of shoddy ethics who overbilled patients and falsified records. She looked for another job and in 1971 accepted an offer from the Harvard School of Public Health.

At Harvard, she worked with other lab assistants in an eight-story building named "Public Health 1," situated to the left rear of the quadrangle. Her boss, a professor of microbiology, had nothing in common with Dr. X, least of all the latter's ethics. Dr. Z could have served as medicine's symbol of probity and correctness. He also dealt with employees in a stiff, old-fashioned way that went to the opposite extreme of Dr. X's chummy behavior. He addressed the research assistants as "Miss or Mrs." and avoided the place where the assistants took their coffee breaks like an admiral would an enlisted women's mess.

"If he had to reach me, he would lean his head in and say, 'Miss Sullivan.' But he would never walk into the room, because he was just above that," Sullivan said. When she became friendly with a young man who was a medical student, Dr. Z took him aside and said it was not appropriate to be friends with a research assistant.

In Dr. Z's laboratory, Sullivan and two other assistants worked on a study of trachoma. They injected guinea pigs with trachoma-like diseases and collected the pigs' tears and vaginal secretions to study the progress of the disease. It was not like doing hard labor in factory conditions amidst dust and smoke, but lab work could be unhealthy. Sullivan proved to be allergic to guinea pig secretions and eventually developed asthma. What bothered her most, however, was the patronizing and condescending way that the men of SPH—faculty members, administrators, and postdoctoral assistants—treated female research assistants. "There was this sort of attitude," Sullivan said, "that if you were at all smart, you wouldn't be here, you would have moved on by now."

Many RAs, it was true, worked only long enough to earn money for graduate school, or to help pay tuition for spouses (usually husbands) who were studying medicine. In the early 1970s, growing numbers of RAs took these jobs as a step toward permanent employment, perhaps a career in medical research. But male officials continued to treat all RAs as part-timers who came to Harvard looking for a husband. As recently as the late sixties, Sullivan recalled, Harvard Medical School ran want ads for research assistants and secretaries with the implicit pitch: "Come work at Harvard. Meet a medical student. Get married!"

Reflecting this demeaning treatment, the RAs called themselves "lab lackeys." The worst of it came from the male managers' view of womanhood. The female's hereditarily determined function in society consisted of giving birth, cleaning house, and accepting male domination. This being the case, why should women workers quibble about taking orders and doing women's work?

Chapter Two

Not long after the aborted lab-cleaning attempt, the male hierarchy came up with an idea for saving money. Every department in the School of Public Health had a few secretaries. It was a relatively thankless job, resulting in an even higher turnover rate than among lab workers. "Secretaries went through our office so fast, you wouldn't even learn their names and they'd be gone," Sullivan said. This state of affairs upset the faculty. A plan was announced. New secretaries no longer would be hired. Instead, each research assistant would draw secretarial duty on a rotating basis one day a month.

The very idea insulted the RAs. Sullivan said, "They just assumed that we're women, we could do this job, we're all the same, you know." The women got together and unanimously condemned the scheme. All signed a letter of protest. Meeting with the department head, the women attacked the "Secretary for a Day" program as "offensive," and in the face of such opposition he canceled it. "We came out of that one again feeling like we really won something, because he had to back off," Sullivan said. "We had cohesion."

But it was a momentary "cohesion," jelling in response to foolish management actions but quickly breaking up when the bosses retreated. Nothing enduring formed. The research assistants had no voice on the job and no reason to believe that they would not have to react time after time to absurd, sexually discriminating orders. Sullivan could see no way out. "You either left or accepted the fact that this is the way it was. You would never make much money. It was a dead end. The work we did was valuable, the backbone of medical research. We did everything and it was skilled, and the more you knew about it the better you could perform. It didn't seem fair that it wasn't seen as a real job, one you could stay at and move up the ladder."

The proponents of "free labor markets" would have shrugged and advised Sullivan to use the one voice that no one could suppress, her "exit voice." If she and all her dissatisfied friends quit the School of Public Health, leaving it disabled, the managers would either change their spots or lose *their* jobs. Sullivan thought of leaving. But where would she go? If she couldn't get fair and equal treatment at Harvard University, the institutional paragon of liberal enlightenment, then where? Where in Boston, or where in the United States for that matter?

CHAPTER THREE

*I*n June of 1970 Kris Rondeau graduated from Whitinsville High School. On her seventeenth birthday a friend gave her a copy of a new book, *Sexual Politics* by Kate Millett. Rondeau tried to read it, but her mind rebelled against entering Millett's abstract literary world. She knew that the book had to do with the male supremacy themes of famous male novelists, such as D.H. Lawrence and Norman Mailer, whose books she also hadn't read, and she had a vague idea of what Millett was getting at. But she gave up, feeling a little guilty, but also feeling that maybe heavy analytic reading was beyond her.

She worked that summer in nearby Manchaug at a small plant that produced styrofoam wigheads. She assisted three older women who stood all day long, shaving excess styrofoam off new wigheads and stuffing them in bags—for $1.60 an hour. A boss named Harry watched them through dirty windows in his office overlooking the factory floor. As they shaved and stuffed, wighead after wighead, the women talked continuously, chattering about their lives outside the plant, health problems, family joys and sorrows. Rondeau listened.

One woman had several children and loved her husband. Another was overweight and had to sit down now and then. She even brought in a note from her doctor. "But Harry gave her a hard time because she had to sit down," Rondeau said. "They all should have been sitting down whenever they wanted to, but the theory was, they didn't work as fast if they were sitting down." The third woman, the mother of two children, disappeared in the middle of summer. She ran away, driven off by some misery in her life, and never came back.

"Every one of them was dealing at home with big important issues—husbands, children, the elders, death, money decisions," Rondeau said. "But they'd come to work and have virtually no power. It was not like I had an analysis of what I saw. But listening to these women was saving me. I knew I couldn't be put into a mold like that."

By the end of summer she still hadn't read Millett's book. But she felt now that its contents said something to her. "By holding it, I could feel what was probably in it, if I could understand it," she said. "I think the women's movement gave me the possibility of not being put into a mold. I went out seeking my fortune because I was told I could."

By 1970 Leslie Sullivan had come to feel part of the women's liberation movement, a sort of free-floating, unconnected part since feminism and "women's lib," as some called it, had little practical meaning for her. At first the term "feminist" had reminded her of stout women in bustles and big black hats, carrying placards in 1890s photographs. As the word returned to general use (it had not been much used for decades) to mean one who believes in the economic, social, and political equality of men and women, Sullivan came to think of herself as a feminist—not a meeting-going feminist, simply a woman who believed in equality.

She had been out of college for three or four years before she saw that the women's movement offered more than political theory. "It was at Harvard," Sullivan said, "that I made the real connection between being a woman and the job we were in. I was more aware that I wasn't the only one. I could see it was no accident that the women were all in these positions. I began to see that it wasn't just me, or how was I going to deal with this. You had to improve the entire system for everybody."

But how? The women's movement offered exciting concepts like *Sisterhood Is Powerful*, the title of a recently published book, and Sullivan supported current efforts to pass the Equal Rights Amendment and win abortion rights. But in 1972 the women's movement and its principal spokeswomen seemed remote from the daily workplace.

The women's movement in America had risen from an unknown place over the horizon like a dawn delayed from prehistoric times. For more than a hundred years occasional piercing rays had shot up over the curvature of society, flaring briefly, causing panic among men. The militant feminism of women who, at the Seneca Falls conference of 1848, called for a restructuring of society to give equal status to women was followed by something else entirely: the women's suffrage drive of the late nineteenth and early twentieth century, culminating in the vote for women; the predominantly female temperance movement which in the 1910s set the nation on an eccentric course leading to Prohibition; and the drive for "protective legislation" (for example, laws banning female employment in certain hazardous industries) spearheaded by Eleanor Roosevelt and others in the thirties. Historians later would argue that these campaigns, whatever their worth in other terms, diverted women's energies from the true feminist goal of equality in all institutions of society.

During World War II, millions of women went to work in defense industries to replace men gone to war. There was nothing remotely equalitarian about this trend. The women for the most part received less pay than their male co-workers. They were endlessly harassed, confined to certain jobs, ignored by their unions, and in the end pushed out of their jobs—with the eternal thanks of a grateful nation—when the men returned from the battlefields. In the fifties, the nation settled into a long retreat from war, economic deprivation, and political activism. Veterans took their families into the burgeoning new suburbs, where everyone set to acquiring possessions and making children. But even in that quiescent period social and economic trends began to force changes in women's role in society. The home became "a concentration camp" for women, declared Betty Friedan in her landmark 1963 book, *The Feminine Mystique*, the title referring to the glorification of motherhood.

By the mid-sixties, some trends had become irreversible. The demand for women workers in typically female jobs had grown rapidly as retail trade and other service industries expanded. The demand for labor, as always, found a willing supply. Given that women who entered the labor force in the sixties were on average much better educated than in the past, it was not surprising that they, in turn, demanded more of work. At the same time, technological improvements in housekeeping and birth control shortened, by some years in the aggregate, the time required for homemaking and caring for children. It was a time of rising expectations in which the desire for self-improvement was not confined to the male half of the population. Inevitably, the conflicting roles of women could be resolved in only one of two ways: a reversion to the past, or a rooting out of inequality in all American institutions. When men on the whole failed either to recognize the role change or voluntarily to relinquish power and perquisites to make room for it, women acted.

Historians have traced the origin of the women's liberation movement, if not back to the very moment of creation, at least to a misty soup of trends and developments in the early sixties. Among those developments were the establishment by President John F. Kennedy of a Presidential Commission on the Status of Women; the related growth of state commissions on women's issues; the passage of two pieces of legislation, the Equal Pay Act of 1963 and, a year later, the landmark Civil Rights Act of 1965 with a section on equal opportunity in employment.

New feminist groups sprang to life, most notably in 1966 the National Organization for Women (NOW), to push for action under the new laws. One result was massive litigation, thousands of sex discrimination suits filed against employers of all kinds by government agencies, women's groups, and individual workers. War protesters and student radicals adopted the feminist cause (if only in theory), and feminists in turn borrowed their methods of dramatizing issues through well-publicized demonstrations. They ridiculed public events, such as the Miss America pageant, and private behavior, like the use of bras, girdles, and false eyelashes, in which women unthinkingly—or with purpose—acted out roles as sex objects that kept them inferior to men.

With the help of new publications like *Ms.*, which first appeared in 1972, feminists brought the issues of rape and husband-battered women to public attention. They called for the establishment of day care centers, protested unequal representation of women in art exhibitions and other areas of public life, insisted that the priesthood be open to both sexes, and demanded that women have the right to deal with their bodies as they wished—that is, have abortions. Most controversial of all, they reached back to the 1920s and resurrected a campaign to insert an Equal Rights Amendment (ERA) in the Constitution. On March 22, 1972, Congress approved the ERA and submitted it to the states for ratification.

By 1972, writes historian Ethel Klein in *Gender Politics*, surveys showed that more than 40 percent of women felt they should have an equal voice with men in the public sphere; only 25 percent believed that woman's place was in the home; and a majority believed that women as a class had common problems. In other words, feminist consciousness had risen to a level where it could be a political force for legislated reforms. Women everywhere began examining their own situations in the light of new insights about women in American society.

In the early phases of the women's movement, television and the press focused on protests and demonstrations, aided by participants who exploited the vulnerability of TV-led media slavishness to images of action.

Opponents could point to women carrying placards reading, "Starve a Rat—Don't Cook Dinner" or "Marriage Is a Form of Slavery" or "Society to Cut Up Men (SCUM)" as proof of a feminist effort to destroy the traditional concept of family and punish men for being men. There was enough silly behavior on the fringes of the movement, and enough real confusion in the minds of Americans about the conflicting roles of women, to nourish this view. Along with many women, Leslie Sullivan laughed at the radical feminists' japes and insults (some *were* funny and carried a nugget of truth). But she did not hate men—continued dating them, in fact—and intended to marry one some day and start a typical American family. Ultimately, however, the radical taint would help opponents kill the ERA.

By the early seventies, no sign-carrying feminists could be found marching through Harvard's "great white quadrangle." But feminist ideas were wafting about. Activists were holding consciousness-raising meetings, especially on the subject of women's health. The notion had been growing for some years that the medical profession, monopolized by men, did not place enough importance on, nor even fully understand, health problems specific to women, such as gynecological malfunctions and diseases. In 1970, a group of laywomen, who later incorporated as the Boston Women's Health Book Collective Inc., produced a book that examined many neglected issues of women's health. Revised and reissued in 1973 as *Our Bodies, Ourselves*, the book won international fame (more than four million copies had been sold by 1996). The book was well known to women in the Harvard Medical Area. A student at the School of Public Health, Norma Swenson, worked on the 1973 revision.

Sullivan and her co-workers were aware of this activity, but it didn't affect them as employees. Their bosses seemed to have learned little from the womens' small acts of protest, and there was no one to teach them. The Medical Area schools had never had women in top-level managerial posts. If there was a women's movement in the area, it needed a leader, or at least a symbol of resistance to the status quo. The Harvard administration almost inadvertently provided one.

Dr. Mary Howell didn't mount a feminist soapbox when she taught pediatrics at the Medical School. But her students came to know pretty quickly where she stood. There was a stand-up-for-what's-rightness about her that could not be mistaken for mere righteousness. She had a Ph.D. in child development as well as an M.D., had studied psychology, had been a practicing pediatrician, had been—and still was—a wife, mother, teacher, writer, mental health consultant, and counselor of young women. What Mary Howell knew was that, with the possible exception of physical size and strength, women were equal to men in all respects and should be treated equally in society. She believed that a deep and abiding sexism pervaded the medical profession, starting with medical education.

The young women Howell taught at Harvard told her appalling stories of discrimination in the daily life of the Medical School. This made her think back to her own student days at the University of Minnesota in the fifties and early sixties. So few women studied medicine in those years that systematic discrimination seemed almost a normal state of affairs. "There was nobody with whom to share it, and no place to put anger if you recognized it," Howell said. Ten years later her students, who had come of age with the women's movement, refused to accept unequal treatment as a necessary cost of entering the profession. Struck by the depth of their anger, Howell decided to conduct a survey of the treatment of women students in American medical schools.

Before she began the survey, however, the unexpected happened. The dean of Harvard Medical School, Robert B. Ebert, asked Howell to take on the job of associate dean of student affairs. The appointment, announced in September 1972, startled many; never before in its century-and-a-half history had the school had a female dean. But the political atmosphere was changing rapidly in the early seventies. A substantial rise in female enrollment had increased pressure on Ebert to eliminate sex discrimination in all its forms. At the urging of feminist students and faculty, he appointed Howell to the new deanship.

While serving as associate dean, she completed her survey and wrote a book sardonically titled, *Why Would a Girl Go into Medicine? Medical Education in the U.S.: A Guide for Women*. Based on a survey of 146 students at 41 medical schools, the book and subsequent journal articles revealed sex discrimination in all aspects of medical training, from the admissions process, to the classroom and dissecting table, to the student health service.

It was common practice, she found, for male medical professors to belittle female students in a way that demeaned all women. One student, for instance, told of her school's graduation ceremonies in which "only the *gentlemen* were invited to take the Hippocratic oath" [emphasis in original]. Like football locker rooms, the men's-club atmosphere of the medical profession brimmed with "humor" directed at women. Male lecturers, giving slide presentations, frequently slipped in pornographic slides to the amusement of many male students. "The only significant difference between a woman and a cow," one instructor told his students, "is that a cow has more spigots." Every woman, Howell wrote, seemed "an appropriate object" for this "male sexual prurience" whether she was a student, a patient, or even a colleague.

Howell concluded that doctors stereotyped women as "possessed by affect, incapable of rational or analytic thought, scheming and opportunistic, and *not worth* the time, energy and thought required for good patient care" [emphasis in original]. Assuming the existence of "psychogenic" problems, physicians frequently misdiagnosed illnesses and prescribed inappropriate treatment such as unnecessary hysterectomies. Howell allowed that "much of this discrimination against women is not malicious by conscious intent." It mirrored what was happening in the society, though one might have expected practitioners of the healing arts to lead the way in rejecting a bias that so obviously inflicted psychological damage.

Believing that Harvard Medical School would not be pleased with her description of medical education, Howell used the pseudonym, "Margaret A. Campbell." Not until she left the dean's post in 1975 was her authorship disclosed. Published in 1973, *Why Would a Girl Go into Medicine?* found its way to medical schools across the country and served as a powerful document-in-evidence for reforming medical education.

Howell knew that sexist attitudes and biased treatment could not be altered by executive order. Reform was unlikely unless women ascended to important faculty positions. The catch was that only tenured professors could vote on candidates for tenure, and in 1973 only 1 of 150 tenured professors at HMS was a woman. So thoroughly had men controlled admission that Harvard Medical School didn't admit women as students until 1945, and then largely because the war had taken a toll of male physicians. In the early seventies, antidiscrimination laws and the women's movement convinced more and more young women that they had as much right as men to be doctors or lawyers. From 1969 to 1973, women as a proportion of students entering U.S. medical schools jumped from 8 to nearly 20 percent. Harvard, slightly ahead of the trend, admitted forty-six women (28 percent of the new class) in 1973, up from twenty-four in 1970.

The two most important deans in the Medical Area, Robert Ebert of the Medical School, and Howard H. Hiatt of Public Health, supported a more open admissions policy. Both were known as social-minded "liberals" in a highly conservative profession. But both had to contend with faculty members who defended the low female admission rate on grounds that it reflected a lack of qualified women applicants. "Qualified," however, was a subjective determination made by the men who interviewed the applicants.

"Those men wanted to admit people like themselves, who would be sort of like their sons, their proteges, assistants, and helpers," Howell said, recalling meetings of the admissions committee that she attended. "The 'girl applicants' didn't fit that picture. Women were refused admission on the basis of qualities that would not have even been part of the discussion if the applicants had been men." More women finally were admitted, partly because attitudes did change, however slowly, and partly because many more applied. In 1972, the Medical School received 524 applications from women, compared with only 84 a decade earlier.

The import of Howell's review was that the medical profession, including its educational institutions, was a great deep well of chauvinism. And if women students were treated badly, Howell wrote, "it is clear that patients who are also women are doubly demeaned." Using the same arithmetic, she might have added that female employees of medical schools, having the lowest status of all, were triply demeaned. Indeed, she said in 1994, she believed this to be true.

Conditions for three of the groups—female students, faculty members, and patients—began to change in the early seventies, largely because of critics like Howell and because of the growing awareness of women's rights promoted by the women's movement. The situation was different, however, for women workers at medical schools.

After becoming dean, Howell came to know and respect workers like Leslie Sullivan. She saw how dissatisfied they were and sympathized with them. Lacking authority in personnel management, she couldn't engage their problems directly. But she began promoting a plan for advancing the interests of all women in the Medical Area through a Committee on the Status of Women. This quasi-official body, operating with the authority of the deans, would gather data on all matters relating to women and recommend action to the deans on issues such as admissions, faculty appointments, maternity leave, and child care. In early 1972, a faculty governance committee in the Medical Area had recommended the creation of such a committee. Deans Ebert and Hiatt supported the idea, but a year had passed with no action being taken.

As the new year 1973 began, Dean Mary Howell and her activist colleagues decided the time had come to encourage the deans to act.

One day in February 1973, Leslie Sullivan spotted an unusual notice on the bulletin board in the lobby of Public Health 1. It announced a meeting to discuss sex discrimination at Harvard, and it invited all women, including employees, who usually were excluded from discussion groups. Sullivan decided to attend.

Fifteen to twenty women gathered in a large lounge area on the ground floor of Vanderbilt Hall, a dormitory building on Longwood Ave. across the street from the medical quadrangle. Sullivan was one of only a few workers. Among the faculty members and students were women whom Sullivan knew by reputation, including Dean Mary Howell and the student Norma Swenson, already known for her work on *Our Bodies, Ourselves*. The candid talk of these women surprised Sullivan. People met all the time in the Medical Area to listen to lectures by outside speakers, or to discuss health and research issues. Following the great tradition of academic free speech, school officials encouraged people to talk all they wanted, provided of course that certain cultural, political, and institutional standards were adhered to. It went without saying that one did not foment institutional distrust by asking searching questions in open meetings about Harvard policy.

In this case anger overcame custom. The university seemed too faint-hearted in attacking sex discrimination. The Medical Area deans, for one thing, had yet to create a Committee on the Status of Women. There was little evidence of plans to promote women to policymaking and tenured teaching positions. With regard to hiring, Harvard University had announced its commitment to equal employment opportunity in late 1969. For three years it had been working secretively on an Affirmative Action Plan as required by the federal government. By now, surely, the plan should be ready. But no such announcement had come from the administration. The women's group appointed a task force to investigate.

Sullivan heard something in the voices of these women that drew her to a second meeting on February 21. The task force made a revealing report. Unknown to all but a few Harvard officials, the university had completed a draft of its Affirmative Action Plan in late 1972 and now awaited the approval of the Department of Health, Education and Welfare. No women's groups had been consulted in formulating the plan, and no one was allowed to view the one existing copy, kept under lock and key in a university office.

Annoyed by this, students and professors brought up other instances of the administration's indifferent attitude toward women. Sullivan mentioned some of the problems encountered by research assistants. It quickly became obvious that all women connected with the medical schools had to cope with discriminatory practices of one kind or another. Everyone agreed that the time had come for the women to band together and press for action. On the spot, they formed a committee, open to all women, which would lobby for women's rights. They named it the Harvard Medical Area Women's Group (HMAWG). One of its main goals was creation of the long-proposed Committee on the Status of Women.

It was an exciting moment. For the first time, women in the Medical Area had put aside their occupational and educational differences to act in concert. Sullivan had known none of these women when she went to the first meeting. Now they all were looking at one another, still guardedly but with some surprise, as if to say, "We have a common interest!" Like an infectious grin, feminist consciousness was breaking out in the Harvard Medical Area.

The core of the Harvard Medical Area Women's Group, about ten to twenty women, met frequently through February to set up and launch the organization. The most influential group, in terms of leverage with the deans, were the faculty members who had jobs ranging from lecturer to assistant professor. Second in terms of influence were several graduate students in the Medical Area. Many had earned a master's degree in a health-related field and now were studying for a Ph.D. or an M.D. Sullivan became a spokeswoman for the third group, the employees, who constituted the largest group of women in the Medical Area but who, paradoxically, had practically no influence with school administrators.

A conflict over goals arose at the very beginning. The faculty and student groups had two primary concerns: enlarging the female student population and getting more and better faculty appointments for women. The employee group, on the other hand, had no need for hiring quotas. "The faculty had too few women, but in the workforce we were already the majority," Sullivan said. The workers, classified by Harvard as "salary and wage" (S&W) employees, wanted nondiscriminatory working conditions, more money, and a career advancement plan. Some professors and students seemed sympathetic with the workers' situation, but many thought it of secondary concern.

It was clear to Sullivan that if the priority items of the three groups were tossed into one big pot containing all women's issues, the workers' heavy proletarian demands would sink to the bottom while the profession-als' issues—floating on top like pretty sprouts and garnishes—would at-tract attention. If the administration acted at all, it would be to spoon up these issues and surreptitiously dump the rest. Only a unified HMAWG could force the administration to deal with all issues, and Sullivan saw that some faculty women and students already had drawn a line between their problems and those of the workers. For this reason, she supported the forming of a separate section to address the "special needs" of the S&W employees. Sullivan and two or three other employees would run this co-terie under the umbrella of the full group. "I liked this idea," she said, "be-cause I saw it as an avenue to improve our situation. Our jobs deserved more than we were getting out of them, and I thought the women's group at least would help us learn more about the entire situation and see what other women were doing."

Sullivan and her little band began devoting part of each workday to recruiting new members and gathering information about the workers' sit-uation. Normally they couldn't have acted with such freedom. But Medical Area supervisors, newly sensitive to women's concerns, may have been un-der orders to accommodate the workers. The administration apparently didn't want to stir up the female student body or cross strong faculty mem-bers like Mary Howell. In early March, Sullivan and three co-workers be-gan publishing a biweekly newsletter of seven or eight mimeographed pages, which they called *S&W Notes*.

Sullivan discovered that she had a knack for committee work—set-ting up meetings, getting people involved, defining issues. She was begin-ning to discover within herself a driving force that had been on idle for some time, lacking a means. It came from who knows what combination of childhood dreams and traumas and victories and defeat, and it sounded windily inflated when spoken out loud, though in fact what moved her was the simple concept that individuals and groups of people should do right by one another. This new desire to organize people was tinged with anger, probably a minute dash of class envy, and a major dollop of naive faith in the American way as taught in school. She had found herself caught in a system that did not work. Like a novice mechanic, she had been searching for a tool to fix it—not a small thing like a wrench, but a large instrument whose name she did not know and a function she could only guess at. The question was, had she now found that instrument?

As office and lab workers, Sullivan and other reporters for *S&W Notes* had a certain amount of freedom to move about and meet other employ-ees. Sullivan herself frequently ran errands for her lab supervisors. "I'd have to deliver one thing for my boss and I'd stop off at six different places on the way and talk to people," she said. She set up a newsletter distribution system by recruiting one or two supporters in each office. And *S&W Notes* began painting a picture of Harvard employment practices.

The three Medical Area schools, *S&W Notes* reported, employed a little more than 1,200 people, including 219 "exempt" employees (professional and managerial workers not subject to wage and hour laws) and 1,000 S&W workers, or "nonexempts." Seventy-five percent of the latter category were women. The newsletter acknowledged that in the past "most women" took these jobs only for a few years and to supplement family income. "Now," it continued, "although more and more women in these positions are dependent upon their own earnings, Harvard still perpetuates the 'non-career' nature of these positions." A personnel officer made the startling admission to *S&W Notes* that Harvard "has no guidelines for promoting people after a certain number of years of service." Nor did it offer incentives to employees to improve job skills through further education. Harvard, in short, had no personnel policy deserving of the name.

Few employees had ever seen the university's personnel manual, which was kept in the personnel office and could be viewed only with special permission. But a sympathetic administrative assistant let Sullivan copy portions of the manual after working hours. As a result, *S&W Notes* of March 23 scored a major coup, publishing a table of salaries and occupational grades never before made public. For the first time workers could view their situation in perspective. The article revealed, among other things, how the university used the short-term work tradition to exploit women workers.

Each year Harvard granted to a selected group of workers small "merit raises," usually less than the annual inflation rate. At the same time, in order to remain competitive in the labor market for new employees, it increased starting minimums by a percentage equal to or greater than inflation. This resulted in an upside-down wage scale on which experience counted almost nothing. An entry-level research assistant hired in 1972 had an annual salary of $6,960. In 1973 the standard merit increase would bring the salary to $7,273. But a newly hired worker in the same position received $7,200, only $73 per year less than employees hired a year earlier. Year by year, under this policy, experienced workers fell further behind, producing the absurd situation of workers with several years experience making hundreds, even thousands, of dollars less a year than a person hired off the street.

Interest in the new women's group expanded rapidly. *S&W Notes* of April 4 noted that seventy women attended a noon meeting on March 28. By the end of the school term, Sullivan's section had put out five newsletters containing more information about employment at Harvard than Harvard itself had ever disseminated. Scores of women had attended lunchtime meetings, and Sullivan herself had struck up acquaintances throughout the Medical Area. Her well-publicized drive, combined with behind-scenes lobbying by leaders of the parent HMAWG, finally culminated in what they thought would be a major achievement.

In July 1973, the deans of the Medical, Dental, and Public Health schools jointly established a Committee on the Status of Women. Feminist consciousness had proved its potency. The women of the Medical Area had won—or at least some of them had.

The Committee on the Status of Women (CSW) began meeting in August. Almost immediately it ran into trouble. The deans had appointed twelve voting members (nine of them women), including nine professors, one student, and two employees. Sullivan was offered a seat but preferred to serve ex-officio along with Mary Howell and two other Medical Area administrators.

Women activists had thought that a CSW with the official sanction of the deans would be able to push reforms rapidly from proposal to practice. But almost all administration-sponsored committees, by their nature, have a "conservative drag," as Mary Howell had pointed out in her book. Not all CSW members wanted to move with equal speed. Furthermore, official committees must produce official minutes to be reviewed by higher-level officials (the Medical Area deans in this case), all of which tends to deaden the level of debate. "I quickly began to feel," Howell recalled, "that the committee meetings were pallid and boring."

But more than that, a corrosive elitism had begun to erode the very concept of female solidarity even before the committee was set up. In small planning sessions of faculty members and students only, Mary Howell was astonished to hear proposals that workers be excluded from the committee. She took the opposite view "against quite a lot of disagreement, especially on the part of women faculty and to a lesser extent on the part of women students." She argued that "it was not right that a committee like this, which we hoped would have some influence, was just going to be people with graduate degrees, M.D.s and Ph.D.s. I insisted that it include the women staff at all levels."

Howell and her supporters won the argument. Formally, the CSW had worker representatives. "But in terms of being a voice for women," she said, "it really was just a voice for faculty and students. Although the little opening had been made for staff, I think they always felt, the ones who attended meetings, that it was not meant for them, or that they were not entirely welcome."

With good reason. Some faculty women could not conceal their condescending attitude. Leslie Sullivan had sensed this in the past. But at an early meeting of the newly formed committee, a raw and ugly elitism smacked her squarely in the face. In debating an agenda for the committee, a couple of professors declared that their issues took precedence over those of the salary and wage workers. Sullivan remembered a psychologist who argued that "secretaries" had not reached a level of accomplishment deserving the same consideration as doctors and students. Her remarks were "unbelievably offensive," Sullivan said. "There was no point in discussing employee issues [her argument went], because any improvements that the group gained for the faculty women would trickle down to the workers."

It was not just a crack that had breached the wall of solidarity, but a gorge. And, as is usually the case in broad groupings of workers, the wall was weakest at the top. Gender solidarity, Sullivan saw then—and would many times in the future—rarely equates with worker solidarity. The problem with identifying a common interest in the face of stiff opposition is that it reveals how downright common everybody is. This is a deeply troubling insight for those with the most earning power—and the highest opinion of themselves. Social movements, however, cannot be blamed for the way some of the people in them behave.

Despite the elitist sentiment, the CSW gave a nod in the direction of helping the workers by forming an employee task force. In the fall of 1973, it busily collected data and identified issues. But the work seemed useless to Sullivan. A legal problem had arisen. Actually, it had always existed, but now that the women's committee was, in effect, an arm of the administration, Harvard administrators and lawyers began citing chapter and verse to discourage activities on behalf of employees.

Under federal labor law, only "nonexempts," or workers with no managerial duties, were eligible to join unions. When the National Labor Relations Act (NLRA) was passed in 1935, it dealt strongly with one of the major problems facing workers at the time. To defuse widespread worker restiveness, many large employers had set up company unions under the guise of providing "voice" to their workers. These were purely and simply manipulative bodies, formed to give workers a sense of democracy where none existed. To do away with "sweetheart" unions, the NLRA sensibly prohibited management from negotiating pay and other terms of work with employees on committees dominated by management.

There could be little doubt that the CSW met that definition. It did not exist until the deans said it existed. And when it started meeting, Harvard attorneys—including General Counsel Daniel Steiner himself—sat in to ensure compliance with the law. There could be no discussion of anything relating to the salary and wage workers' pay and working conditions or personnel problems.

"It was clear from the beginning that our needs and concerns were not going to be addressed," recalled Edie Brickman, an employee member of the committee. She was a research assistant, for years an antiwar activist in the Medical Area, who had joined the CSW after its first few meetings. She remembered a meeting when the company union question came up.

"Dan Steiner was there and said, 'We can't deal with employee issues because that would be considered a sweetheart union.' I said to him, 'Then you're asking us to have a regular union? That would be fine.'" Except that there was no union and little chance of getting one. Steiner later confirmed that the administration took this position. He couldn't recall the particular meeting cited by Brickman, though he remembered her.

Nothing in the law prevented Harvard from acting voluntarily to correct the more egregious pay and workplace problems that Sullivan's group had exposed. Nor was there anything to prevent faculty and student women from lobbying on behalf of their sisters in the work force—nothing except custom, tradition, elitism, and American reality.

In everyday life, employers rarely took voluntary action to improve pay or workplace conditions beyond the level needed to "compete in the labor market," as if this phrase alone—clanging with the simple clarity of free markets economics and a misplaced social Darwinism—should be the determining factor in management–worker relations. In class relations, those who have made it in America, boosted up in many cases by working-class parents, rarely extended a hand down to help others up the ladder.

Chapter Three

If Leslie Sullivan hadn't understood this reality before, she did now. Sometime in the autumn of 1973, she lost faith in the Committee on the Status of Women, and in the idea of female unity in the Medical Area. She saw that women workers—the "lower-level employees," as the elitists referred to them—were not likely to win equal treatment through "voluntary" means, or with the help of other women acting as a group. Perhaps nothing could be done.

The curious thing was that women workers in other parts of Boston seemed to be finding a way to make change. A citywide organization of women was fighting discrimination in government jobs, other groups were filing suits for back pay on behalf of female victims of bias, the Massachusetts legislature approved the ERA, and a handful of women in Boston-Cambridge founded what became the nation's largest advocacy organization for female office workers. Women seemed to be on their way, making progress everywhere, except at Harvard.

CHAPTER FOUR

*K*ris Rondeau began her senior year at Windham College in September 1973. Located in Putney, Vermont, Windham was a small school with a student population of several hundred. She had enrolled at Windham because it *was* small and far enough away, but not too far away, from her hometown. She had never spent more than a few nights outside Whitinsville. "It was a hard place to get away from," she said, "and when you did, you had to learn about the whole world outside."

She had to learn, for example, about cheese and black-and-white movies. Growing up in lunch-bucket Whitinsville, she had assumed that from the world's supply of cheese you could choose either Velveeta in chunks or Kraft individually wrapped slices, to be consumed with soft white sandwich bread. Attending social get-togethers at college, she saw people standing around with glasses of wine and dainty crackers topped with wedges of cheese that came in many varieties, ranging from hard and sharp to soft and smelly. This astonished her. When she first went with college friends to a Friday night movie, she thought they should ask for a refund because the movie wasn't in technicolor. "At the end everybody sat for a long time watching the credits, and then they went out and talked about it. This was far beyond my experience."

In the early seventies Windham was "a hippie place, sex and drugs and rock and roll," Rondeau recalled. She had some good times, intermixed with episodes of ill health. She had suffered bouts of depression since her teenage years, and after an emotional breakdown in college she began therapy with a psychologist. In her junior year she began concentrating on science courses. "I had done well in science in high school, but it had never occurred to me it was okay for a girl to do science," she said. With the encouragement of her instructors, she began reading on her own and became fascinated with evolutionary biology, psychobiology, and ethology.

"It kind of hit me at Windham that I needed to think about some kind of path. I had to think up a career. I wanted very much to have a job in which I wouldn't be bored, and I thought about being a doctor. So I decided to prepare for that somehow."

Leslie Sullivan and many other women of the sixties had discovered there was little you could do to prepare for slamming into a brick wall. The corporate world (encompassing business, academia, government, and organized labor) did not take well to the idea of women having careers. Neither antidiscrimination laws nor education, that great American antidote for all social diseases, were having much effect on virulent male chauvinism. Not that every last American male had broken out in gruesome sores. Some had overcome the malady while others carried it passively.

But the disease affected systems of thought as well as people. Centuries ago its spores had wormed their way into the basic premises upon which men built their great corporate and government bodies. These included assumptions about "women's nature" and "women's place" in society, assumptions accepted by most men (and many women) and incorporated in man-made systems such as hiring and personnel policies. At one time these systems may have reflected the way society actually worked—a time when people owned slaves; when women, assumed to be inferior biologically to men, had few rights under the law; and when the U.S. economy operated with relative efficiency on the labor power of full-time work by most men (and all slaves) and short-term work by some women.

By the 1970s, the days when a minority of young, mainly impoverished women worked for a few years in factory and shop before marriage had passed, probably irretrievably, into history. This was not the doing of feminists but rather of powerful economic and demographic trends. Now the nation *needed* the labor of women, and most families *needed* the income of mothers and wives to supplement the stagnant wages of working-class and middle-class husbands. Starting in the sixties, women began piling into the labor force in record numbers. Between 1950 and 1970, the percentage of women working or looking for work (the so-called labor force participation rate) increased from 33.9 percent to 43.3 percent.

There was nothing new in women working, but there was something revolutionary in so many women working for so long and for so many good reasons. In corporate America, however, the personnel policies and management methods still operated as if economic conditions and society's values remained the same as a century ago. Employers figured on hiring women on the same old terms, at below-standard wages, and keeping them in thrall. Women rebelled, or tried to rebel, and nowhere did more of them try harder, in as many different ways, as in Boston.

❦

On November 22, 1973, the *Boston Globe* carried the first public mention of what would become the most famous organization of female white-collar workers. "Hub Women Office Workers Unite for Higher Pay," said a headline over a story about a YWCA forum attended by two hundred women and sponsored by a group calling itself 9to5. One of the women quoted in the story was a young Harvard secretary named Karen Nussbaum. She would become a well-known advocate of women workers and, eventually, director of the Women's Bureau of the U.S. Department of Labor, an agency made prominent during the New Deal by Eleanor Roosevelt's enthusiastic support.

In 1973 Nussbaum had no such aspirations. She had taken a job at Harvard Graduate School of Education, on the Cambridge campus, at about the same time that Sullivan went to work in the Medical Area. Working in the same office with Nussbaum was Ellen Cassedy, a friend she had met in the late sixties while attending the University of Chicago. Both found themselves stuck in dead-end jobs. With a few other frustrated Harvard secretaries, they formed a weekly discussion circle. Cassedy and Nussbaum also got in touch with groups of female workers in other Boston workplaces. In 1972, the women formed a committee of ten from various industries and began circulating a newsletter, *9to5 News*, which eventually had a distribution of about six thousand throughout Boston. It attracted so much attention that the group decided to set up a citywide organization. Thus, in November 1973 was born 9to5: Organization for Women Office Workers. Cassedy resigned from Harvard and became the first full-time staff member, and Nussbaum followed within a few months.

9to5 operated largely as a lobbying group, campaigning for the passage of measures like maternity benefits and an Office Worker's Bill of Rights. The group also filed lawsuits and won a $1.5 million back-pay award for employees of three publishing firms. It established committees in several employment sectors—such as insurance, publishing, banking, law firms, universities, and temporary work agencies—and developed data on wages, benefits, and personnel policies in each area. Each committee advised workers in its sector on work-related issues. When it came to getting changes made, 9to5 was somewhat at a loss, for it had no leverage to persuade or force employers to do anything. For a while it tried public confrontation, demanding meetings with business groups like the Chamber of Commerce. These attempts brought publicity but no changes in employer policies. To keep interest alive, the leaders had to claim victory in situations where, as Nussbaum put it, "if you got the meeting, *that* was the victory. Having the meeting was the victory."

One significant thing that 9to5 and other women's groups did, however, was to make many thousands of working women aware of the problems they had in common and to focus public attention on discrimination in the workplace. In the early 1970s, Boston became a hothouse of organized efforts to improve women's jobs. The Boston YWCA lent its established presence and strong political support for this movement, serving as a headquarters for 9to5 and other organizations. One of these, City Women for Action, founded in 1971 to aid government employees, won major lawsuits against city agencies engaged in massive violations of laws requiring equal pay for equal work. Lawyers for City Women for Action, such as Betty Gittes, led a fight in the Massachusetts Legislature for repeal of protective legislation, state laws originally passed to protect working women but which had come to be used by employers as a cover to exclude or exploit women.

In Massachusetts, women workers were banned from a number of hazardous industries, such as mining; they were not allowed to work more than forty hours a week (no jobs requiring overtime); they were not allowed to lift objects weighing more than forty pounds, and so on. The premise underlying this body of legislation was that major biological differences separated women and men, a long-accepted theory that served as a justification for keeping women in secondary roles. The women's movement of the sixties and seventies worked hard to discredit the idea, with considerable success; most of the old women-only laws were struck down at that time.

Within a year or two, 9to5 began establishing chapters in other cities. Similar organizations also sprang up to do essentially the same thing. Among them were Women Organized For Employment in San Francisco, Women Office Workers in New York, and Women Employed in Chicago. 9to5, with a short and pithy name that resonated with meaning, grew into a national organization. Its success inspired a popular movie of the same name starring Jane Fonda, Dolly Parton, and Lily Tomlin.

From the beginning, however, 9to5 could do little more than offer advice and sympathetic support to women who wanted to reform their working conditions. Nussbaum and Cassedy soon began to perceive, as Sullivan had in the Medical Area, that when the women's movement descended to the workplace, it did not bring—because it did not possess—a means of negotiating with the employer. Only a union had standing under the law to bring an employer to the bargaining table. "In 1973 the concept of union was on our mind, but we didn't have a clear idea what to do about it," Ellen Cassedy conceded. "I guess we saw that some day everybody would want a union, but we also saw a long-standing need for an organization for random individuals."

The 9to5 leaders also sensed, correctly, that organized labor was not a friend of the women's movement. Some unions had constitutional provisions declaring opposition to discrimination by sex. But these ideals were more observed in the breach than in the practice, and male union leaders were as chauvinistic as men anywhere else. Many women office workers wanted no part of unions for other reasons. They had read and heard too much about corrupt union leaders, strikes and other kinds of strife, and they felt themselves above, or at least different from, industrial blue-collar workers. Adriana Nasch Stadecker, an MIT graduate student, interviewed women office workers in Boston for a 1976 doctoral dissertation, *9to5: Women Office Workers Interpret a Social Movement*. Many women, she writes, believed that they could "raise the consciousness" of male bosses on a one-to-one basis without union intervention. Others saw unions as "male-dominated bureaucracies." As Nussbaum put it, "We built an organization that we thought people like us would want to join."

Stadecker found that even those women who would be willing to join a union thought they would have to change its structure in some way to make it more responsive to women's concerns. When Nussbaum and Cassedy formed their Harvard discussion group in 1971, they were encountering the same problems as lab workers in the Medical Area: widespread discriminatory practices cemented in place by outdated sexist and elitist attitudes. Their jobs were regarded as "female jobs" which by tradition commanded lower salaries than male jobs that required equal, or much less, skill and ability. Women office workers wanted better pay, as well as improved benefits such as maternity leaves and day care programs. But these bread-and-butter issues constituted only part of the problem.

What fired up the women even more than the economic concerns was insulting male behavior, coupled with a myriad of discriminatory work practices, all of which added up to grossly unequal treatment. To male bosses and union leaders, many of the complaints in this category seemed petty and insignificant. One incident would always stick in Nussbaum's memory as representative of the type. It occurred one day when she worked in an office at the Harvard School of Education.

"I had no work space of my own, and so I was working in the hall, putting together notebooks for a committee meeting. I had work all over the place. I was trying to keep track of it, and a male professor came by and said, 'Why aren't you smiling?' It was that kind of stuff that just drove us wild. I felt that I was a professional, not an 'office wife,' which was kind of the language that we used at the time."

Management took the attitude, how could Harvard secretaries possibly complain about such trivial items? After all, their jobs posed no threat to life or limb or kept them in chains. They worked in pleasant surroundings with very bright people. What more could they want? For one thing, the women would reply, they wanted recognition that they also were bright people, despite being *only* secretaries. They had brains and wanted to use them. They *didn't* want to be expected to keep the boss's coffee cup filled, or to run to the photocopier every time someone brought a single piece of paper to be copied. In those early days, the Harvard secretaries thought, naively, that the women's movement would alight upon Harvard and magically transform the university into a place that actually practiced gender equality in the workplace while teaching it in the lecture halls.

When the secretaries began signing petitions and demanding action, they learned where the real sources of control lay in workplace relations. The first lesson came in 1971 when five secretaries in a research center at the School of Education sent a memo to management listing all the "trivial" things they wanted changed. They emphasized that secretaries should be able to control the flow of work to avoid duplication and to adapt old procedures to new circumstances. As an afterthought, the women mentioned that a salary increase would be nice, too. It was the afterthought that the director picked up on, Nussbaum recalled. He granted them a $1,000 raise, buying off the secretaries to retain control of the work process. The women took the money and abandoned the other ideas. "They felt defeated," Nussbaum said. "They had no concept of a larger movement and longer struggle."

When Nussbaum and Cassedy, as 9to5 organizers, began advising workers in other industries, they ran into the same obstacle. Although the pay issue was important everywhere, the real battles—in a sense, the entire war—would be fought over work practices and procedures and the trivia of discrimination embedded in them. How work was organized, job descriptions and classifications, job postings for promotion and transfers, training for higher level skills, and grievance procedures became the crucial issues. "We thought," Cassedy said, "that the last thing employers would be willing to give was money. We thought we'd be able to get all these less important, symbolic things, like job descriptions, job posting and things like that. But when we showed up at the door, they immediately threw money at us. It was the power that they didn't want to give up. The ongoing involvement in employment decisions—that was the most threatening thing as employers saw it."

Without a voice in workplace decisions women could not root out discrimination as they knew it. Even if a company had a grievance procedure (few nonunion employers did), the machinery did not recognize most complaints about sexist practices as *real* grievances. A real grievance involved being fired without cause or being unfairly passed over for promotion. Few employers in any sector—university, industry, or government—understood or gave heed to the family of grievance that came to the fore with the women's movement.

Yet, ironically, it was a management official, at MIT, Mary P. Rowe, who first developed ways of handling women's special concerns. As special assistant to the president and chancellor of MIT, starting in 1973, Rowe headed an office called "Women at Work." Though not a union organizer or the leader of a group like 9to5, Mary Rowe was one of many Boston women—Mary Howell at Harvard Medical School was another—who in the early seventies began forging crucial links between the women's movement and the workplace. The holder of a Ph.D. in economics, Rowe had had wide experience in human relations. She had worked with refugee groups in Europe during the fifties and later with women's groups in Cambridge as an expert on day care programs. When feminists at MIT urged appointment of a senior female administrator, Rowe got the job.

In her role as ombudsperson, investigating and resolving employee complaints at MIT, Rowe perceived that the problems experienced by women in white-collar jobs could not be resolved by applying rigid bureaucratic rules. Everything had to be open to change with the involvement of employees, including the structure of jobs and management style. She discovered, in interviews with hundreds of employees, that women were exposed to various degrees of sexism ranging from unconscious slights to conscious harassment to deranged behavior and illegal acts of discrimination.

Illegal acts were relatively easy to deal with since they were, in legal terms, actionable. But no good mechanism existed for resolving complaints in the first three categories, which occurred daily, in unlimited numbers, and were of infinite variety. These constituted what she came to call the "minutiae of sexism." Rowe identified this family of problem in a paper published in 1973. One of the most common of the unconscious slights involved the "invisible secretary" problem. Women workers could be invisible to bosses, co-workers, even customers in the same way that Ralph Ellison described his hero's plight in *Invisible Man*: "I am invisible, understand, simply because people refuse to see me."

Rowe remembered in particular a black female secretary who disliked her job because it was *cold*. She had no specific complaint about a supervisor or co-worker but said that everything connected with her job was . . . *cold*. Rowe asked her to keep a log of everything that anyone said to her over the course of a month. "She came back at the end of a month with an empty notebook," Rowe said. "Nobody had spoken to her. They would put jobs in her in-basket, take jobs out of her out-basket, write her notes. But nobody spoke to her. She was the only woman and the only black person in the lab. Racism and sexism. Cold."

The two devised a plot. The secretary would speak cheerfully to everybody who came into her office. She would put flowers and photographs of her children on her desk. The plan worked, though it took a while. The men in the lab began speaking to her. Eventually they hired two more black women.

Rowe came across countless problems in this category, problems that could not be resolved by resorting to personnel rules or grievance procedures. Each case had to be treated individually, with the involvement of the worker, supervisor, and sometimes co-workers. The organization of work frequently had to be altered, and Rowe had authority from top-level management to negotiate such changes. She eventually formulated a general theory of sorts out of her practical experiences as ombudsperson. Any minority in a workplace, not just women, was subject to subtle discrimination. There also existed a "minutiae of racism" and "minutiae of anti-Semitism." She later used a more general term. "Microinequities," Rowe says in a 1990 paper, "are fiendishly efficient in perpetuating unequal opportunity, because they are in the air we breathe, in the books we read, in the television we all watch, and because we cannot change the personal characteristic that leads to the inequity." This kind of discrimination, she continues, "is now, in most workplaces, the principal scaffolding for segregation in the United States, the framework for discrimination against everyone who is obviously 'different' from the person making decisions about whatever is the matter at hand."

In 1973 the term microinequities had not been invented, the "minutiae of sexism" concept was unknown to corporate personnel offices, and it was a rare employer who had a Mary Rowe in a position to make change happen. Yet Mary Howell and Leslie Sullivan in the Medical Area, and Nussbaum and Cassedy at the Harvard School of Education, had all cited examples of subtle but vicious discrimination. The question was, what to do about it. They had no Mary Rowe to appeal to.

After about a year or so of working for 9to5, Cassedy and Nussbaum gradually came to the conclusion that they were stirring up a lot of excitement without producing much real change in the workplace. "We had this tremendous power in ideas of women's equality and no institutional framework for it," Nussbaum said. "It wasn't until 1974 that we began to realize that we could take people through repeated campaigns, winning this or winning that, and still never change power relationships in the workplace. It occurred to us that there should be a law that allows workers to bargain over these things. And then we realized there was a law, the labor law." In this account, Nussbaum exaggerated the group's naivete for effect; 9to5 leaders did not suddenly discover the existence of labor law, but they did realize that without the bargaining leverage of a union their movement had reached a dead end. They began searching for a national union that might be interested in forming an alliance with 9to5.

In the Harvard Medical Area, meanwhile, Leslie Sullivan also had come to a dead end.

National and international events overshadowed doings at Harvard that fall. America's attention was focused on a foreign cartel named OPEC, a confirmed enemy of the people, and on a home-grown suspected villain, the President of the United States, Richard Nixon. The latter stood accused of concealing the White House's involvement in a burglary of Democratic Party headquarters, the so-called Watergate affair. He appeared well on the road to impeachment.

OPEC was an organization run by a group of oil-producing Arab nations. To punish the infidel Western world, they raised prices on their precious oil and slowed shipments to a trickle. In the United States, many service stations closed down and others sold gasoline only sporadically. When they opened, motorists would form blocks-long queues. The duty of sitting in line fell to those whose time was deemed least valuable to society, namely wives, secretaries, and a goodly number of Harvard research assistants.

Not Leslie Sullivan. In the biological world, many creatures possess a physical feature—a brilliant color, or set of spiny scales—that warns off predators. Something about Sullivan, her demeanor perhaps or the prominent cheekbones on her Irish face, performed a similar warning function for male professors: None of them asked or ordered *her* to tend a fuel-starved car in a gas line. She felt a sense of outrage nonetheless, knowing of several women who had to do such a thing. You didn't have to be a radical feminist to want to reform this system.

But she saw no hope. The marvelous energy and promise of last spring had been smothered in the somber deliberations of the Committee on the Status of Women. The committee might do good work for faculty women and students, Sullivan thought, but for employees it was a sham. She refused to pretend that working women really had a strong, independent voice on a committee that existed at the pleasure of the administration. Sullivan began thinking again of looking for another job. And then, quite unexpectedly, she made a new friend, thanks to Mary Howell.

Sullivan and Howell had gotten on well during the formative days of the women's committees. One day in November, Howell introduced her administrative assistant, a young woman named Deborah Hiatt, to Sullivan. The two struck it off and began eating lunch together or taking noontime walks. They talked constantly about women and work in general and what could be done to change matters at Harvard.

A recent graduate of Macalester College, where she was involved in the women's movement, Hiatt applied for a job as Mary Howell's assistant because she knew of Howell's writings about women in medicine. It so happened that her father, Howard N. Hiatt, was dean of the Harvard School of Public Health. But she got the job on her own. Harvard always had openings for young women. "I didn't come to Harvard Medical School because it was Harvard Medical School," Deborah Hiatt said. "I came because it was Mary Howell."

What Hiatt observed in Harvard's administrative offices both fascinated and repelled her. "A lot of women had been working for their bosses for a long time, and a certain amount of pride in what the women did came from the successes of the men they worked for. I think most of the women that had that kind of relationship would say that they liked it. And Harvard encouraged the idea that you were lucky to work for Harvard, no matter what your job was, or how much you got paid, or how you got treated."

Young and idealistic, Hiatt offered to enlist in the work that Sullivan had started the previous spring. She was impressed by Sullivan's knowledge of the Medical Area and her ability to organize a committee and distribute a newsletter. That was the key to any movement—communicating with women, making each aware that hundreds of other women had the same vital interest in improving their lives at work. Hiatt urged Sullivan to return to the crusade.

Sullivan was reluctant. "I wasn't sure I wanted to stay at Harvard," she said. "I wasn't sure that I wanted to put so much energy into it." But Hiatt's enthusiasm forced her toward a decision that she had been putting off. "I felt at that point," Sullivan said, "that a union was the only way to go." Not that she knew much about unions. Her mother always spoke well of her teacher's union, but Sullivan had no idea how a union operated. Instinct told her one thing: a union could act independently of the administration.

One day, as they chatted in Hiatt's office, Hiatt pressed the point with particular insistence. Why didn't they just do it, whatever they had to do—form a committee or put out a newsletter . . . whatever?

"Well," Sullivan remembered saying, "after all this time and all the mistakes we've made, I know how to do it. But I'm not sure I want to do it."

"I don't know how to do it," Hiatt said, "but I really want to do it." She paused. "Why don't we just give it one good try?"

Sullivan laughed. "Okay, we'll give it one good try."

At the beginning there were just the two of them, Leslie Sullivan, the disaffected research assistant, and Deborah Hiatt, the idealistic daughter of a Harvard dean. They started a union drive. Sullivan, at least, thought of it as a union drive. Hiatt viewed it more as a women's movement. In any case, their first objective was to rejuvenate last spring's network of women workers.

They put out a one-page newsletter under the name of the now-defunct Harvard Medical Area Women's Group. "Vol. 2, No. 1," of S&W News appeared in mid-December 1973, pretending to be a natural sequel to the old newsletter. It contained no mention of "union" and merely summarized the work of the old women's group. Referring to women workers, the newsletter said, "The common feeling that we have no recourse—that there is nothing we can do but tolerate bad situations (or leave)—is simply untrue. We can effect changes if we are willing to work for them."

Sullivan and Hiatt recruited a few other women and began assembling an organization. In the first three weeks of January 1974, they put out two more issues of *S&W News*, each slightly more militant in tone than the previous one. The word "union" had yet to appear. The Harvard administration was not evil, merely ignorant, *S&W News* suggested, in that it had failed to regulate its own workplace with comprehensive personnel policies. Pay raises, promotion, action on grievances—all depended on "your boss's benevolence," the newsletter said, adding: "In regard to working conditions the employee's dependence upon her boss's benevolence is even more pronounced. If you don't wish to bring your boss his coffee and wash his cups, you can refuse—or can you?"

The newsletter spoke of trends in the national women's movement and noted the formation of 9to5. "Women workers are standing up for their rights all over the country," declared the issue of January 18. "Even more exciting, in many cases, they are winning." All advocate groups exaggerate, and this amounted to extreme exaggeration. Apart from a few well-publicized lawsuits over discrimination, women were not winning many victories in the workplace.

Nonetheless, women in the Harvard Medical Area began responding to the promise of change. On January 23, about seventy-five employees, including a few men, met in an amphitheater classroom during lunch break. For the first time in a public forum, Sullivan posed the idea of "unionization as a possible solution." The audience didn't bring down the rafters with demands for a union. It was decided that the leaders should find out more about unions and labor laws.

You couldn't live in Boston for long and not learn something about organized labor merely by absorbing city life. Boston was a citadel of unionism on a par with Pittsburgh, Chicago, and New York. Well over half of all blue-collar workers in the city belonged to unions—municipal unions, state employee unions, construction unions, factory unions, transportation unions, hospital unions. As a consequence, unions were always in newspapers and on TV. But the media, preoccupied as usual with consequences rather than causes, tended to portray organized labor as doing little else than demanding huge pay raises, negotiating, striking, protesting, and being investigated for corruption.

Boston also had a thriving community of labor consultants, law firms, academic experts, and even spiritual advisers. Many church groups supported organized labor (or at least the process of collective bargaining), and none more strongly than the Roman Catholic Archdiocese of Boston. An arm of the Archdiocese, the Boston Labor Guild, for years had offered evening courses in industrial relations taught by professionals. Sullivan and two other Harvard women enrolled in such a course early in 1974.

At the same time the women continued recruiting workers in the Medical Area. By the middle of February, they had formed a "core committee" later named the Harvard Medical Area Employee Organizing Committee. A tightly knit group that eventually had about twenty members, it met weekly under rotating chairpersons and made all decisions by consensus. The presence of one or two men at the early meetings did not change the committee's orientation toward women's issues as reflected in the views of Sullivan and Hiatt. Both thought of themselves as feminists, but they avoided characterizing their movement as "feminist," knowing that the term carried many shades of meaning.

"I was a feminist, but I would not use the word 'militant,'" Deborah Hiatt said later. "I read articles now [1993] about women who think the term is synonymous with hating men. That is not what it meant to me. I believed that women were not being treated as equals in this society. My philosophy was the women's movement first. Leslie's ideology was union first. She was more of a pragmatic union organizer than I was."

Sullivan agreed with this distinction. "Deborah," she recalled, "was coming at it more from a women's consciousness point of view than I was. For me it had a practical side. I just felt we were treated unfairly, and I wanted to make a practical move to change things."

In a sense it was a perfect fusing: a strong feminist viewpoint welded to a very pragmatic goal of creating an organization that could deal with down-to-earth workplace problems. Coming together from various workplaces in the Medical Area, the first women members found that most had to put up with daily indignities, such as taking the boss's shirts to the laundry or gassing up his car. Few had Sullivan's ability to just say "no" to such demands. The women talked often about these things in the early meetings.

"It was a kind of group therapy," remembered Marlene Goldman, who joined the core committee in the spring. "By talking about it, we would learn to say, 'No, I'm not going to do that today.' At first it was a joke. You know, 'Get your own coffee.' It soon became something that you wanted to say."

The next step, and the most difficult one, was selecting a national union to affiliate with. The Harvard group needed money, professional organizing guidance, and paid legal help (not just advice) to go up against

Harvard University. But they had to be discriminating in their choice because, as Hiatt pointed out, "Just saying the word 'union' was a daring thing in our environment and would turn off a lot of women." The union they chose must be democratic, honest, clean, and knowledgeable about working women. Searching for such a creature would be like advertising in the personal columns for a strong, sensitive-to-women's-issues mate interested in having a long-term relationship. Even with a hundred-plus unions affiliated at the time with the AFL-CIO, the pickings were slim. Other groups of women were running into the same problem. When Ellen Cassedy of 9to5 asked an official of the Office and Professional Employees International Union for help in organizing women office workers, he said, "Great idea! If I could get a girl in here to do my typing, I'd be out there with you." And Karen Nussbaum remembered a Teamsters leader in Boston who growled at a 9to5 leader, "You can't organize women. They think with their cunts, not their brains."

Sullivan and Hiatt set off on a union search with only a vague definition. They wanted a union that knew "how to organize women workers in service or office occupations." Did this mean using special techniques that appealed to the female psyche? No. Nothing so sophisticated (or improbable) had crossed their minds. They simply assumed that any union with a significant female membership must be sensitive to women's concerns. The Service Employees International Union (SEIU) and District 1199, both of which represented women in health care institutions, leapt to mind. But they were locked in a nasty jurisdictional battle involving Boston-area hospitals. Sullivan and Hiatt crossed them off the list.

They found an intriguing lead in a *Ms.* article published in 1973—during *Ms.*'s early days, before it lost interest in the unglamorous world of ordinary working women. The author, Margie Albert, a union organizer and former secretary, described the choices facing women workers in a realistic way. Women's organizations, she noted, were pushing a narrow workplace policy aimed at getting women into top-level corporate positions. But most women workers neither had much chance of advancing into managerial ranks nor really wanted to. The women's movement, Albert wrote, "can work for secretaries, too. By uniting on the job for our mutual benefit, we will move up—but it will be up with our sisters, not up from them."

The moment they read her piece Sullivan and Hiatt became potential disciples. They got in touch with Albert in New York City, where she worked for a union known as District 65. On February 11 she came to Boston and spoke to a group of Medical Area employees.

In the late sixties, Albert had organized one of the earliest unions of female office workers, about twenty women in her New York law office. Later it had affiliated with District 65, the Distributive Workers of America. At Harvard, Albert spoke with detailed knowledge of social relations in an office staffed with women but controlled by men. Then in her forties, she radiated a warmth and experience that captivated the younger women. Twenty years later, long after that unexpectedly brief association and long after Albert had died of cancer, Sullivan remained captivated. "Margie Albert," she said, "was a great woman."

To find out more about District 65, the committee sent a small delegation headed by Sullivan to New York in early March. The union owned a handsome, eleven-story stone building on Astor Place on the edge of Greenwich Village. The entrance way had a charming art deco facade with a sign on a marquee proclaiming "District 65" in a bright, always-lit electric sign. Most of the building was given over to the welfare of District 65 members. In addition to staff offices, it contained meeting rooms, a large area for social events, an oldtime "hiring hall" where members reported for job referrals, a bar, credit union, dental clinic, pharmacy, and offices for legal aid and vocational services.

"I was pretty impressed," Sullivan said, "that they had this huge building with so many services for their members. And they made a big point of telling you all they had." What she learned of the history of District 65 also impressed Sullivan.

From its founding in 1933 on Manhattan's lower East Side, the union grew as a polyglot, welcoming all comers regardless of race and occupation. Jewish dry goods workers, who formed the original core, merged with groups of shoe salesmen and textile workers. This union became Local 65 of a CIO organizing committee in the mid-thirties, and the name stayed with the core of the union as it went through an amazing number of transformations, mergers, affiliations, disaffiliations, and reaffiliations into the fifties. In 1954, it became part (for a second time) of a large national union, the Retail, Wholesale and Department Store Union (RWDSU), where it became known as District 65. From its beginnings, 65 had ties with the Communist Party (as did many unions at the time) but broke with the Party in the early fifties.

At various times District 65 included department store clerks, gas and chemical workers, and agricultural employees as well as the original dry goods workers. But at no time did it represent a significant segment of any one industry, like únions in steel or autos or newer ones in health care. Lacking such a base, it never grew into a national union or received much recognition outside of New York City. But it was unusual in a number of respects, including its leadership.

By the 1960s, one of the original organizers of 65's textile section, David Livingston, had emerged as president. He was an extraordinary man, both in his strengths and weaknesses. More than most union leaders in the affluent fifties and sixties, he understood the need to organize new workers on a continuous basis, and he hired many talented organizers. Under Livingston's bold, quirky leadership, District 65 had grown to about thirty-five thousand members, mostly in New York City and New Jersey, by the seventies. It was a pariah in the American labor movement but a darling of the political left. In 1968, it became the first union (and ultimately one of the few) to oppose publicly the Vietnam War. A year earlier, the union had pulled out of the AFL-CIO, following the lead of Walter Reuther's United Auto Workers. Reuther criticized the federation's hard-line stance in foreign affairs and its timidity in organizing workers at home.

These actions earned District 65 a reputation of being "democratic" and "progressive" in the leftist political lexicon, which meant that Livingston took positions on external issues that pleased the left. What went on inside the union was a different matter. In its first thirty years, 65 was a shining exemplar of vibrant, shop-floor democracy. It developed a system which encouraged rank-and-file participation through strong shop stewards in every plant, warehouse, and office. The stewards, in turn, vented their members' concerns in a monthly meeting of the General Council presided over by Livingston. The union provided for members' welfare through a variety of programs and activities headquartered in the building on Astor Place. There were meetings every night, programs for children on Saturday mornings, and dances for adults on Saturday nights in the union's "night club."

"That building was rocking seven days and nights every week," recalled Moe Foner, a former District 65 staff member and well-known unionist in New York for half a century. Foner directed publicity for District 1199 during its rise to prominence as a hospital union. In 1995, he still served as director of its acclaimed cultural affairs program, "Bread and Roses." He worked for District 65 in 1949–50, at a time when the union played a central role in most members' lives. "I never knew another union that could mobilize its members the way 65 did," he said. "It was a model of democracy in those years and the most effective and unusual union that existed in the labor movement at that time."

The union pioneered in negotiating for medical and hospital benefits, establishing a "cradle-to-grave" program as early as 1945. Named the District 65 Security Plan, it was a self-insured plan financed by employers who contributed a percentage of payroll to a central fund. The union itself administered the plan from offices that occupied an entire floor in the building on Astor Place. Long before unions in other industries won limited coverage under Blue Cross and Blue Shield, District 65 provided fully-paid medical and hospital benefits to members and retirees. It was a wonderful scheme for a relatively simple era of low-cost health care. Livingston regarded it as 65's crowning achievement. It would become, unfortunately, too heavy for the wearer, a crown that toppled a kingdom.

Livingston, Foner said, was "a brilliant tactician" (many former associates used the adjective "brilliant" in describing him). An open-minded man who personified the "social justice" side of unionism, he believed that unions should embrace all workers without regard to race or sex. From the 1940s on, District 65 opened its arms to black workers and employees in small shops usually ignored by other unions. Cleveland Robinson, a black organizer who rose to secretary-treasurer, one of three top offices in 65, was an authentic hero of the civil rights movement and a close associate of Martin Luther King.

But Livingston had a fatal weakness. A dictatorial leader, he surrounded himself with sycophantic "yes" men and allowed the democratic structure of the union to deteriorate. Cliques developed in secondary leadership tiers, preventing the rise of fresh talent from the ranks. Personally, Livingston was difficult to get along with. In dealing with staff members, Foner said, "he would cut you to pieces in front of other people. He had a wicked thing in him." Other associates recalled this behavior. "David did not like people to disagree with him," said Eugene Eisner, who served as general counsel of the union for thirty years.

But the deterioration was not evident in the early seventies. This is when Livingston's vision might have turned the union around if the structure had not decayed. By then, organizing opportunities in the largely male, blue-collar industrial world seemed to be vanishing. When corporations built new plants, they located them in the nonunion South and Southwest. The growth of manufacturing jobs had slowed almost to a stop, while employment in the service industries—what everyone thought of as "female jobs"—expanded at a fast rate. Union leaders knew of this change, but most assumed that women either could not be organized or would not make good union members.

Livingston, however, hired several women and began organizing women office workers in publishing houses, book stores, and colleges and universities. He put Margie Albert in charge of a publishing industry drive. At about the same time, Leslie Sullivan made her decision. She wanted to be part of 65, and she wanted to work with Albert.

Young people who migrate to social activism are by definition impressionable: all ships appear seaworthy if they're headed in the right direction. This was especially true for the generation of the sixties, which had been weaned on gratifying hopes of instant reform and easy revolution. When you are young, you believe in your ability to distinguish the real thing from the impostor even if both fly the same flag, not understanding that all human organizations are a bit of both, impostor and real thing.

As she later admitted, Sullivan wanted to jump on a fast boat to union organization. She liked District 65's diverse membership, its leftist political stance, and its opposition to the Vietnam War. Although the shooting was over by 1974, the ideals of war resistance remained strong. Perhaps most important to Sullivan and her friends, District 65 had Margie Albert.

With the agreement of her committee, Sullivan began negotiating with the union. She made only two demands, that District 65 allow the Harvard women freedom to conduct their own affairs and that it hire a full-time organizer from within the organizing committee. The obvious candidate, of course, was Sullivan herself.

To Sullivan's disappointment, a male organizer, not Margie Albert, came to negotiate the agreement. "They sent us Herman [fictitious name] who would 'yes' you to death," Sullivan said. "He was very slippery." Herman agreed to her conditions but refused to put anything in writing. This worried her, but she pushed the concerns to the back of her mind. "District 65 was all we had at that time . . . and I wanted to do it so badly."

CHAPTER FIVE

*E*ven for a Boston end-of-winter, Tuesday, March 19, 1974 was extraordinarily chilly. Early that morning, Sullivan, Hiatt, and about twenty other activists stationed themselves at all entrances to the Medical Area on Longwood Ave., at Brigham Circle, and on Huntington Ave. As their ears turned pink in a frigid wind, they passed out leaflets to Medical Area employees arriving for work. Barely a month and a half after its first open meeting, the Harvard organizing committee was proclaiming its existence.

This was traditional organizing. You developed a core of support, handed out leaflets and flyers, and asked workers to sign union authorization cards. With cards signed by 30 percent of employees, the union could petition the NLRB for a representation election. There was some danger in this approach. Giving out campaign literature was like revealing a sniper's position to the enemy, the employer. Much later, the Harvard union would reassess this tactic. But in that first campaign, in all innocence, the women followed accepted practice.

Antiwar sentiment had whetted a hunger for writings critical of established authority, and Medical Area people snapped up whatever was handed to them. Reading the leaflet, they encountered a style more akin to scholarly discourse than to hard-hitting pamphleteering. It began with a long excerpt from a 1937 Supreme Court decision upholding the law that gave workers the right to form unions (National Labor Relations Act). Labor unions, the court said, arose because "a single employee was helpless in dealing with an employer." The leaflet concluded, "We believe a union at Harvard Medical Area is not only necessary, but possible." This come-reason-with-us style contrasted with the slam-bang attacks on employers that were traditional in union organizing.

The tenor of the campaign changed dramatically on May 2 when Sullivan and her group hit the street with Leaflet No. 5. By then Sullivan and Herman had come to an agreement on affiliation. "District 65 Is Our Choice!" declared the headline. Through the magic of mimeograph, the amateur Medical Area Employees Organizing Committee had metamorphosed into a real union. But even after affiliation, there were two distinct bodies. One was the local union, which the women called "Medical Area 65" and which for the most part ran its own affairs and made its own decisions. The second body was the national union, District 65, which paid for organizing expenses (up to a point) and proffered advice (good and bad) but otherwise maintained a remote presence. In ensuing months Harvard administrators would try to blur this distinction with misleading statements. From their version one might think that District 65 agents, operating out of a foreign territory called New York, had parachuted into the Medical Area and subverted innocent, Harvard-loving employees.

The passing out of lapel buttons put the final stamp of authenticity on this new union. In crimson letters on a white background were the words "We Can't Eat Prestige." No one could remember where the phrase originated. A saying embodying this sentiment, perhaps with slightly different wording, had been floating around Harvard for some years. Sullivan and other committee members talked it over, trying different words, and used the phrase for the first time in their February 6 newsletter. It caught on, not surprisingly, given its expression of a literal and symbolic truth, and the committee decided to make it their official slogan.

On May 14, *The Harvard Crimson* published the first news account of the union activity. Quoting a Harvard official, it reported that the university would oppose a union representing workers only in the Medical Area. Harvard contended that the union should be university-wide, not that it *wanted* to deal with a union covering the entire support staff. University officials thought it would be nearly impossible to organize on two geographically separated campuses at the same time.

One thing lacking, from Sullivan's point of view, was the advice of an experienced woman organizer, specifically Margie Albert. Sullivan couldn't understand, never would understand completely, why the union would not delegate Albert to supervise the Harvard drive. Although Sullivan saw her from time to time on trips to New York, the older woman—who had so captivated the young women of Harvard and who had been the main reason they chose District 65—never returned to Harvard as an organizer. "We kept asking for her, but they wouldn't send her," Sullivan said.

For the women of Harvard, however, there was reason to celebrate. They now had support from a bonafide union, a source of funds (however limited), an engaging slogan, a send-off of positive publicity, and a cause worth fighting for.

Meanwhile, what was going through the minds of university officials as they contemplated the beginnings of a union campaign? Sullivan and her friends, gazing up at the executive-level windows in Building A, could only speculate. They could assume that a group of deans and administrators, sitting in conference room chairs embossed with the ancient Harvard motto *Veritas*, had engaged in a collegial discussion and arrived at a knowledgeable, reasoned decision on how to respond to the union phenomenon.

One of the most famous human skulls in U.S. medical history sat in a display case on a fifth-floor gallery overlooking the main hall of Building A. It had belonged to one Phineas P. Gage of Cavendish, Vermont. In the fall of 1848 Gage had the misfortune to be standing over a drill hole, tamping down a charge of blasting powder, when the charge exploded. The tamping bar, two feet long and a quarter-inch thick, shot straight up through his head, entering under the left jaw and exiting over the right forehead. A physician applied balms and dressings, observing the wound through the aperture at each end. A hearty man of twenty-five, Gage recovered within a few months, appearing none the worse for the spearing. For years he earned a living driving a coach and exhibiting himself to curious audiences.

Baffled experts questioned how Gage could function with a hole in his brain. Although he became "fitful, vacillating, obstinate and profane" and died of a "fit" in 1861, he had retained speech, memory, and motor skills for many years. Anatomists began rethinking prevailing assumptions about the structure of the brain. In due course they discovered that different regions of the organ controlled different functions and emotions.

For several generations, the display of Gage's skull and tamping bar had amused, informed, and puzzled medical students. It also illustrated the need to be humble in the face of biological mysteries. Humility forces you to explore the causes of a phenomenon, rather than merely accept unproved assumptions. Medical science, and Harvard Medical School, had thrived on this belief in the scientific method, and humanity has been all the better for it.

But social phenomena such as union activity did not provoke an equal exploratory fervor on Harvard's part. Authorities assumed they knew why the Medical Area women were acting so rebelliously. It was easily explained: a misbehaving boss or two, a moderate pay schedule (perhaps even a bit on the low side), the frustrations of overqualified lab assistants. Put these elements in a pile, soak with feminist anger, toss in a fiery union organizer from New York . . . poof! There was no need to look closer at the causes or to question what kind of union the women wished to form—that is, how it would behave if Harvard granted recognition. All unions behaved the same, didn't they?

Medical Area administrators did what American management generally does when workers talk of organizing. They called in the lawyers. Not that this proceeded from choosing between many options. By this time in the history of labor–management relations in the United States, it was an automatic, pragmatic response conditioned by decades of making assumptions about how to prevent workers from behaving in their own interests. How could salary and wage workers even know what their best interests were?

Almost from the moment Sullivan spoke aloud the word "union" at the open meeting on January 23, Medical Area administrators had kept their deans informed about the nascent union drive. The deans maintained an official silence on the issue. Behind the scenes, however, "there was great consternation," recalled Howard H. Hiatt, then dean of the School of Public Health. Personnel officers and lawyers began scurrying about, writing memos and holding strategy sessions with the deans. The course of action was to speed up implementation of an antiunion policy adopted by the university in about 1970.

In that year, the National Labor Relations Board had asserted jurisdiction over the employees of private colleges and universities. (State-related university systems were covered by state laws.) At the time, few unions existed in the private institutions, with the minor exception of those representing handfuls of building trades and dining hall workers. The NLRB action set off scattered organizing efforts. Two brief, unpublicized attempts on Harvard's main campus in 1970–71 caused the university to reassess its personnel policies, according to Edward W. Powers, who then was associate director of personnel. Officials found that pay levels varied widely from school to school. "People were paid what their supervisor wanted to pay them," Powers said. "There were tremendous inequities, not only among the faculties, but within each faculty. We discovered a really horrendous situation." They saw that union organizing could erupt anywhere in the decentralized university over the salary issue. One or more unions might attack Harvard in several different areas, organizing it faculty by faculty. Powers and others designed and put in place a uniform salary program for the entire university.

But more had to be done. The administration wanted to avoid any unionization of clerical and technical workers, believing it would bring factory-type work rules into an academic setting. This presumption apparently led to the adoption of an antiunion policy by the Harvard Corporation, an entity like a board of directors which consists of the president and treasurer of Harvard and five other members known as fellows. Since the Corporation does not preserve a record of its deliberations, whether it did, in fact, establish the antiunion policy could not be verified. Daniel Steiner, who became Harvard's first general counsel, said he believed that the policy was in place when he took office in 1970. To carry it out, the university asked its outside law firm, Ropes, Gray, to explore ways of making the university immune to piecemeal union organizing. Its recommendations included administrative changes in the Medical Area.

Ordinarily, the deans of the Medical Area schools resisted incursions into their territory. Harvard, after all, operated in decentralized fashion, more so than any other university. In academic and financial matters, the deans of Harvard's professional and graduate schools captained their own vessels. Each school was supposed to finance its own operations through tuitions and fund raising, a tradition captured in an old saying, "every tub on its own bottom." First used by a Harvard president in the early nineteenth century, the expression was so idolized it might have been graven in Harvard brick. Even in the 1990s, people at Harvard actually went around saying, " 'every tub on its own bottom,' you know," in response to centralizing trends they disliked. For a hundred years, Harvard University had found this principle to be sound, sensible, and convenient, except of course when it was deemed inconvenient and therefore unsound. It would be most inconvenient to have "every tub on its own bottom, with its own union."

Dean Robert Ebert had raised the old battle cry of autonomy from the bridge of the Medical School as well as any dean at Harvard. Quite frankly, though, he was relieved to have union relations taken out of his hands. In his nine years at the helm, Ebert had had to deal with a great deal more social turmoil than he had signed on for. When he became dean in 1965, Harvard Medical School was a relatively sleepy place. Then came—not even in succession but all in a lump—the student free speech movement, the civil rights movement, the antiwar movement, the women's movement, and the mini-movement of the SDS (Students for a Democratic Society).

"This was a tough time," Ebert recalled. "I got a lot of harassment from students. Had my office occupied. They got out, but I had to meet with protesting students, the SDS. This whole thing [student revolts] spilled over onto the medical campus. They raised the Vietcong flag on the flagpole. I was kept pretty busy for a while. It was hairy in 1970."

Even before the political tumult, Ebert could not have been characterized as an unworldly academician. A graduate of the University of Chicago Medical School, he had served as a Marine Corps battalion surgeon in several South Pacific island invasions during World War II. As a surgeon and teacher at Case Western Reserve, Ebert began to espouse ideas that were anathema to most physicians, such as group medical practice, which in the sixties still had the taint of socialized medicine. He wanted to experiment with prepaid medical plans but ran into opposition on the Case medical faculty. Ebert then moved to Boston and Harvard Medical School.

"I knew Harvard was conservative," Ebert said, "but I also knew that Harvard wouldn't care what anybody else thought. They were too arrogant." With the help of the Harvard faculty, in 1969 he founded the Harvard Community Health Plan, a pioneering and highly successful prepaid medical plan based on the group practice concept.

When the union threat came along in 1974, Ebert had already fought a number of political and administrative battles over sociopolitical issues and didn't feel much like taking a strong position for or against. He didn't consider himself to be antiunion. As a student in Chicago during the thirties, he had seen the great surge of industrial unionism, had grown angry about the use of police against labor in the steel towns of the region. "My background as a sort of a liberal Democrat was to be sympathetic to unions," he said in 1994.

But as dean of the Medical School in 1974, Ebert presided over an antiunion policy. In his view, he was merely carrying out a decision by the Harvard Corporation. "The whole issue of unionization was up to, basically, the Corporation," he said. "And clearly, like any other big corporation, they didn't want a union. But I didn't align myself one way or another. Frankly, I stayed out of it, partly because it was a university matter and not mine." Ebert, however, did not stay completely out of it. As he conceded, letters opposing the union went to employees over his signature.

Only a good stone's throw west of Dean Ebert's office in Building A, Dean Howard Hiatt of the School of Public Health faced the question in quite a different light. Everybody knew that his daughter Deborah was one of the principal union organizers. Her name appeared on all the union literature and she could be seen passing out leaflets with the rest of them. He knew that she didn't feel entirely comfortable in a role that might embarrass him. On the other hand she had been brought up to act on principle. While he might have been embarrassed at first, more important was that his daughter was doing what she thought was right. In discussions with her about the need for a union, "she provided me with insights that I hadn't had previously," he recalled.

When Hiatt attended meetings during that time, "I saw my fellow deans sitting all around and imagined them to be looking at me with some discomfort," he said. "I'm sure they were. There I was in this highly suspect position and feeling rather proud of my daughter for what she had done or what she was in the process of doing."

Hiatt nonetheless had ambivalent feelings about unionism in a scientific institution. A 1948 graduate of Harvard Medical School, he spent much of his early career as a physician-scientist, working both in clinical practice and in research, specializing in molecular biology and biochemistry. Before becoming dean of Public Health in 1972, he had served as physician-in-chief of Beth Israel Hospital. In his research lab at Beth Israel, Hiatt worked with a principal technician, a woman whom he considered a colleague. She worked under his direction but contributed much in the way of technical expertise. She helped with his journal articles, and he made certain that she received a credit line. The two of them frequently had to work twelve-hour days to complete projects.

"If she was in the middle of the experiment at five o'clock," Hiatt said, "it wasn't a matter of my asking her not to leave at that time. She never would have asked to leave. The experiment was as much hers as mine." During slower periods, he encouraged her to take days off during the week to attend to personal matters. "Not only did I encourage it, but I was resentful if she had to get permission from some kind of personnel officer to do that."

Hiatt continued: "When you have that kind of a relationship with a colleague who technically is an employee, you're very apprehensive lest a union or for that matter a management enter with ground rules on working conditions that don't lend themselves to codification. Were there people who took advantage of this situation? Of course there were. I'm sure the relationships ranged from the most collegial to outrageous exploitation." The only way to control the bad actors (and his daughter assured him there were bad actors), he reluctantly concluded, was to have a strong management personnel policy, or a union.

Hiatt expressed his opinions in meetings with the Medical Area deans and Harvard President Derek Bok. When his view did not prevail, Hiatt said, "as a member of the administration I had two choices. One was to accept the university's position or, second, to resign. I couldn't in good conscience fight [the policy decision] from inside." He adopted a personal position of neutrality and put responsibility for union issues in the hands of an associate dean who kept him informed.

And so the antiunion policy was put in motion under the direction of Dan Steiner and his staff, working with personnel managers and administrative deans in the Medical Area. Ebert and Hiatt were not involved, but their noninvolvement was quite different in nature. Ebert did not disassociate himself personally from the policy but Hiatt did—and the women who organized the union would always remember him for this. Even so, Hiatt said in 1993, "When I look back, I wish I had been more, rather than less, vigorous in addressing these problems."

Not long after organizing started, Hiatt attended a meeting on the matter with the two other Medical Area deans, top-level administrators, and Harvard lawyers. Dan Steiner made a presentation, informing the Medical Area deans and managers how the university proposed to fight the union. He discussed the organizing effort in general terms and did not—perhaps in deference to Hiatt—name any of the employees who were leading the charge.

Hiatt then spoke, and later remembered his words. "I am appreciative," he said, "that none of the union organizers have been mentioned by name or dwelled upon individually." He smiled at his fellow deans and added, "Perhaps some of you feel that my daughter is at a confused stage in her life. Personally, I'm proud that she has been instrumental in bringing us together in this meeting."

Leslie Sullivan, union organizer—as of July 1 she went on the payroll of District 65 after quitting her Harvard job. One day she got out of bed and realized that she and George Meany were part of the same thing, this *organized labor*, which demanded above all else loyalty to the organization and its leaders. This gave her contrary feelings. When Meany, as head of the AFL-CIO, went in front of the TV cameras and urged that President Nixon be impeached, she was proud to be a part. When Meany, on the other hand, defended practices that kept women and blacks out of high union office, she was glad that District 65 had withdrawn from the federation.

But she was not happy with Herman, her union supervisor who traveled from New York to Boston a few times a month to look in on her activities. A man in his late fifties, Herman had no special knowledge of white-collar women's issues. Worse, said Sullivan, "He was very, very untrustworthy, and I tried to cover this up. I didn't want people to know how bad he was." One thing he did right, for whatever reason, was to stay out of the Harvard campaign. He never appeared on campus but met with Sullivan in an office she opened for District 65 in downtown Boston.

She could not understand how David Livingston could think of Harvard as a leading-edge campaign and send a hack like Herman to supervise it. It was also annoying that the union wouldn't give her a budget for the Harvard drive. She had to pay many expenses out of her own money and wait for reimbursement by the union, often for months. She gave only fleeting thought to these concerns during busy months in the summer and fall of 1974. By late summer Medical Area 65 had "signed up" about four hundred employees and set its sights on doubling that number before seeking an election. It had begun putting out a bimonthly newsletter, *Medical Area District 65 at Harvard*. The initial letters of the first three words were highlighted to emphasize an acronymic meaning, *MAD*. It was written in a lively, tongue-in-cheek style but, despite the acronym, did not contain derogatory material aimed at "polarizing" the work force into pro- and antiunion groups, as opponents charged.

With District 65 contributing only a distant muttering of advice, worker activists in Medical Area 65 did all the actual organizing. Decisions were made by a committee of about twenty members, of whom a smaller core group did most of the work. Deborah Hiatt left Harvard in the summer of 1974 to attend law school. There would be many such losses, to further schooling, or marriage, or motherhood, or other jobs. But a continuing supply of new employees brought new activists to the fore, overlapping with the old.

The first committee developed a distinct personality, or culture (to the limited extent that a small group can be said to possess a culture), which established a template for all that would follow. "It was a remarkable joint leadership," Sullivan said. "We were a group of people who worked together easily, who didn't feel particularly turf protective, who had no particular axe to grind. There was seldom any tension. Somehow we just clicked. It was unusual."

Marlene Goldman was a member of the core group. A twenty-five-year-old research assistant at the School of Public Health, she also was studying in a graduate program and eventually received a doctor's degree in epidemiology. She became a feminist and unionist because of her boss. "He was only an assistant professor," Goldman said in 1995, when she herself taught at the School of Public Health. "I don't consider that very powerful, being one now, but at the time he seemed a semi-God. He was a bastard, actually." He expected Goldman to get his coffee and lunch and go to his apartment and water his plants when he went out of town. "He might 'ask,' but you would not feel comfortable saying 'no.' When the power differential is like that, you sort of want to do it. But this was the least of our complaints. More important was having no say in anything that was decided." She thought that the civil rights movement of the 1960s inspired her group in fighting Harvard. "We didn't really know if we could [bring about change]. But we were young, and we felt we were entitled to try—and *that* came out of the sixties."

Of the first core group, political activism came most naturally to Edie Brickman. Her mother had been that rarest of all creatures, a white female civil rights worker in the South during the 1930s. A graduate of Boston University, Brickman went to work at Harvard in 1965 and got caught up in antiwar activities. Other members of the group were Karen Fischer, Janet Tice, Nancy Clifford, Paula Heckman, and Sue Torrey, each of whom threw herself into the effort for several months and then departed. Later arrivals included Barbara Costa, Kristin Mahon, and Jeanne Lafferty. The last two would be important figures in union efforts at Harvard for several years. Both became feminists and antiwar militants in the sixties and bounced around in jobs and leftist politics before coming to Harvard, where they discovered that the union movement provided more than endless debating and resolving.

Although the Harvard union drive drew its original inspiration from the women's movement, it lost its for-women-only allure within the first month. There could be no union without men, since men constituted 20 to 30 percent of the work force. In a relatively short period of time, the union converted itself from a pressure group riding on a powerful but narrow geyser of feminism to an organization of both sexes motivated by a sense of broader social injustice. A few men became leading activists, working on an equal footing with the women. The men came for varying reasons, including a desire to improve their own pay and working conditions, a belief in gender equality, and a belief in the labor movement as a progressive force. The prospect of working with a group of attractive young women also had a certain appeal. John Rees, a 1971 graduate of MIT, joined the union out of political conviction despite the fact that his job as computer programmer probably would be classified as "professional" and thus not part of a clerical bargaining unit. He belonged to the Socialist Workers Party, which in the early seventies was in a phase of building "mass movements" for social and political reform rather than engaging in narrow radical activity. Rees saw that the Harvard union was "clearly a women-dominated effort." But this didn't bother him. He and Sullivan eventually were married.

Drago Clifton, a German-born research assistant, grew up in Western Europe's postwar tradition of democratic socialism and simply believed that workers should belong to a union. Richard Pendleton, one of the few black employees in the Medical Area, worked in the basement bindery of Countway Library, one of the largest medical libraries in the nation. He wanted a strong union for two reasons, to halt the demeaning treatment of women and to goad the university into improving its own operations. Two men who came later were Jeremy Pool and Ross Schubarth.

Contrary to what some feminists might have expected from the history of groups like SDS, these men didn't attempt to take over the committee. They accepted female leadership. "The women's movement was in its insurgency," Rees said, "and it seemed proper for women to lead the union campaign."

Unlike many political groups, the union committee remained free of factional quibbling over the finer points of feminist or political theory. Once, in the very early days, a member wanted to change all "he's" to "she's," even in quotes extracted from books and articles. Sullivan and others rejected the idea of putting words into the mouths of long-dead authors. After that, the group avoided debates over such issues and concentrated on organizing. "We kept it very concrete," said Marlene Goldman.

"We had a goal of forming a union, and we each kept to the goal. We were not coming out of ideology." Recalled Kristin Mahon, "It was made clear when you joined the committee that 'we're here to work on the union. Any other political agenda you have, keep it outside.'"

Sullivan was the linchpin of the committee. "Leslie and her lists" is how they thought of her. She carried lists of everything: lists of employees to be organized, lists of committee members, lists of things to do, and lists of issues to be negotiated—when and if the union got in. She was fearless in approaching strangers, like new employees, and excellent at taking control of a meeting and explaining, in a "genuine, convincing way," what had to be done, as Jeremy Pool put it. Goldman said, "Leslie was a role model. She believed it was possible. And she was the strongest woman I had met. For me, knowing a strong woman was a big thing. I have become much more like that, but I wasn't like that then."

The committee had a great deal of fun being together, laughing and joking. This set a pattern of behavior that would last for years. Social lives, even love lives, centered on the committee. "It was a wonderful, wonderful time," Edie Brickman said, looking back on the mid-seventies. She remembered that Harvard administrators grumbled about the union's unexpected progress. "They were saying, 'How can these people do this, taking time off from their work.' They didn't realize, we just didn't sleep for three years." Success in organizing seemed to spill over to work in the lab. "Sometimes your experiments work and sometimes they don't," Brickman continued. "But during this period everybody's work was fabulous. All our experiments worked fantastically well."

By chance, fortune, or predestined fate, Kris Rondeau entered the world of working women at the very gates of Harvard University. In the summer of 1974, after graduating from Windham College, she moved to Cambridge and began looking for a job in the Boston area. She and her college boyfriend, who had enrolled in a graduate school at Harvard, settled into an apartment on Mt. Auburn St., two blocks from Harvard Yard. For several months, she made do with temporary jobs, answering telephones or running switchboards. During her off-hours she took college extension courses in physiology and biology. She still had thoughts of becoming a doctor.

During her first years out of college, she learned much more about urban living than about career and work. She enjoyed living in Cambridge with its odd mixture of Puritan tradition, historical ambiance, and New Deal liberalism. It was a place where people danced in the streets when Nixon resigned the Presidency. There was white male elitism, it was true, but also a tolerance for racial and ethnic diversity and a belief in the importance of education. "I had assumed I was a country girl," Rondeau said, "but I discovered right away, living in Cambridge, that I really was a city girl. I loved everything about it." City life gave her access to museums, art galleries, libraries, places of historical importance, and 24-hour convenience stores and movie houses. In her free time she often took long walks through the city, five to seven miles, sometimes along the Charles River but more often along streets that ran through many neighborhoods so that she could observe different ways of life. Except for scientific subjects, her reading ran to fiction and some poetry. Her favorite novelist was Dickens, her favorite poet W. B. Yeats.

In 1975 Rondeau landed a job with the U.S. Department of Labor in Boston. Her office administered a compensation program for government employees injured on the job. It was mainly a clerical job, but she learned valuable lessons about work and health and especially about psychological stress. By the mid-seventies, the effects of race and sex discrimination at work were beginning to dominate claims for stress-related illness. "A person would be harassed on the job, like the first woman postal worker in such and such a town," Rondeau said. "And she would just be treated so badly that eventually she would crack and they would pay her to go out on disability."

In the spring of 1976, Rondeau saw a want ad for lab assistants at Harvard Medical School. She immediately applied. She had no idea that deep in the recesses of that marble edifice there seethed anger and resentment and a silent clash of interests that had degenerated into a year-long legal battle.

CHAPTER SIX

In the year 1783, at the prompting of faculty members who had served in the Revolutionary War, Harvard College established a department of anatomy and medicine. The war had stimulated great interest in new medicinal and, especially, surgical methods. Many a maimed soldier and sailor would not have returned alive but for a valiant hacking and hewing of limb under fire by courageous surgeons. The first chairman of the new department, himself a former war surgeon, conducted classes at dissecting tables set up in an unused chapel in Harvard Yard. As the number of students grew, the community of Cambridge was hard pressed to provide an adequate number of sick, dying and dead on which to practice. The great hospitals of Boston offering an unlimited supply of the necessary, Harvard professors and medical students began traveling to those places in pursuit of learning. Within a short time, a not insignificant part of each day was spent on horseback, crossing and recrossing the Charles River. Finally, in 1810, the professors packed up their instruments and skeletons and moved the entire Harvard Medical School to Boston, where it thereafter remained in various locations. School officials could not foresee, of course, that this logistically-correct decision would give rise, nearly two hundred years later, to elaborate legal proceedings under a then-unknown branch of the law dealing with a then-unknown entity called a labor union.

Richard Levy would always remember the first morning of the National Labor Relations Board hearings in Boston. It was Monday, March 17, 1975. He and Leslie Sullivan arrived early and took seats at the union's table in the hearing room. In the rows behind them sat about a dozen union members wearing "We Can't Eat Prestige" buttons. When Harvard's legal team filed into the room, Levy could only think of the journalistic term "battery of lawyers." First came the attorneys, wearing dark gray business suits, striding in unison like an elegant horse troop. They included Dan Steiner, Harvard's general counsel, and three or four men from Ropes, Gray, a law firm that handled most litigation for the university. Next came a line of foot troop carrying bulging valises, boxes, rolled-up maps, and easels for mounting exhibits.

As the lawyers took seats at the opposing counsel's table, Sullivan turned to Levy. "Are you going to do this alone?" He laughed. As a union lawyer, he usually worked alone against big corporate law firms. But he had never seen anything quite like the legal manpower that Harvard threw into this NLRB proceeding. Ropes, Gray was a prominent Boston firm noted for thorough, exacting work, high fees, and a staff largely composed of Harvard Law School graduates. (Indeed, this entire opening scene resembled a scene in a much later movie, "The Verdict," in which Paul Newman plays a Boston lawyer struggling against a powerful institution represented by an influential law firm said to be modeled on Ropes, Gray.)

Levy had come up from New York to represent the Harvard women in their bid for an NLRB representation election. Sullivan had filed a petition for the election in mid-February, but Harvard objected on grounds that the scope of the proposed unit—the Medical Area only—was too narrow. Only a university-wide unit of clerical and technical workers would be appropriate, Harvard contended. The NLRB now was convening hearings to collect evidence and arguments on the issue.

Only thirty-two, Levy already was a partner in a New York firm, Eisner and Levy, which represented District 65 (his senior partner, Eugene Eisner, was general counsel of the union). Levy had appeared many times before the NLRB, usually on behalf of low-wage workers. The Harvard case presented similar issues in an entirely different atmosphere. "It wasn't like the usual tumult of New York labor cases in the garment industry, involving ordinary folks with scrappier kinds of lawyers," Levy recalled. The Harvard lawyers were "cool and distant, very methodical and precise, and there was no end to the resources they devoted to this thing." He was referring mainly to two Ropes, Gray attorneys, Thomas L. P. O'Donnell and Nelson G. Ross, who handled the hearing work. Steiner appeared only occasionally. (What the Ropes, Gray attorneys thought of Levy remains unrecorded. Citing lawyer–client confidentiality, they refused to talk publicly about the case.)

With Levy arguing for the union, Sullivan felt confident about the outcome. The problem was time. If the hearings dragged on too long, turnover in the Medical Area would undermine the workers' unity. District

65's president, David Livingston, had pushed her to file for election sooner than she had planned. Instead of going to the board with authorization cards signed by 60 to 70 percent of employees, she had "barely a majority"—a fact that she carefully concealed from everybody but her committee. She could win an election tomorrow or next week, but after that . . . who could tell?

For this reason, Harvard obviously wanted to put off an election, or avoid one altogether. Yet in contesting a vote among Medical Area employees, the university had brought up a legitimate question. If a union expects to negotiate for a group of workers in a large organization, it must be decided who belongs in that bargaining unit. Where the union and employer are unable to agree, the NLRB must make a decision based on evidence submitted in hearings. This seemed sensible enough to Sullivan. What didn't seem right was that the NLRB's cumbersome procedures allowed Harvard (or any employer) to draw out the hearings for many months.

The Medical Area workers had abided by the law in requesting an election. Yet they couldn't *have* an election. Not just yet. Wait for a while: four, five, maybe six months. But the thing about democracy is that people want to vote when the question is paramount in their minds, before it is dulled by time and distorted by demagogues. History showed that the longer the delay between petitioning for an election and actually voting, the greater the opportunity for an employer to instill doubt or fear in the minds of employees.

The proceedings were held at the NLRB's Boston offices, in a sort of deflated courtroom. It lacked oaken balusters and a black-robed judge sitting in magisterial isolation, but it had a bench up front for the hearing officer, whose function was more procedural than judicial. There was a modest witness stand, attorneys' tables, and several rows of audience benches.

Levy led off the union case by calling several workers to testify about their jobs. In election cases involving large employers with geographically separated offices and plants, the board had developed criteria for determining whether any one work site, or group of sites, constituted an *appropriate bargaining unit* under the law. The primary test was whether the workers shared a *community of interest* in wages, hours, and working conditions. This involved seven or eight factors, including work duties, skills, the extent to which employees worked in more than one location, and the degree to which the plants or offices operated under centralized or autonomous management.

Levy argued that the Medical Area was "a whole different working world" from the rest of Harvard. His witnesses described their job duties and responsibilities, emphasizing that they had nothing to do with supervisors or employees in other parts of the university. Forty percent of the Medical Area workers were classified as "technical," compared with only 5 percent elsewhere. The medical research assistants, Levy contended, had special knowledge and skills and faced health hazards in working with diseased tissues and research animals.

O'Donnell and Ross called several witnesses of their own to contest Levy on each and every point. Not only did technical assistants work in other parts of the university, the Harvard lawyers argued, but some were exposed to occupational hazards every bit as dangerous as the medical assistants. Witness the poisonous brown recluse spider known to inhabit a university museum in Cambridge. Museum employees testified in detail about, first, the brown recluse's potentially harmful sting and, second, care of the spider which entailed no small risk. Detail was piled upon absurd detail, all in an effort to crush the union. In its surreal way, it was hilarious. Long after the hearings ended, Sullivan and her friends would counsel one another, "Watch out for the brown recluse spider!"

As the hearings continued through March and into April, workers were stunned by the vigorous legal battle being waged over their rather simple desire to have a union. At the beginning, Sullivan had predicted in a *MAD* article that the NLRB would issue a decision by late summer 1975 and conduct an election shortly thereafter. Now her faith in speedy NLRB justice was evaporating. The hearing process, in fact, was one of many weaknesses in the law governing elections, the National Labor Relations Act (NLRA).

With lawyers offering voluminous amounts of evidence, the hearings consumed more than twenty days. Labor law was a hungry fat man who demanded seven-course meals with all the trimmings of a legal banquet: rules of evidence, technical points of law, partisan witnesses, aggressive cross-examination, court stenographer, hundreds of exhibits, extensive briefs. In the hands of skillful lawyers on both sides, and in the absence of systemic restraint, the fat man gorged on a plate piled high with stupefying detail.

Lawyers will do what lawyers do. The trouble was that the NLRB allowed them to do it. The board had dealt with thousands of "multiple site" cases in private industry since the 1930s and in a large majority of them had approved a bargaining unit for a single location. On the basis of this broad experience the board could well have devised rules of thumb for examining some of the seven or eight factors that went into a finding of *community of interest*. But it had not. After forty years of experience, board procedures still required unions and employers to litigate each of seven or eight factors as if it involved wholly new issues of law. This is what took so much time.

The board could have adopted rules to speed up the hearing process. But the larger problem, the necessity of holding pre-election hearings in the first place, would require changes in the law itself. The law required the board to address legal issues raised by the employer or union before the election occurred. This often meant that workers had to wait months, or years, to exercise their right to vote. There was more than a little inconsistency in a law that created a right but effectively denied its exercise.

A better way, as many labor law scholars had suggested, would be for the board to conduct an election two or three weeks after receiving a petition. Following the election, the board could hold hearings on unit "scope." If it concluded that the unit was ill-defined, some workers might have to be excluded or added, or the election voided or rerun. But there would be many fewer hearings under this plan; whichever side won the vote would no longer need to press its legal case. Most important, the workers would vote shortly after asking for an election, not months or years later.

A change of this magnitude required amending the NLRA. But business interests and their allies in Congress always marshaled enough votes to defeat reform proposals. When originally passed in 1935, the NLRA had been called "Labor's Magna Carta." By 1975, after forty years of board rulings and court decisions chipping away at workers' rights under the law, it promised much more than it delivered.

The more than three thousand pages of transcript produced during the Harvard hearings testify to the redundancy of detail. In Sullivan's view, "Harvard just dragged it out forever. We had testimony on endless items." But neither did Levy make brevity a virtue. In his view, each time a management witness made broad statements about Harvard operations, he had to counter with several workers who cited exceptions to ambiguous statements. Even the *Harvard Crimson*, which began daily coverage with some fanfare, eventually became bored with the event and stopped publishing stories long before the hearings ground to a halt.

There was one day, however, when everybody in the audience snapped to attention. On this occasion a mysterious document—referred to darkly in the press as a "secret memo"—made its appearance. A worker sympathetic to the union had found three pages of a memo in a mimeograph machine on the main campus and had turned them over to Leslie Sullivan. The fragment seemed to be part of a document outlining a strategy to avoid unionization of the Medical Area.

"Our April, 1971 memorandum," the memo said, "indicated that the university's ability to sustain the position that only a universitywide bargaining unit or units are appropriate among supporting staff personnel was in need of strengthening." One strengthening measure was to change the Medical Area Personnel Office from a relatively independent branch of the central office in Cambridge to a "subsidiary" of that office.

When Levy produced the partial memo one day in the hearing room, the Ropes, Gray lawyers jumped up in protest. They argued that the document could not be introduced into evidence because it was part of a memo they themselves had written for their client, Harvard, and therefore was protected by lawyer–client privilege. The hearing officer agreed. But Harvard's "secret" had been exposed. As early as 1971, as MAD charged, the university had paid the law firm "to devise a sophisticated, well-coordinated plan to stop employees from organizing a union." This accurately described the situation. But Harvard's action was not illegal and much less lethal than the steps taken by many employers to avoid a union.

The "secret memo" episode left the Ropes, Gray lawyers red-faced but did not really harm their case. To counter Levy's argument that the Medical Area essentially ran its own affairs, Harvard presented a parade of financial and personnel executives who testified that the university operated in a highly centralized fashion. This assertion would have astonished all who knew even a little about Harvard. In every other forum, and for all other purposes, the university made a virtue of its *decentralized* structure, arguing that the autonomy given to individual colleges and professional schools resulted in academic excellence. "Every tub on its own bottom" was virtually a university motto.

But in the NLRB hearing room, Harvard lawyers argued that only academic management was decentralized. All important services such as funding, budgeting, accounting, payroll, maintenance, dining facilities, utilities, and custodial services were furnished and controlled by a central Harvard management. This argument proposed the peculiar view that the university's organizational philosophy and culture flowed from the provision of services, not from the academic structure. To support its position, Harvard cited personnel management in particular. Salary levels, benefits, and other employment policies were applied uniformly across the university under the direction of a personnel office in Cambridge. But this fact in itself proved little. All corporations establish and monitor personnel policies from a headquarters post.

The question was whether the Medical Area Personnel Office (MAPO) operated with enough independence to support the notion that Medical

Area workers had a separate community of interest. This would become a central issue in the case. Harvard had converted MAPO, with the advice of lawyers, to a "subsidiary" of the central office in Cambridge. But it still retained some independent functions. While department heads in other parts of the university had to seek approval of the Cambridge office on hiring and salary matters, MAPO served in that capacity for the Medical Area.

It was a complex set of facts that seemed on the surface to add up to six of one and a half-dozen of the other. On the one hand, Harvard administered itself on a vague pattern of centrality relating to services. It was also a point in Harvard's favor that a few existing unions, which represented dining hall and maintenance workers, were organized across the university. On the other hand, by its own attempts at reorganization, Harvard implicitly acknowledged that Medical Area employees formed a separate "community of interest." This could not be wiped out, as the student editors of the *Harvard Crimson* noted, merely by changing an organization chart.

Understandably, the university did not want to be broken up into several unionized pieces. Yet the NLRA directed the board to "assure to employees the fullest freedom in exercising rights guaranteed by the Act." The NLRB long ago had interpreted this to mean that there could be more than one appropriate unit among the work sites of an employer. The board was not mandated by law to approve the *most* appropriate or *most* comprehensive bargaining unit possible, only *an* appropriate unit. The Medical Area seemed to qualify on this ground, if no other.

Harvard looked at the unit issue from the point of view of an employer that wanted to run things as "efficiently" as possible, with as little interference as possible. Workers looked at the same issue as a matter of rights. The questions of which view better reflected national labor policy or which better enabled industrial democracy were not answered in the Harvard case. When the hearings ended in June, board employees packed the stenographic transcript into cardboard boxes and delivered them to the office of the NLRB regional director, who was responsible for making a decision. And so the case of the Harvard women who wanted more out of work than trickle-down prestige passed into the hands of The Law, and no one knew when The Law would give it up.

Many a fledgling union had died this way, denied life-giving purpose. Sullivan and her committee found it hard to suppress their anger, but they tried to channel their energy toward an eventual victory at the NLRB. Devising stratagems for keeping interest in the union alive, they invented things to do. Some activities amounted to little more than survival games for a long voyage on a life raft. The committee seized on issues that it could do nothing about and made a show of concern as if it *could* do something about them. In April, for example, *MAD* criticized new administration plans for employee parking and suggested alternative ideas. The administration gave no indication it had been listening.

There were more meaningful things to do. Up to now, Medical Area 65 had functioned as an organizing vehicle. Now it took steps to behave like an established union. The union held elections for a 13-member executive committee which replaced the organizing committee. Then it went a step further and elected stewards, one for each fifteen employees in the Medical Area. With some training in handling complaints, the stewards actually began to function as unofficial grievance representatives, backed by a provision of the NLRA which says that in any workplace a worker has the right to present a grievance to management in the presence of other workers.

Sullivan's faith in the law had been shaken but not her determination to press ahead. From her courses in industrial relations, she knew that American workers had never had an easy time of it when their right of freedom of association collided with owners' property rights. Harvard's attempt to evade the union had driven her deeper into the heart of the labor movement. Now this became her life.

"I just really believed," she said, looking back at that time, "that organizing workers was the right thing to do and that District 65 was the right union and that we would make it work. I was very clear in my mind where we were and where we should go, but I'm not entirely sure how I got that way."

While awaiting a decision on Harvard, Sullivan spent less and less time in the Medical Area. District 65 wanted her to organize elsewhere in the Boston area. Clerical workers at Boston University had formed an organizing committee, and Sullivan went there to help a co-worker, Kathy Kautzer, the second staff member hired by 65 in Boston. This drive was energized in the summer of 1975 when BU faculty members voted to be represented by the American Association of University Professors.

Meanwhile, the women's movement was faltering in the workplace. For all the promise of its early months and its continuing popularity among office workers, 9to5 still hadn't achieved any widespread change in "power relationships," as Karen Nussbaum phrased it. After a long search for a union ally, 9to5 entered an alliance with the Service Employees International Union (SEIU). A few years later they would form SEIU Local 925, with Nussbaum as president, to engage in traditional union organizing among office workers. The original 9to5, still led by Ellen Cassedy among other women, remained independent but agreed to direct groups of workers seeking a union to Local 925.

For workers in the Harvard Medical Area, the days drifted on, late summer passing into early fall. No word came from the NLRB, no hint of imminent decision. Not even a rumor lay in sight. Becalmed on the ocean of The Law, no hope on the horizon, defectors slipping over the side: would it be death in the doldrums?

The Boston office of the NLRB, headquarters of Region 1 covering New England, was one of the agency's largest and busiest regional headquarters. Its director in 1975 was Robert S. Fuchs, sixty-five, a board attorney since 1948 and regional director since 1971. A likable, easy-going man, Fuchs was known by colleagues more for his social skills than brilliance as a labor lawyer. "His strength was getting along with the parties rather than deciding complicated legal issues," said a long-time board official in Washington who dealt with all regional directors. This was not unimportant for an agency whose success depended largely on its reputation for integrity and impartiality. By having good relations with both union and management officials, a regional director could strengthen a perception that the NLRB staff did not play favorites.

This Fuchs had done well. Making a decision in a tough case, involving one of the most prestigious institutions in the country, was another matter. After closing briefs were submitted in August, Fuchs, following his normal procedure, assigned the case to a staff lawyer who would draft an opinion to be issued over Fuchs's name. What happened then was never fully explained. It is known that Fuchs wavered. In early October, he announced that his office was unable to reach a decision and would forward the case to Washington. This action mystified everyone. Except in extraordinary circumstances, it was a regional director's duty to decide cases that arose in his or her region. Had Fuchs been intimidated by one side or the other? Perhaps he simply had passed the buck on a difficult case. Fuchs did not respond to the rumors and remained silent about his actions until long after he had retired.

In a 1994 interview, looking back nearly twenty years, Fuchs recalled that the Harvard case confounded him. "It was so very, very close and in my opinion almost unprecedented," he said. The five-member NLRB in Washington had not yet decided many cases involving the scope of bargaining units at universities. Why should a regional director venture into virgin territory, given the certainty that the losing party would carry an appeal to the full board? "It was such an important question, I felt the board would have to treat with it anyhow," he said.

It took six weeks for the Washington office to respond to Fuchs. In late November, the board replied that it would not accept the case. A staff member who was present during a discussion of Fuchs's request recalled the tenor of the meeting. "One board member said, 'You tell Fuchs he should decide this case or we'll get a new regional director.'"

Fuchs had to decide, and did, though how is not clear. In 1994, he admitted being confused about the sequence of events. He recalled with certainty that in the end he received separate opinions in the case from two of his staff attorneys, both of which came down on Harvard's side. He could not remember if both opinions were drafted after Washington ordered him to make a decision or one before and one after. The important thing was that Fuchs had two opinions with the same outcome: the Medical Area would *not* be an appropriate bargaining unit in which to conduct an election. On January 15, 1976, he dismissed District 65's petition for an election in the Medical Area.

The decision was based primarily on the centralization of "operational matters, including labor relations" under university vice-presidents. The Medical Area's branch personnel office was no more than a "satellite" of the central personnel office, Fuchs's ruling said. In conclusion, it continued, Medical Area employees "do not share a sufficiently special community of interests which would justify creating a special unit for them." There would be no election unless the union won an appeal.

Fuchs's ruling staggered the members of Medical Area 65. "I was warned that we'd have a unit fight with Harvard," Sullivan said. "But I thought that any person who reasonably looked at our situation would see we were a union." She could not help but feel that undue influence was brought to bear by Harvard. "Such an extraordinary wait didn't seem like it could be a coincidence," she said in 1994. "Dragging it out so long really took its toll on us."

The NLRB is highly vulnerable to criticism in one respect. The ideological leanings of the five political appointees who serve as board members change with administrations, producing startling inconsistencies in the interpretation of labor law and, in some periods, long delays in case-processing. In the area of influence-peddling, however, few federal agencies that have existed since the 1930s can cite a cleaner history than the NLRB. In the Harvard case, Fuchs in 1994 denied that he had felt pressure from the university, and Dan Steiner said none was exerted. The record supports their stories.

But it was crime enough for the board to countenance such a long delay. Shortly after Fuchs released his ruling, District 65 filed an appeal with the board in Washington. It would take some time for the board merely to decide whether to review the case. Eleven months already had passed since Sullivan petitioned for an election. Another fourteen months would pass before a final decision came down. And this would be only the first of several times that the NLRB would attempt to dispense justice in various cases involving Harvard University and this very same group of women employees. The board would advance and retreat, advance and retreat, and ultimately it would take ten years to make up its political-judicial mind about relatively simple issues.

The legal relationships thus prolonged would not quite match in length those in Dickens's famous intergenerational *Jarndyce v. Jarndyce*. But what became a series of Harvard cases lasted through three presidencies and innumerable wars, police actions, and economic recessions. The first round of hearings was still under way on April 30, 1975, when helicopters pulled the last American soldiers off the roof of the American embassy in Saigon. U.S. manufacturing was preeminent in the world, with high-paying factory jobs that set the standard for what work should be. Six years later, and again nine years later, long after the Vietnam War had become a bitter memory—with Ronald Reagan in the White House and corporate raiders swashbuckling up and down Wall Street and a million manufacturing jobs gone for good and with America converting swiftly to a postindustrial service economy—even then, District 65 lawyers would face Steiner, O'Donnell, and Ross in an NLRB hearing room for the several dozenth time, on the very same issue as in 1975. And that would not be the end for the Harvard lawyers. Four years later still, with Communism in worldwide retreat and the Cold War nearly at an end, they would be contending yet with union attorneys on the question of whether Harvard workers should have a union.

In the first episode, the wait endured by the Harvard workers would be, as Sullivan said, "outrageous."

CHAPTER SEVEN

*I*n January 1977, stagnant arctic air lay like a frozen tarpaulin across the entire Northeast for many days. Powerhouses ran short of fuel, forcing factories and offices to close for lack of heat. Homeless people froze to death in the streets of big cities. In Boston, snow that had fallen earlier now froze solid.

The cold crept into Kris Rondeau's lab room in Building C, turning frigid to the touch all objects with a metal surface, which is to say most laboratory equipment. Yet winter seemed almost a redundancy in the Medical Area. When it came to social relations, the entire place was cold the year round.

By early 1977, Rondeau had worked there the better part of a year but had come to know only a few of the hundreds of people who entered and left Building C every day. She liked some things about her job. She got along well with her co-workers, especially two in her physiology lab, a male graduate student and a young woman lab assistant. Lunchtime was the best part of the day. The three of them would sit in the lab room, eating and chatting. "We had a little frying pan that we used over a Bunsen burner," Rondeau said, "and we would sometimes make what we called Bayonne steaks, which is fried baloney. We really enjoyed these lunches."

Lab supervisors treated her well enough, though some were annoyingly patronizing. But she and her co-workers became increasingly concerned about pay. Rondeau had advanced only a little from her starting salary of $8,600, which was low for someone with a college degree in 1977. She realized that regardless of education most women suffered from a tradition of underpayment. More than 80 percent of all regularly employed women made less than $10,000 a year in 1976, compared with only 38 percent of regularly employed men.

The limitations of her job also had taken the edge off the early thrill of working at Harvard. She had learned pretty much all there was to know about slitting open rats' skulls and implanting electrodes. "After about six months I'd reached a point of real boredom," she said. "I'd worked in factories, and I knew what was good about this job. The research probably was important, and there was more freedom on the job. But it was a low-level science job and not much more interesting to me than putting wig-heads in bags."

The coldness of the Medical School bothered her most. It seemed to come from the very organization of work. Building C housed dozens of research units, each with its own one- or two-room laboratory, outfitted with its own technology, its own scientific reason for being. It was not a place where people formed a community of the whole. It was divided into cells of research. Walking through the hallways, she would see inside each lab room the same general configuration of island cabinets and shelves of glassware and counters crowded with measuring, gauging, probing, recording machines, with electrical wiring, and large sinks. The people who worked in the next cell were only a wall's width away, but she rarely met them unless by chance she found herself standing with them during a fire drill.

Defenders of this arrangement would say (Rondeau often heard the argument) that it simply reflected the nature of scientific research; that true science, the study of natural phenomena, was a highly individual thing; that the microscope eyepiece accommodated only one eye; that only one hand, operating as the extension of one mind, could finish the unfinished equation on the blackboard; that Einstein was one man, not a pool of female research assistants; and that, ergo, only men had the capacity to do incisive mathematical analysis and inductive reasoning necessary to science. It did not have to be said, therefore, that not everyone (not even every man) had a creative mind; that there had to be principal investigators, who by a twist of natural selection turned out to be mostly men, and there had to be people who performed the experiments and cleaned the glassware, who by a reciprocal twist happened to be largely women.

Rondeau acknowledged that there had to be a research leader and research assistants. But the RA position ended in a cul-de-sac; no more to be learned and no way out except by going backward. There should be some way to make the jobs expandable to fit a growing person, she thought. Why not continuous education at work? If the bosses wouldn't put in training courses, why couldn't workers teach one another? Indeed, she herself undertook to teach her skills to a young man who cared for the lab animals—and was severely reprimanded for it.

By early spring Rondeau still hadn't attended any union meetings or met the "Leslie" that Ross had talked about. Other things occupied her attention, including her night courses in physiology. She and her college boyfriend had taken separate paths, and now she lived with four other women in a house on Oxford St. in Cambridge. She had signed a District 65 union card, though not out of a strong belief in unionism. She simply gave in to the persistence of Ross Schubarth, the friendly electronics repairman. The NLRB had taken the Harvard case under advisement a few months before she came to Harvard and had yet to deliver a decision. Every two weeks or so she read the union newsletter, *MAD*, which always spoke of a decision coming from the NLRB, soon . . . "any day now." It had been "any day now" for several months. You tend not to think much about a distant acquaintance who has been in a coma for two years, which was more or less how Rondeau thought of Medical Area 65.

At the NLRB offices in Washington, Harvard was one of thousands of cases lined up in an orderly decision-making queue. The board was working its way through a backlog which said much about a significant change in the tenor of labor–management relations in the United States. In the forties, fifties, and sixties, American employers had more or less accepted unions, albeit grudgingly. Hardly any company ever *wanted* a union, but organized labor in those decades had seemed too powerful to resist beyond putting up a token fight in organizing campaigns.

Sometime in the late sixties employers began realizing that the balance of power was shifting. Business competition had become more intense. It was no longer as easy as in the first decades after World War II to raise prices to cover wage increases won by unions. Public attitudes about organized labor had turned negative. Many unions, feeling impregnable in their industrial fortresses, practically gave up organizing the unorganized. Loopholes in the labor law, which had always been there, began to look more enticing to corporate lawyers and antiunion consulting firms. Employers perceived that it could make "good business sense" to fight harder against unionization, even push the boundaries of the law. The cost of committing an "unfair labor practice," such as firing employee activists to kill a union drive, could be inconsequential compared with the benefits of not having a union.

By the mid-seventies, unfair labor practice charges against employers had mounted exponentially. In fiscal 1977, the record would show, the NLRB received 42,802 such charges, a sixfold increase from the 7,451 of 1955. Only a small percentage of these charges reached trial or appeal level, but those that did consumed more staff time than ever before. At the same time, cases involving disputes over representation elections also increased in number.

For these reasons, Case No. 1-RC-13715, *The President and Fellows of Harvard College, Employer, and District 65, Distributive Workers of America, Petitioner*, had to wait its turn. After Fuchs dismissed District 65's election petition in January 1976, the union requested a review by the board in Washington. A special unit of staff lawyers had to prepare a summary analysis of the case so that a panel of the five-member board could decide whether to consider it. Harvard's willingness to spare no expense in building a 3,000-page record in the 1975 hearings made the going rough for the analysts. Not until the middle of 1976 did the board finally agree to review 1-RC-13715. Then began a new process involving submission of briefs by the two parties and further analysis by NLRB staff and board members themselves.

By the early spring of 1977, more than two years had elapsed since the workers asked for an election, and still no decision had been made. But Medical Area 65 refused to die. "It was our feeling," said Leslie Sullivan, "that we had to keep people busy and keep people signing cards. We never stopped signing cards. We organized by department, and we tried to sign up every new person who came to work."

MAD exhorted members to think of ways to "keep our name alive," to maintain "visibility." The union sponsored after-work social hours, flea markets, picnics on the quadrangle lawn in good weather, occasional lectures by outside speakers. Now and then, when a health and safety problem arose in the labs, the union seized on it and inflated it to the size of an issue worthy of a workshop, or at least an angry series of articles. Towards the end, *MAD* showed signs of scraping the bottom for causes.

The heart of the Harvard union was the organizing committee, which continued to throb with life. The legal delay lasted so long that several of the strongest committee members were promoted to jobs that probably would exclude them from an eventual bargaining unit. These included Edie Brickman, Drago Clifton, and Marlene Goldman. But they kept working on the committee, as did John Rees and Jeremy Pool who, as "professional" computer programmers, most likely wouldn't be in the clerical union.

In early May 1977, the saying "any day now" began to mean, literally, any day now. The board could not be so insensitive as to let another school year slide by without acting. A ruling *had* to be imminent. People began talking more about the union question.

In the physiology lab, Rondeau could feel it closing in around her. Union supporters began urging her to take a more active role. Some of her friends favored the union but were too passive to lead the way. They told Rondeau that she had the guts to stand up for what they believed in. She felt an almost tangible change in atmospheric pressure, the way it is when, at the end of a long flight, you descend from cruising altitude. You take out the ear plugs, the clouds fall behind, and there below, spread out in all its glory and perversity, is the every day world where you have to choose sides.

Rondeau hadn't fully decided what to do when word finally came from Washington. On May 11 the NLRB issued a decision reversing the Boston regional director. The employees of the Medical Area did, indeed, constitute "a separate appropriate unit for the purposes of collective bargaining," the board declared in a 3-2 split decision. It ordered Fuchs to meet with the parties and prepare for an election.

"We have won an historic victory," said the May 19 issue of *MAD*. Understandable euphoria, but a more cautious assessment might have noted that split decisions could be overturned when the political coloration of the board changed. Generally, board members were characterized not so much as Democrats and Republicans but rather as prounion or promanagement in outlook. In the Harvard case, the board's two decidedly prounion members, John H. Fanning and Howard Jenkins Jr., decided in favor of the union. They were joined in the majority by Chairman Betty Southard Murphy, known as a swing voter. In their majority opinion, these three indicated that the key factor against Harvard's position was the existence of a personnel office in the Medical Area, which "gave recognition to the separate character of the Medical Area." No other graduate school within Harvard had its own personnel office. The majority also relied on the geographical separation of the two campuses, the lack of interchange between Medical Area workers and other university employees, the medical orientation of the work in the Medical Area, and the fact that District 65 had organized a majority of the Medical Area workers.

The two dissenting votes were cast by promanagement board members, John A. Penello and Peter D. Walther. "Today's decision," they said in a lengthy dissent, "represents nothing short of board sanctioning of piece-meal department-by-department organizing of nonprofessional employees on campus—a result which on this record, we submit, is consistent with neither board precedent nor with sound collective-bargaining principles." Such strong language had the look of a minority opinion that could switch easily to the majority column when, and if, a Republican President changed the composition of the board.

As appalled as they were by the decision, university officials decided not to protest but to bring the matter to a head in a certification election. Their electoral position had improved markedly in the two years since Medical Area 65 asked for an election. The work force of 1975 had turned over at least by half, with a substantial number of workers who had signed cards in 1975 having left the university. Meeting with Fuchs's people in the Boston NLRB office, Harvard and the union agreed on certain rules for an election, including precisely who would be eligible to vote. The election date was set for June 29.

The time had come for Rondeau to make a decision. A passive vote for the union did not seem sufficient. She thought she owed it to herself to decide if she *really* wanted the union. What it came down to was the people on either side and not what the union would "get" for her at the bargaining table. It seemed to her this should not be a political choice—the power of organized labor versus the power of capital. Rather it ought to be a moral choice, just as making friends was a moral thing. Her early years in Whitinsville served as a frame of reference in making this judgment. She had grown up among working people who scraped along without wealth or luxuries. The Harvard environment in contrast reflected "tremendous privilege," she said. "Many people had had easy childhoods and wonderful educational opportunities. I believed that this would cause these people to be morally superior. I thought that pettiness, cheating, and dishonesty were caused by not having enough money. I was wrong."

The deans, administrators, and professors at the Medical School had money and education; their manners and way of speaking were polished to a high gloss. But they acted out of values no worse and no better than those of the meanest villager in Whitinsville. Many were sympathetic with union aims and had an enlightened, egalitarian outlook in general. Others, like the two principal investigators who led the research projects she was assigned to, had a narrow perspective on social relations. They will be called here Dr. A and Dr. B. Rondeau respected them for their scientific abilities. They seemed ignorant of, and oblivious to, the situation of the workers. Yet they made it very clear that they looked darkly on the union idea, implying that a worker who supported unionization didn't know what was good for her. This irritated Rondeau more than anything else.

Dr. A was a man in his sixties who had visited England and imitated English mannerisms and speech. He took a negative attitude about the union. "Dr. A thought I was outrageously radical, some kind of leftist horror show," Rondeau said. "And so he wouldn't talk to me about the union." But one day he remarked that she ought to know about a certain matter because she belonged to the Teamsters, didn't she? In another conversation, he revealed that he had no idea how much RAs were paid. "He thought we all had 100 percent employer-paid health insurance."

But it was Dr. B who came to personify for her the elitist, condescending attitude of some administrators and faculty members that detracted so much from Harvard's good qualities. One evening Dr. B sat down with his lab assistants and began telling stories about his own undergraduate days at Harvard. He portrayed himself and his friends as rebellious "liberals" who engaged in wild and glorious pranks, such as climbing through dorm windows. "Ah," he added, with a sigh, "those were the days when Hahvad was Hahvad."

Rondeau remembered rolling her eyes in disbelief. The man was serious! Telling this story, she added, "There *was* a Hahvard experience, you know. The Medical School was very much a Hahvard experience. And if you went to a party, people would say, 'What do you do?' 'Well, I work at Harvard Medical School.'" She mimicked the way an incredulous person's eyes would bulge as he or she emitted an admiring "'Ooohhh!'" Rondeau laughed at the recollection. "I could have said, 'I shovel shit at Harvard Medical School,' and they'd say, 'Oh, really! That must be good shit.'"

The other side, the union side, affected her in a quite different way. The first time she attended a committee meeting, in late May, Leslie Sullivan spoke at some length, summarizing unsettled legal issues. Rondeau was impressed. "She was very clear and articulate," Rondeau said. "Later on I got to know her really well, and I saw other great things about her. But initially I was amazed at her ability to speak." Someone introduced the two women after the meeting. Sullivan, ever the practical leader, did not dawdle over the introduction but assigned a task to Rondeau.

Over the next few weeks Rondeau saw more and more of the core activists, like Edie Brickman, Jeanne Lafferty, Kris Mahon, John Rees, Jeremy Pool, and Richard Pendleton. She accompanied them on organizing trips through the Medical Area. She not only enjoyed being with them but also admired them. As she put it, "I thought they were brave people. Building a union is not entirely selfless, but it's an expression of caring. I wanted to be like that. A person who took care of herself but whose sense of responsibility included helping others. I thought that was the best way to live."

Rondeau didn't like to think of the administrators and professors as constituting a "class" of people. She knew that one should not generalize, and yet she could not help generalizing. There was no doubt in her mind that *they* generalized when thinking about the workers, especially the women workers, and that *they* thought of the workers as a class distinct from themselves—distinct in terms of education, perhaps also in terms of social class, career possibilities, and an indefinable lack of mien (natural or affected) that stamped one as a member of the academic elite.

She often heard elitists declare that any union, which represented the "narrow" interests of one occupational group, was out of place in an institution dedicated to the selfless advancement of knowledge. But Rondeau saw other groups of individuals touting their interests in a collective voice. Faculty members certainly did this. The deans did it in their councils. Top-level administrators did it in meetings of subordinate deans and personnel officers. Students did it in their student bodies and newspapers. Each of these interest groups practiced collective bargaining of one kind or another. It was okay to be part of a collective if you were in any of those groups but not if you were a worker.

Rondeau became a unionist. Although she still would suffer what she called "a crisis of doubt," her conversion to the union cause was essentially complete by about the second week of June. By then Harvard's antiunion offensive campaign had sprung into action.

At every level of command, Harvard University's antiunion campaign abounded in irony. At the highest level, President Derek Bok strongly defended the concept of collective bargaining and the right of workers to negotiate through a union. Yet he bore ultimate responsibility for carrying out a policy of avoiding unionization. Under Bok, the two men who did most to devise and direct the antiunion strategy, General Counsel Daniel Steiner and an associate general counsel, Ed Powers, thought of themselves politically as liberals.

Born near Philadelphia in 1930, Bok graduated from Stanford, received a law degree at Harvard, and began teaching there in 1958. Only ten years later, Bok was named dean of the Law School and three years after that, in 1971, president of Harvard University. Meanwhile, he had married into, if that is the way to put it, one of the most famous intellectual families in the world. His wife Sissela, herself a philosopher and writer, was the daughter of two Swedish Nobel Prize winners, Alva and Gunnar Myrdal.

As a legal scholar, Bok specialized in labor law, studying under Archibald Cox among others. Cox, a noted labor law theorist, became something of a national hero in 1973. Appointed as independent special prosecutor in the Watergate case, he was fired by President Nixon's Justice Department when he refused to take orders from the White House. Cox was one of two men that Bok regarded as mentors of a sort. The second was John T. Dunlop, an economist with vast practical experience in labor relations, who served as a Harvard dean in the early 1970s. "Archie taught me about labor law," Bok said in a 1993 interview, "and John taught me about labor unions." Both would play important advisory roles when Bok had his ultimate confrontation with Harvard's white-collar union.

Bok coauthored two books on labor law and collaborated with Dunlop on *Labor and the American Community* (1970), a scholarly, yet pragmatic, work that describes the benefits and disadvantages of unions. Though its tone is academic and objective, the book clearly implies that unions often are good for workers and should be accepted by society as valued institutions.

As Harvard president, Bok imposed a new administrative system on an old pyramidal structure in which faculty members occupied most official posts. He divided Harvard's command structure into functional lines that reported to five new vice presidents. The reorganization enabled faculty to concentrate on academic matters and gave over the running of the university to administrators—a revolutionary change that would pose problems. He also presided over a project on academic reform which produced the concept of the "core curriculum." By 1977, Bok was regarded as an effective president during a troubled transition period.

Bok came to rely especially on his general counsel, Dan Steiner, a 1958 graduate of Harvard Law School. In 1970, Steiner was named as Harvard's first in-house general counsel. When Bok moved up to president the following year, Steiner became a valued confidante and troubleshooter. A self-described liberal, he was active in Democratic politics, often working on the same side as unions in political campaigns. But as Harvard's chief lawyer, he was deeply involved in implementing Bok's antiunion policy and became even more involved in 1975 when Bok put the personnel and labor relations function under his command.

Steiner, in turn, rehired a former Harvard personnel officer, Ed Powers, to oversee labor relations and the union avoidance campaign. Powers grew up in the union game, the son of a longtime UAW local union officer at a General Motors plant in Lockport, New York. Young Powers intended to follow his father into the labor movement. By 1956, when he received a law degree at the University of Michigan, he had changed his mind. Switching to the management side, he worked for several years in labor relations at American Airlines. He moved to the Harvard personnel department in the late sixties, and after a two-year hiatus returned in 1975 as associate general counsel in charge of labor relations under Steiner. Powers was not an antiunion idealogue. He got along well with local labor leaders. But he believed that unions polarized a work force and created a "poor working environment" without improving the lives of members.

It went without saying that Harvard would not engage in physical abuse or intimidation to encourage employees to vote "no" on election day. The antiunion campaign designed by Steiner and Powers focused on getting information to employees in three ways. First, there would be one-on-one sessions between individual supervisors and workers. Powers himself took on the task of meeting with groups of supervisors to advise them on what to say and how to say it. Second, Steiner and personnel officers would address large worker–management meetings at the departmental level and higher. Finally, the administration would inform employees of its position in memos and letters.

The entire campaign was directed at the union's most vulnerable point, the credibility and reputation of District 65 itself. "Much of our strategy in the beginning was to attack District 65," Powers said. "We said to the employees, 'Maybe you want a union, but you don't want this union.' Fundamentally, we didn't want workers to be unionized at all, and we certainly didn't want them to be unionized separately."

But Powers instructed administrators not to denounce unionism per se. It would not look good for a university to condemn freedom of association. Harvard also did not wish to damage its image of academic neutrality in labor–management affairs. Since the 1930s, it had supported organized labor as an institution and had been allied with unions in education programs. The best known of these was the Harvard Trade Union Program, which had been conducting annual, ten-week graduate-level sessions for union officers and staff members since 1942.

Harvard's attack on District 65 involved four main points: that this "industrial" union knew nothing about universities; that it viewed Harvard workers merely as a source of dues income to be used in propping up its shaky financial structure; that it would not allow local autonomy in bargaining and other matters; that it would discard the health insurance plans provided by Harvard and force workers into the union-administered, financially unstable District 65 Security Plan.

In order to make this pitch, Harvard first had to plant the idea that outsiders, not Harvard employees, were behind the union drive. As early as 1975 the administration distributed a letter that started, "Dear Harvard Employee: District 65 of the Distributive Workers of America, whose headquarters are in New York City, has been passing out leaflets at Harvard . . . " In other words, barbaric invaders from Sin City were disrupting an otherwise idyllic relationship between management and workers. Harvard officials knew very well that the unionizing effort had originated among a group of their own employees, now known as Medical Area 65.

During the weeks leading up to the June 29 election, it was this local group—Leslie Sullivan and the members of her committee—that still led the union campaign. The records clearly show that they wrote and distributed all the newsletters and leaflets and made all the presentations and talks, with the exception of one or two inspirational speeches by District 65 leaders. The national union did not send in organizers or dictate strategy and tactics. Indeed, Sullivan came to regret a lack of advice from experienced organizers.

No record exists of the vocal assault on District 65 made by Harvard administrators. But the same allegations were issued in a barrage of letters and memos distributed to workers in June 1977. Powers himself produced most of the written material based on his own research. District 65 was, in his words, "an easy target." Quoting from government reports and the union constitution, he selectively dissected the financial and political makeup of the union.

In a four-page analysis dated June 10, for example, he pictured the union as a hodge-podge of "non-skilled and semi-skilled" blue-collar workers whose interests would predominate over those of a female white-collar university group. District 65, the analysis charged, periodically "finds itself in a financially precarious position" because job-cutting recessions halted dues payment from the unemployed, forcing other members (like Harvard employees) to take up the slack. "You might ask yourself: This union needs me, but do I need this union?"

On the issue of local control, other Harvard memos quoted from the District 65 constitution which invested a policy-making body called the General Council with the power to issue "final and binding" decisions on all matters. What Harvard failed to say about local autonomy was that all unions, indeed all private organizations, have rules governing the behavior of members. To undecided voters who knew nothing about unions, it might very well appear that if the union won, workers would find themselves under the thumb of unknown officials in New York.

Years later, Powers acknowledged that Sullivan and her friends were sincere in declaring that they would be independent. But in 1977 Harvard chose to represent them as being deluded. "You may think you're going to control," he said in 1994, paraphrasing Harvard's approach in 1977. "But once you get in, you'll find the decisions are not going to be yours. I think that's generally true."

On the union side, Sullivan argued heatedly that Harvard was clouding the issue. But she regretted not having insisted, back in 1974, that District 65 sign a written agreement guaranteeing local control. She personally had no doubt that Medical Area 65 would run its own affairs. Livingston and his top leadership rarely got involved in the affairs of locals outside of New York. Nor did District 65 have economic reason to try to impose specific wage levels or work rules. It was not as if the union had to keep up the integrity of a nationwide wage-and-benefit pattern like those that existed in the steel and automobile industries. The steel and auto unions represented a high percentage of workers in these industries and made every effort to prevent any one company or plant from undercutting the national wage pattern. In contrast, District 65's university membership in 1977 constituted less than 0.5 percent of university workers nationally. There was no university wage pattern to be maintained.

Harvard literature raised a number of quasi-legal questions meant to arouse fears about losing individual rights. The District 65 constitution actually aided them in this respect. The union had failed, through carelessness or inattention, to eliminate outdated and even illegal provisions. The constitution still contained, for example, a statement dating from the early 1930s favoring "closed shops." The closed shop arrangement, under which an employer agreed to hire only workers who belonged to a union, had been illegal since 1947. No employer would agree to such a requirement, even if 65 tried to impose it. No matter. There it was, overripe and obsolete, in the constitution, and Harvard cited it as an example of how the union would force people to join.

The item of central concern was the District 65 Security Plan, the union's self-insured program that provided health care benefits to active members and retirees. Financed by company payments, the plan was running into trouble as employers with the bulk of 65's membership went out of business. To keep it viable, District 65 tried to negotiate the plan with as many employers as it could. The Harvard administration banged away repeatedly with the charge that if workers voted in District 65, they would have to scuttle their current health insurance plans and be part of the Security Plan.

"The union needed a very large unit to salvage their health and welfare plan," Powers recalled. "It was in serious financial trouble. The whole union was in financial trouble, because they organized too many small units. Their average unit was under twenty. It was to their credit in a way, because the other unions wouldn't even organize these shops with a large number of minorities. Politically, I'm quite a ways on the left. So I admired this policy, but it created a financially unviable organization and unviable health plan."

But the parent union could not impose the Security Plan at will. Local unions had the right to negotiate and ratify whatever terms suited them best. And, of course, the employer could reject such a demand. In reality, Sullivan and the committee long ago had decided it would be foolish to cast out Harvard's existing plans. But the local union left itself open to criticism by not stating definitively enough that it wanted no part of 65's rickety program.

Harvard was right to point out the pitfalls of the program. The university did not want to toss money down the drain; nor did it want its employees to get involved in a highly risky plan which could (and ultimately, years later, did) collapse. The controversy came to a head only a week and a half before the election, and it taught the union that when it came to trading charges and counter-charges in print, Harvard had the faster printing press. Rondeau, by then an active member of the committee, remembered what happened.

"Fools that we were," she said, "we put out a letter, saying, 'No, you don't have to belong to the Security Plan. You have a choice, and here are some examples of places that were organized by 65 where the workers had chosen to stick with their current health plan.'" One of these was Harper & Row, the New York publisher that had been organized by 65 in 1974. In reply, Harvard put out a memo questioning the inclusion of Harper & Row. "So the next day," Rondeau continued, "we idiots, answering *this* charge, put out a letter from Harper & Row employees."

Signed by ten Harper & Row workers, the letter confirmed that they had rejected the Security Plan in favor of keeping Harper & Row's Blue Cross program. " . . . we want you to know that with District 65 we were completely free to determine for ourselves what we wanted to see included in our contract," the letter said. But Harvard responded with another letter, questioning the reliability of the Harper & Row letter.

The fusillade of letters, presenting two irreconcilable versions of the situation, undoubtedly irritated Harvard employees far more than it educated them. As Rondeau later reflected, "We got ourselves into, not just a paper war, but we also put the workers into the middle of a fight between the union and Harvard. It was a deadly thing." This episode taught her the futility of trading charges in print, and she would never forget the lesson.

In the final two weeks preceding the election, employees came under a daily assault of antiunion letters and memos pointing to seeming contradictions between statements by the local and parent unions. The plan worked to a large degree. "Even though we had been warned about the antiunion campaign," Sullivan said, "we really hadn't truly anticipated the intensity of it. There was one after another, every day. We were going around trying to put out fires. We would barely respond to one and there was another one."

During June, the antiunion offensive all but drowned out the union's positive voice. Time had taken the edge off some of the women's issues that had been a major spark for unionization in 1974. As for demeaning treatment of women, the flagrant practices had all but ceased, or at least become less visible. The union still made a major issue of salaries, particularly the salaries paid for "female jobs." It continued to demand child care facilities and improved benefits. Harvard at the time did not provide a dental insurance program.

By 1977 something interesting had begun to happen. Perhaps weary of listing the same specific demands on salaries, benefits, and working conditions over and over again, Medical Area 65 had adopted a more general approach. "We want a voice in the issues that affect our working lives," it said. There was a hint here of seeking something more than a seat at a negotiating table, an unstated, unspecified demand for a role other than the narrow one of bargaining traditional bread-and-butter issues. Preoccupied with defending itself, the union never got around to defining this inchoate feeling in practical terms. But the idea would be revived in the future and eventually translated into an innovation in union organizing.

In this first Harvard drive, the organizers did characterize worker–management relations in a fairly novel way. Recognizing that employees generally enjoyed working at Harvard and respected their supervisors, the union did not conduct a traditional hate-the-boss campaign. "The union does not exist in opposition to supervisors," said a *MAD* article in December 1976. "The union exists in opposition to Harvard's autocratic administration and its archaic personnel policies."

Near the middle of June, workers in Building C received a "Dear Employee" letter inviting them to a meeting on the union issue. Several such meetings already had taken place in the Medical Area. The union called them "captive audience" meetings, implying that workers had to attend and drink in whatever potion management chose to dispense. Harvard administrators later would argue that attendance was not mandatory. The letter did not say that all employees *must* attend. Of course not, union leaders responded; it didn't have to. How many souls would be foolish enough to reject an invitation from the boss to attend a meeting on an issue known to be of critical interest to the boss?

So sensitive was the issue of compulsion at Harvard that nearly twenty years later Dan Steiner and Ed Powers would vehemently object to use of the term "captive audience." Said Steiner: "There were no 'captive audience' meetings to the best of my knowledge. Some people left during the meetings. Union people came to the meetings and argued. When the employer takes a position, I agree there is some possibility that that has an intimidating effect. I also would say that I know for a fact that some employees at Harvard felt intimidated by the union. They felt the atmosphere was hostile. That if they expressed themselves as being opposed to the union there'd be a kind of ostracism. So I think there's the possibility of people feeling intimidated by both sides."

In the case of the Building C meeting in June 1977, Rondeau could not recall anyone who entertained the notion of *not* attending. Indeed, when the time of the meeting arrived, "department administrators went around to each lab and office and cleared the area. You were kind of picked up and brought to the meeting."

Rondeau and about two hundred others were herded to a large amphitheater classroom used for lectures. She noticed that *everybody* was there—not just union-eligible workers but also supervisors, administrators, a large number of faculty members, and even postdoctoral students who worked in the labs but were not classified as employees. Climbing the

Chapter Seven

steps in the amphitheater, she had the impression of being shuffled in a stacked deck. People were supposed to voice their opinions, but the eminence and power of the professors and administrators far outweighed the feeble voice that lab assistants and secretaries could muster in such a gathering. Whatever their private beliefs about unions, faculty members were not likely to oppose the administration line on the District 65 drive.

The first speaker was Vivienne Rubeski, a well-liked personnel officer in the Medical Area. Although she thought of herself (she later told Rondeau) as being rabidly antiunion, union activists in fact considered her the least rabid, altogether a very decent person. Rubeski spoke in a low-key manner, "kind of walking back and forth and saying nice things about Harvard," as Rondeau described it. Next came Daniel Cantor, director of personnel in the Medical Area. He took a somewhat tougher line than Rubeski. The third speaker, Steiner, escalated the rhetoric. He talked about "how District 65 only wanted our dues money, and how we'd all have to belong to the Security Plan," Rondeau said.

At the conclusion of his talk, Steiner asked for questions. Rondeau had a question, one fed to her by Sullivan. Union leaders felt it was important not to leave the impression that Harvard had cowed union supporters. She couldn't remember, in 1994, what question she asked, but she did remember Steiner's response when she raised her hand.

He pointed to her and said something like, "Yes, Kris. Kris Rondeau, isn't it?" She had never met Steiner. Obviously, he had been well-briefed. Anticipating hostile questions from union activists, the administration used the name-calling tactic as a method of gentle intimidation.

Management countered the union-fed questions with setups of its own. Exempt employees stood up and gave testimonials for Harvard, Rondeau remembered. "And then there were prize-winning scientists," she added, "who said it'd be awful if the union got in. You know, 'We're trying to cure cancer and these [union] people are out for themselves.' This was effective in scaring young technicians. But I don't think the faculty thought of this themselves. The lawyers put it in their mouths."

Rondeau left the meeting feeling that the union had been outclassed by a considerable margin in the propaganda battle. A meeting like this, she thought, was "frightening in some really deep way about the use of power." She got on an elevator with several other employees of her own department. "One woman was sobbing, and the others wouldn't look at me. When I saw these women shaking, not speaking to me, averting their eyes, crying, I knew we had lost them, and I don't think we ever got them back. That's when you cry, if you're going to cry, when you're changing your mind from 'yes' to 'no.' "

On the day before the election, each worker received a letter at home from Derek Bok. The man who knew more about labor relations than any of his subordinates, certainly more than any Medical Area dean, had stayed aloof from the conflict. He had never appeared at a meeting and never been implicated in the antiunion campaign. And now came this letter from "Office of the President" and addressed to "Dear Staff Member." It was like Zeus reluctantly coming down from Mount Olympus to straighten out the affairs of men.

The letter started, "Since I have been quoted in the union literature over the past couple of years, I thought you should know how I feel about this particular election." As if the union had reached out to an innocent bystander and dragged him into it. Of course he had been mentioned: he was the president. And as the president of Harvard University, he almost had to fill the role of moral superiority that academia has chosen for itself. University professors, you see, do not act out of self-interest like ordinary mortals. They alone have the ability to ponder and come to objective conclusions about issues that affect everyone, including themselves. He was "not persuaded," he wrote, that "the choice of this union would be in your best interest." His letter raised the specter of outside control, noting that most of District 65's members lived in the New York City metropolitan area. "I question whether it serves you best to delegate such power to a remote union leadership with so little experience in higher education."

On election day, June 29, everybody was talking about Bok's letter. He was highly respected throughout the university, and Sullivan knew that he had hurt the union cause. Even so, she thought the union might win by a couple dozen votes. By the end of the vote count that evening, however, it was clear that she and her committee had underestimated the power of the antiunion campaign. Workers had voted against union representation, 436 to 346, a ninety-vote margin.

Later, the committee analyzed what went wrong. Whether intentional on the part of the university or not, the NLRB delays from 1975 to 1977 had cost the union hundreds of votes—the prounion workers who had left Harvard during that period. It was evident, moreover, that large majorities of two categories of employees voted against the union. One group worked at the New England Regional Primate Research Center, located in Southborough, Massachusetts. Administratively linked to the Medical School, the Primate Center employed sixty to seventy workers who mainly served as animal caretakers. In 1975, Medical Area 65 had wide support among these workers. But in the ensuing two years, while NLRB offices bounced the Harvard case back and forth, most of the prounion people had left.

A second source of "no" votes was a group of lab workers who had supervisory duties and were classified as Research Assistant II. The union realized that they likely would be excluded from the bargaining unit but mistakenly agreed to have their votes counted in the final tally. The RA IIs tended to see themselves as part of management and undoubtedly voted against the union. The Powers-Steiner onslaught on District 65 and Bok's last-minute letter also probably turned many "undecideds" to a "no" vote.

No one could think clearly about what to do next. "We were too stunned," Sullivan said. "We were so disappointed and so overwhelmed by what had happened. We were worn out, emotionally worn out."

CHAPTER EIGHT

*T*he first time she lay down in front of a truck on a picket line, Rondeau realized that she had found her calling. Not the act itself; she had no intention of becoming a professional picket. On that pre-dawn morning in 1979, she was one of four pickets blocking a driveway at Boston University during a strike for union recognition. Each woman trusted and drew strength from the others. This is what appealed to Rondeau, the acting in concert with people in whom she had absolute trust.

Rondeau still worked at Harvard Medical School but frequently lent a helping hand in District 65 organizing drives around Boston. In May 1978, clerical and technical workers at Boston University had voted for the union, but a year later BU still was trying to have the vote annulled. Now the predominantly female office workers were striking for union recognition. So it was that Rondeau found herself standing with three BU strikers on a driveway at three in the morning. When a delivery truck turned into the driveway, the pickets waved their "On Strike" signs. The driver stopped but did not retreat. The women promptly lay down in the driveway. Rondeau felt the cold concrete through her jacket and jeans. After a few moments, the driver backed out and drove off.

"I was scared but not *that* scared," Rondeau recalled. "I was with people I trusted, and I didn't really think that truck was going to roll over me. I would have to test my depth of commitment on something else." She would.

As a volunteer picket, she played only a bit part in the drama of the BU strike, which ended when the university recognized District 65 as bargaining agent for clerical and technical workers. It was an impressive victory, and Rondeau and her friends at Harvard could not help feeling a bit envious. The June 1977 election loss in the Medical Area had demoralized union supporters. Shortly after the election, the organizing committee disbanded. Some of the strongest members, who had stayed at Harvard only to see the union through the election, left the university.

Rondeau and other 1977 activists remained good friends and saw each other frequently at lunch and social gatherings. They discovered that collective action had been so deeply implanted that even when the organization died, evidence of it remained. When a blizzard hit Boston in January 1978, a half-dozen or more old union activists gathered with skis and sleds and had fun in the snow for a few days while the Medical Area remained closed. "We played outside all day and at night we'd make dinner together and sit around listening to music and go home late," Rondeau said. "It was a nice feeling to have so many friends."

The election loss had been a shattering experience, but a mere political disappointment compared to the psychic pain that Rondeau had lived with since her teenaged years. Perhaps this was why losing the election didn't seem to affect her as profoundly as others. During this period, aided by therapy, she continued to emerge from the deepest recesses of her depression. On nice days she often walked to work. One spring morning, as she approached a bridge crossing the Charles, she noticed flowers on the river bank. She had seen flowers there before, but now she *noticed* them. Where before there had been only black and white, now she saw vivid hues, reds, greens, yellows. "I thought, 'Oh my God! I'm seeing color for the first time in my life.' I wondered what was it in me that had been closed down so that I hadn't known the color was there."

Her growing involvement in union activities stimulated a desire to do other things. She volunteered to work at a battered women's shelter in Cambridge. As her interests broadened, she became less satisfied with her Harvard job. It had become obvious that her lab assistant skills provided no entry into high-level medical research. She found herself increasingly in a financial pinch what with the cost of living rising at about 10 percent a year in the late seventies. Rondeau's starting salary at Harvard in 1976 was $8,600. By the end of 1978, she still made less than $10,000 despite three annual raises. Her third raise, in July 1978, fell well below increases in her rent and other living expenses that year.

"When I got my check," she recalled, "I was standing in the hallway with a woman who was a dishwasher in our lab. She looked at her check and kind of shrugged. But when I looked at mine, I started to cry. I realized I was trapped. I thought, 'This is your life, this is how it is, and it's going to be like this for a long time.' I began to think of unionism as being a solution for lots of problems, especially that heavy feeling that workers have of being a small, insignificant, struggling person."

Rondeau was ready for something new.

❧ ☙

Sullivan was determined to lead another drive at Harvard when the time was right. Meanwhile, she worked on other District 65 campaigns, including the one at Boston University, the nation's fourth largest private university. BU clerical workers had begun preliminary organizing in 1974 and had chosen District 65 to finish the job. The BU president, John Silber, ran his ship in a highly authoritarian manner that invited rebellion. Despite, or because of, his implacable hostility to employee representation, even BU professors had voted in a union, the American Association of University Professors (AAUP).

As at Harvard, women comprised more than 75 percent of BU's clerical and technical staff, and many were just as wary of unions as the Harvard women. But the existence of the faculty union made a major difference. Barbara Rahke, a clerical worker who chaired the BU organizing committee and went on to become a union organizer herself, recalled that the BU women "looked up to the faculty, for better or worse, and saw them as the ultimate professionals. The attitude was, if a faculty person could go out on strike, certainly a clerical worker could. That had a tremendous impact."

An election for BU's clerical and technical workers in May 1978 was clouded by challenged ballots. Months later, the NLRB declared District 65 the victor by about twenty votes. Silber threatened to carry on a legal fight. The case might have dragged on for years had not the AAUP, bargaining its own contract with Boston University, called a strike of professors in April 1979. Hitching a ride on the faculty strike, the women office workers also walked off the job and demanded that Silber recognize District 65 as their bargaining agent.

With thousands of professors and clerical/technical workers on strike, Boston University practically ceased operations for a week. It was one of the rare instances in university labor relations when employees as dissimilar as professors and lowly faculty secretaries and assistants formed a coalition of sorts. But it did not last long. Offered a three-year contract with an immediate 7 percent wage increase, the 900 faculty members voted to return to work after a nine-day walkout.

The clerical workers mobilized community support with a clever publicity campaign, and public opinion turned against Silber. After all, the underpaid support staff wanted nothing more than recognition of a union that they had chosen in a vote certified by the NLRB. How could Silber, as head of an institution that professed to value the democratic process, deny this much? Apparently he could not. After two weeks of strike, the university agreed to recognize and bargain with District 65.

Silber dropped the legal fight against 65 but not his hostility to unionism. The union had to strike again in the fall to gain a first contract for its 800-plus members. Still, the clerical union survived while the faculty union eventually succumbed to continuing attacks by Silber. (He was aided by a 1980 U.S. Supreme Court decision, considered faulty and wrongheaded by many labor law scholars, in a case involving Yeshiva University. The court ruled that professors in private universities should be classified as managerial employees and thus ineligible to bargain through a union. Using this ruling, Silber and his attorneys won a long NLRB and court fight to decertify the AAUP. The final ruling came in 1987.)

In 1979, however, the women clerical workers at BU won what had become a moral battle with Silber. They seemed to have disproved the old axiom, taken as a biological given in many quarters of the male-led union movement, that women office workers would not strike. Women might resist making aggressive displays just to feel good, but they would hit the bricks if circumstances demanded it and if they had capable leaders.

The breakthrough at BU put District 65 in the vanguard of organized labor's effort to secure a foothold in private universities. The union already had small units at Barnard and Teachers Colleges in New York City, and Julie Kushner, a District 65 organizer, was leading a drive at Columbia University which, in 1985, would produce a 1,000-member unit for 65.

The successful BU campaign also seemed to justify 65's expansion into the New England area, an advance owing much to Sullivan herself. The first organizer hired in the region, she had worked largely on her own for about five years. After the defeat at Harvard, she had conducted many other organizing drives around Boston and throughout Massachusetts. By early 1979 she had begun thinking seriously about returning to Harvard. She wanted to hire and train a Harvard activist to develop a new committee and to assist her elsewhere in the region. District 65 leaders always were reluctant to commit money, and Sullivan had to argue her case over and over. "They didn't care what or where I organized, as long as it didn't cost a lot of money," she said. Harvard, however, presented an especially attractive target, and Livingston approved her plan to hire an assistant.

Sullivan already had chosen a candidate. Kris Rondeau was bright, personable, and very good talking with workers. She had a properly skeptical attitude about management and appeared capable of resisting intimidation. Most important, Rondeau was eager to do it. "Kris was the only one who had a feeling for it," Sullivan said. "She hadn't gotten involved until the end of the first campaign, which might explain why she still had a lot of energy left for the second campaign. It took a lot out of you. You had to believe in it, and Kris believed. When I started to think about going back to Harvard, she was the one who responded."

Despite an interval of two years between campaigns and a turnover of roughly 50 percent in personnel, the Medical Area staff was as restless as ever. Harvard had done little to improve its salary and benefits policy and nothing to change the coldness that pervaded the institution. Rondeau and Sullivan developed activists among the new employees, brought them together with veterans of the first drive, and formed a new committee. It began meeting in March 1979. On May 1, Rondeau quit her Harvard job and began working for District 65.

Transformations in America can be amazing. Three years before, Rondeau had come to cosmopolitan Harvard on the glistening Charles River as a slim, shy, uncertain girl from a feudal mill town in a forgotten valley of central Massachusetts. Now she was an independent, self-assured woman bent on instructing Harvard University, one of the oldest institutions in the New World, on the proper conduct of employee relations.

This would not be immediately. As Rondeau and Sullivan slowly rebuilt support in the Medical Area, they worked as partners on many other projects. They become close friends. Sullivan introduced the younger woman to the fast-moving, often grubby, sometimes dangerous, always stimulating world of the labor organizer. One could picture the two young women flitting about in a sort of worklife underworld, meeting clandestinely with frightened workers, walking on rain-soaked picket lines, talking themselves hoarse over coffee and sodas at diners.

It also was very much a man's world, a huge cock-fighting arena, this world of corporations, trade unions, and union-busters. It always had been. But from the early days there had been pioneering women organizers.

࿇ ࿇

As early as 1834, a few "factory girls" in the Lowell, Massachusetts textile mills organized co-workers and led a "turn-out," or strike, to protest a speedup. Though brief and futile, the strike demonstrated that women could be united over work issues. Labor organizations, however, did not employ female organizers until much later. In 1868, Kate Mullaney, the head of a laundry workers union in Troy, New York, was appointed as a "national organizer" by the short-lived National Labor Union. Leonora Barry, a hosiery mill worker in Amsterdam, New York, was appointed in 1886 "general investigator" of the Knights of Labor, which succeeded the NLU as a national federation of unions. She traveled through the United States and Canada, organizing women and lobbying for labor legislation.

These women and others like them worked in unimaginably hostile surroundings. They received little help from men but much abuse. The prevailing belief of male unionists was that women should stay in the home instead of competing with men for scarce jobs. Society looked down on union organizers in general, and female recruiters in particular. Barry, though a deeply religious woman, was denounced by a Catholic priest as a "lady tramp." The women's suffrage movement of the late nineteenth century drew particular scorn from men. When Susan B. Anthony, one of the most notable feminists of the nineteenth century, proposed merging labor reform and suffrage through working women's associations, male unionists rebuffed her.

Not all female labor militants were suffragists. The legendary "Mother Jones" (Mary Harris) believed that the task of unions was to win a living wage for men so their wives could stay home and raise children. Nonetheless, she inspired men and women alike with her fiery speeches in West Virginia and Colorado mining camps for more than fifty years. She orated and organized, went to jail, and returned to the fray over and over, even as a nonagenarian in the 1920s. Other well-known women organizers of the twentieth century included Rose Schneiderman in the needle trades; Mary Anderson who organized among clothing workers and in 1921 became the first director of the Women's Bureau of the U.S. Department of Labor; Mary Heaton Vorse who wrote about and helped organize laboring women; Elizabeth Gurley Flynn, an organizer for the International Workers of the World (Wobblies) who turned to Communism in the 1930s; and innumerable staff organizers of the Women's Trade Union League, a privately funded organization which conducted social and economic uplift campaigns among women workers (usually, but not always, in alliance with unions).

After World War II, women's interest in union work seemed to decline, though there were notable exceptions, until the late sixties. Political ferment and the women's liberation movement then created both union demand for and a supply of idealistic young women. They filtered into organizing jobs in textiles, the needle trades, electrical equipment, electronics, telecommunications, schools, government offices, hospitals, and other health care institutions. Although unions made use of female talent, they kept women in relatively minor positions. In this respect organized labor differed not a whit from corporate and government employers. In most unions, the practice of electing regional and national officers in convention only impeded the rise of women because men controlled a majority of convention votes. By the early seventies, women served in relatively high-level jobs in only a few major unions, including the United Auto Workers (UAW) and the Communications Workers of America.

To correct this situation, union women started a sort of mini-movement within organized labor. In 1974, about 3,200 trade union women attended the founding conference of the Coalition of Labor Union Women (CLUW). "It is imperative," declared CLUW's statement of purpose, "that within the framework of the union movement, we take aggressive steps to more effectively address ourselves to the critical needs of 30 million unorganized sisters and to make our unions more responsible to the needs of all women . . . ."

Many male union leaders looked with scorn on the founding of CLUW, thus the famous comment by a veteran woman unionist, Myra Wolfgang of the Hotel and Restaurant Employees Union. "When you go back to your unions," she told the huge gathering of union women, "you'll be able to tell Meany and Woodcock and Fitzimmons that 3,200 women met in Chicago—and we didn't come to swap recipes." Meany and Frank Fitzsimmons, president of the Teamsters, did not respond. UAW President Leonard Woodcock sent a good-wishes telegram to the conference.

When it became apparent that CLUW was bent on reform not revolution, the male leadership of the AFL-CIO began to soften its attitude. Meany himself appeared at a CLUW conference in 1977 and said: "If supporting a living wage for all workers makes me a feminist, move over sisters; I've been called a lot worse." In 1980, the AFL-CIO for the first time elected a woman to sit on the policymaking executive council, until then restricted to the heads of major unions, all male. The next year the council created a second at-large position for another woman.

CLUW raised the level of awareness of sex discrimination in unions and goaded male leaders into thinking of reform. But as good as CLUW's intentions were, by 1979 it had not accomplished much. Women still were treated as second-class citizens in most unions and rarely rose to policy-making positions. Leslie Sullivan attended a few CLUW meetings in Boston in the mid-seventies. "It was not a coordinated organization," she recalled. "It provided a way for union women to get together, but I don't think CLUW had any impact on union leadership." CLUW gave her no help in dealing with problems in her own union, nor could it without doing what would be perceived as "meddling" in the affairs of individual unions. Perhaps little more could have been done from within.

By the time Sullivan and Rondeau began organizing together in 1979, labor history offered many tales of women who preceded them. There was nothing new in having to fight battles on two fronts, with employers on one side and their own unions on the other. The earlier women had it harder, working in times and places that posed far more hazardous conditions for women activists. But Sullivan and Rondeau were breaking ground in one sense. They—and Sullivan in particular—were in the first generation of women organizers who began work with heightened expectations. First the women's movement and then society itself, in the form of antidiscrimination laws and regulations, had started them off with a strong sense of moral and legal backing.

The two women were together much of the time, working on dozens of different campaigns ranging in duration from a few days to a year or more, some successful, many not. They organized mainly among workers in service occupations at day care centers, book and other retail shops, with occasional attempts at small industrial shops. They passed out leaflets, introduced themselves on sidewalks, held small meetings in workers' homes, listened to workers' complaints over coffee, negotiated contracts in smoke-filled rooms, vied with lawyers in arbitration hearings, addressed large groups of women, and now and then picketed an office or store.

Rondeau learned by watching Sullivan. She learned to do "cold organizing," or approaching one or a group of workers without preparation or introduction. She learned to form and develop a committee of activists. She learned how to address a meeting and deal with rebellious members and how to distinguish members who criticized constructively from dissidents pursuing a different agenda. In a small union like District 65, a "general organizer" had to do much more than proselytize, recruit, and bring about an NLRB election. Once organized, the new members had to be "serviced," and in a regional office like Boston administrative duties fell to the organizer. While working practically alone for several years, Sullivan had negotiated contracts, handled grievances for all members in the Boston area, and contended with management lawyers in different forums. Now Rondeau learned about the business side of unionism.

The two women agreed on many things but differed in outlook. Where Sullivan was a programmatic liberal-leftist, a believer in following the organization wherever it went, Rondeau took a more eclectic approach. She was loyal to the union but not as intensely loyal as Sullivan. Neither woman would follow foolish leaders down disastrous paths, but of the two Rondeau had less patience with organizational shortsightedness. The idea of a "labor movement" as national revolution-in-process did not have as much meaning for Rondeau as Sullivan. "I was a Harvard worker organizing Harvard workers," Rondeau said, explaining the difference, "but Leslie was a trade unionist."

"It was a very demanding job, both emotionally and physically," Rondeau said. "But it was also fun and satisfying beyond explanation. You don't have to win all the time, but if it's going well, it feels great. We were doing something that we really cared about, so we would be working day and night. We'd build close relationships with the people we were organizing, and this felt good."

The union itself threw many impediments in the path of its own employees. District 65 appealed to women who were strong, idealistic, and highly motivated, precisely the qualities needed to be an exceptional organizer. The trouble was, these same qualities put the new women of 65 into conflict with the union's old-line male hierarchy.

❦

Sometime in the early seventies, David Livingston decided to throw District 65 into white-collar organizing. Within a few years, he hired several women organizers, including Sullivan, Kathy Kautzer, Barbara Rahke, and Carol Knox in Boston and, in New York, Margie Albert, Ellen Harper,

Bernice Krawczyk, Kitty Krupat, and Julie Kushner. The first major development occurred in 1974 when 65 gave aid to an independent union on strike at Harper & Row.

The strike lasted three weeks, ending when Harper & Row withdrew concessionary demands. Later in 1974, the Harper & Row workers voted to affiliate with District 65. The local president, Bernice Krawczyk, resigned her editor's job and joined a District 65 task force that was mounting a publishing-industry campaign headed by Margie Albert. Although District 65 would invest a considerable amount of money and energy in the publishing campaign over the next three years, it would be, on the whole, a failure. The union managed to organize small units at Prentice Hall, Viking Penguin, and New American Library. The staff of *Village Voice*, the New York weekly, joined en masse when press magnate Rupert Murdoch bought the paper. But 65 lost many more NLRB elections than it won and eventually shut down the publishing effort.

The women organized successfully elsewhere, including the Museum of Modern Art. Krawczyk moved up through District 65 ranks, becoming director of the Technical, Office, and Professional Department, before leaving in 1983. During her ten years on the 65 staff, she had an inside view of the union leadership and came to understand the powerful cross-currents that sent confusing signals to far-flung organizers like Leslie Sullivan.

On the one hand, Krawczyk said, Livingston was a "brilliant, brilliant" man who "recognized where the future of the union was and tried to take it there"—that is, into white-collar service industries with predominantly female work forces. But this was an unpopular move among other 65 officials and staff members. Coming out of industrial backgrounds, this middle tier of leaders begrudged what they regarded as different treatment accorded to white-collar workers in general and women in particular. Livingston himself did not seem to act out of sexist tendencies; he acted the dictator with everybody. But many of his subordinates came from a world in which the view of women as the inferior sex, ordained by nature and God to bear and raise children and stay out of men's way, hadn't changed in the century since a priest labeled Leonora Barry, the early female organizer, as a "lady tramp."

"They resented us because we were getting things," Krawczyk said. "We got an office, we got equipment, we got this and that, and what were *they* getting? They were in industries that were dying. They could see that. It was very difficult for them to organize, and they wanted more resources. Instead, it was going to these snot-nose kids coming in the door . . .

114

women on top of that, 'the girls,' you know, and I think they wanted us to fail." Kitty Krupat encountered the same problem with men at every level of leadership. "They were often inhospitable and threw all kinds of obstacles in our way," she said. Livingston's failure was that he put up with these men because they did not threaten him politically.

During the years that Sullivan worked alone, she had only occasional problems with union officials. They were in New York and she was in Boston. Her first supervisor, Herman, was fired by Livingston for various wrongdoings. She didn't get along any better with other men who occasionally visited Boston from the New York headquarters. Sullivan felt that Livingston distrusted her, possibly because she tended to speak her mind. She also discovered that District 65 leaders invariably blamed election defeats on the organizer heading a campaign, and Harvard had been a large loss. Although she directed many winning drives, no one in the union ever congratulated or thanked her. They could not possibly complain that she didn't work hard enough. Yet the men who ran 65 usually ignored her advice and treated her and other women in a manner approaching contempt.

Sullivan was used to male chauvinism. She had experienced it for years at Harvard. She had thought it would be different in District 65, but it was not. "They wanted women," she said in 1994, referring to Livingston and other male leaders of 65. "They thought it was nice to have us there. But they didn't want us in any position of power. They liked to think of us as their 'little girls.'"

It is almost a natural condition of working in a far-flung office that you feel singularly ill-treated. People working at home base may be equally put upon, but being close to the source of foolishness somehow makes one more tolerant of it. District 65 women based in New York certainly had to cope with sexist behavior. Living in the eye of the storm, women like Krawczyk, Krupat, and Kushner learned how to sidestep the worst buffetings. Krawczyk came to see the behavior of the men in a cultural context. Older, blue-collar Jewish men tended to settle differences of opinion by "yelling, screaming and stamping around," she said. "You were expected to fight for what you wanted. Margie Albert showed me the way. She would go to Livingston and yell at him, and they would carry on and even be yelling in the hallways. He would call you a traitor to the cause. But the next morning, everything was fine and it was forgotten, and you went on to the next thing. That was the way they sorted things out."

For the most part Sullivan operated on her own initiative, choosing where and when to mount campaigns. She began organizing workers at day care centers, a swiftly expanding sector of the services industry. Working alone at first, later with the help of Rondeau and others, she signed up workers at about a half-dozen private day care agencies across Massachusetts. Although classified as private agencies, these firms received much of their funding from state government because they provided services for poor working families. Sullivan formed one local union for all day-care members, hoping eventually to amass a group large enough to lobby state government for improved funding. She saw this as a way to expand a vitally needed service for working mothers, to help low-paid workers, and to open up a new area for District 65.

When the New York office assigned her to campaigns, things began to go wrong. There seemed to be no logic in their choice of organizing targets. Someone determined that it would be smart to organize bookstores and other retail shops, many of them with no more than a half-dozen employees. She tried to convince her leaders that recruiting at small shops made little economic sense for the union or for the workers. With high turnover, the employer would be able to prod new employees to vote the union out after a year or two. The pittance of dues income received from a small shop could easily be wiped out in the cost of going to arbitration over one grievance. The contracts negotiated by District 65 improved wages and benefits only minimally for the workers because the employer did not have much to begin with.

"These little places had so few people, but you had to spend as much time negotiating a contract as with a large employer," Sullivan said. "They [District 65 leaders] didn't care that I was putting in a hundred hours a week to organize a small shop because they didn't see my time as valuable in the first place. In the second place, they didn't care what kind of crummy contract you got for the workers. They were not willing to spend the time and effort to really go in and do their best. The fact is we didn't have much leverage in the smaller shops. We couldn't get the workers very much. But the union was never honest with people about what they could do for them."

Sullivan had some horrifying experiences. On one occasion the New York office decided to sign up workers in a shoe factory in Lawrence, Massachusetts. Several male organizers led by a man who will be called Eddie "would fly up from New York and rent a long, fancy car," she recounted. "These guys in the slick suits and black shoes, they just looked so New York. They would pick me up and we would drive to Lawrence. They would park outside the factory and get out in their suits and give out leaflets to these poor immigrant workers. We looked absurd."

Eddie hired a local worker and ordered him to collect cards in the shoe factory to seek an election. One day, this man appeared at Sullivan's office in Boston with a large number of cards he had received in the mail. He was mystified. "They were coming in batches, hundreds of them," Sullivan said. "They were all signed, but they all had the same handwriting and the same misspellings. I called Eddie and told him that the same person had signed all these cards. They were forgeries. He mumbled, 'No, no.' It didn't matter, he said, the cards were fine." She suspected that either Eddie or one of his subordinates had signed the cards and driven to Lawrence to mail them so they would have the proper postmark.

Eddie arrived in Boston a few days later. Brushing aside Sullivan's concern, he insisted that they take the cards to the NLRB to file for an election. The board agent who met with them was an older man who obviously had been around. After examining some of the cards, he stopped and wiped his glasses. "He told Eddie that his eyesight wasn't very good and that he couldn't see the cards too clearly," Sullivan said. "But he thought we should take them back. He was being real nice to us because he saw immediately that the cards were phony. That was the end of our petition for the shoe factory. The fact is we never got more than a dozen legitimate cards from that factory. It was a joke."

It was with a deep sense of regret that Sullivan, in 1994, talked frankly about her experiences with the union. "I should say that I developed these opinions about District 65 later in my history with the union. I was much more starry-eyed and naive in those early years. I really so deeply believed in unions, and I deeply believed in District 65 in particular. It took a lot to disillusion me. It's not like I became cynical about this union overnight. They had to pound it into me."

Speaking of Sullivan, Rondeau said, "She really was in a laboratory, more or less by herself. She didn't have any resources from the union. She had to make it up as she went along, and I think that that's an awful position to be in."

Both women were sexually harassed. Rondeau had been in her new job for less than a week. She was alone in the District 65 office when a strange man walked in and acted as if he belonged there. "I was brand new, twenty-seven years old, and I didn't even know who this man was," Rondeau recalled. "I was standing by my desk, and he put his hand on my ass. I picked up his hand, and I pushed it away and said, 'Don't touch me!'"

A short time later Sullivan introduced him as a union man visiting from New York. He regarded Rondeau coldly, as if she had wronged *him*.

She had reacted swiftly, and the moment always stuck in her mind. "I was really proud of myself," she said. "It was one of those perfect moments when you do the right thing, and I wanted to call my shrink. That man hated my guts from then on."

Sullivan also had a confrontation with the same man. One day he and Sullivan traveled separately to Northhampton, Massachusetts, to meet with employees interested in forming a union. They decided to stay overnight and meet again in the morning. The two went together to a motel, where the man asked for a room for both of them. Sullivan said, "I was appalled. I said 'no' and checked into a room of my own. My relationship with him was downhill from then on."

This incident was, Rondeau believed, the beginning of the end for Sullivan at District 65. The man's dislike for her would be communicated upward in the union. Regina Little, a lawyer who came into District 65 as a member of an independent union and later served as executive assistant to Livingston, said there were other examples of this kind of behavior. Livingston himself was "a very gentlemanly guy," Little said. "He would never say 'broad.' He was always completely professional and businesslike and never did any of that stuff himself. But he had these men in important positions who were doing it and he didn't do anything to stop it."

Rondeau once complained to Livingston about the man who harassed her and Sullivan. "David could be quite cruel in the way he talked to staff members of either sex, but he wouldn't swear in front of a woman," she said. "He found that too embarrassing. But when I told him, 'This guy is sexually harassing us,' well . . . I don't think David listened to stuff like that very well. The meeting was uneventful and useless."

The very survival of District 65 began to preoccupy Livingston in the late 1970s. The times were not right for a union that tried to operate like a social welfare agency on dues income from poor workers in small shops in declining industries. As 65's garment and textile employers went out of business and jobs melted away, revenues going to the union's multi-employer pension fund and the Security Plan also declined. Fewer and fewer active workers supported a rising pool of retirees. Livingston tried to bring in new members with aggressive (and costly) organizing programs in white-collar areas, but he had less and less money with which to do it. District 65 was withering away.

In June 1979, Livingston entered into an agreement to affiliate with the United Auto Workers, one of the largest American unions with more than one million members. But he refused to be, like so many smaller unions that merged with giants, swallowed up and digested and never heard from again. There was this about Livingston: he had a force of personality and chutzpah that would not be denied. He wrested from the larger union a highly unusual compromise. Instead of being divided up into separate UAW locals according to industry and location, District 65's 35,000 to 50,000 members would remain a single unit, or an "amalgamated local union," within the UAW. Even more unusual, the UAW would refund to 65 nearly the full value of the per capita tax that the smaller union paid to the parent.

District 65 thus was able to operate independently with its own paid staff until the merger was completed. The smaller union had to amend its constitution to conform with the UAW's, and many organizational differences had to be worked out. Livingston was not in a hurry. Although sixty-four, he did not want to retire, and he assuredly did not want his union to disappear. There now began one of the longest merger processes in the history of labor organizations.

In the meantime, the UAW subsidized the smaller union. The UAW International Executive Board was divided over the merger, but supporters like President Douglas A. Fraser saw tangible benefits in the future. They thought that 65's organizing vigor in white-collar areas such as higher education and publishing could help the UAW as its own industrial membership declined. In 1994, recalling that period, Fraser said, "A lot of excellent people came out of 65, excellent women organizers, dedicated people who worked like hell."

Sullivan and Rondeau received news of the merger with enthusiasm tempered by realism. From everything they had heard, the UAW was more democratic than most unions and free of corruption. It stood against race and sex discrimination, dealt honestly with its members, performed notably well in wage negotiations, and paid its bills (including organizers' expenses) on time. No other large union had done as much to promote sex equality. In 1968 the union created a position for a woman on its executive board and elected to that seat a vice-president, Olga Madar. This was at least a decade ahead of most unions. The UAW had endorsed the Equal Rights Amendment in the 1970s. In the automobile plants, while men dominated and controlled local unions, some women had played very strong roles as shop leaders since the 1930s.

But Sullivan and Rondeau knew by now that an organization's reputation rarely reflected reality. They didn't believe that their own working lives would be much changed as a result of an affiliation agreement most of whose terms remained to be fulfilled.

District 65 was on the steep end of a slope carrying the entire trade union movement into possibly permanent decline. For women workers, this trend was even more fateful than the stalling of the women's movement. For all their ambivalent attitude toward sex equality, unions were the only institution that could negotiate power and participation for workers of any sex. In this time of management ascendancy, Sullivan and Rondeau charged again into battle with Harvard University. It would be the fight of their lives.

CHAPTER NINE

One morning in March 1981, Rondeau drove out to the Primate Research Center in Southborough. It had always been difficult to keep up support at the Center because of its geographical and cultural distance from other Harvard work sites. The animal caretakers, mainly white men, had no connection with Harvard workers in Cambridge and Boston and more than a little suspicion of women organizers. In recent months, with frequent visits, she had begun developing a band of activists. But on this day, a month before a second representation election at Harvard, something was wrong. As soon as she walked in, workers began scattering.

"I knew these people really well," Rondeau said, "but when I went in there, Vroom! they're gone. They just disappeared. I saw a bunch of guys go into the men's room. I stood outside the door and said, 'Come out, talk to me.' I felt humiliated standing there."

Finally, "one guy got up enough courage and came all the way out and told me a story that was going around. He says, 'We were told that District 65 has lots of blacks and Puerto Ricans in New York City. If we join the union, you'll make us go out on strike, and then you'll bring busloads of blacks and Puerto Ricans from New York to take our jobs.' This startled me, but I said, 'C'mon, think about it!'"

The man acknowledged this was a crazy rumor. Rondeau couldn't find out where it had begun, but the story was so specific to the Primate Center that it must have been started by an antiunion supervisor or worker. She couldn't blame management for the foolish things that people believe, but she could blame them for creating an atmosphere in which frightened and confused workers would take such nonsense seriously.

It was that kind of campaign. Rondeau later would term it the "most disgusting, intense and sophisticated antiunion campaign I have seen or heard of." It was true, as before, that Harvard did not fire union enthusiasts or subject them to physical threats, but in her view a university should not receive good grades for *merely* conducting a campaign of psychological pressure and disinformation. The university, of course, contended that it employed only reasonable, legal means of persuasion. It went about this business with the intention of pulverizing a small union movement—and succeeded, though the residue was not so much dead dust as true grit on which the next movement would be built.

The drive had started in the fall of 1980, at about the time that an enormous wave of popularity was sweeping Ronald Reagan to victory over incumbent Jimmy Carter for the Presidency. The Harvard organizing committee had been working for a year and a half since being reconstituted after the 1977 defeat. The time was judged right to intensify the campaign, and District 65 agreed to put in a little more money. Leslie Sullivan, busy on other union projects in the Boston area, continued to supervise Harvard operations but put Rondeau in charge of daily activities. In December 1980, Rondeau filed an election petition with the NLRB, submitting cards signed by slightly over half of about eight hundred employees.

She soon realized this was a grave tactical mistake. The board scheduled an election for April 9, 1981, giving both sides most of three months to do their proselytizing. For an employer with the resources of Harvard, three months was more than enough time to ram home a powerful antiunion message. Both the union and the employee activists perhaps were too eager to try again. But Harvard's failure to fulfill promises it had made during the 1977 campaign angered many workers, who felt their economic status had continued to deteriorate.

Martha Robb, a leading activist in 1980–81, explained why the demand for unionization swelled again in the Medical Area. "During the antiunion campaign in seventy-seven, we heard from them [management] every day, sometimes twice a day," Robb said. The administration promised to address issues raised by the union if the workers voted it down. "Right after the election, they sent us one letter with 'WE HEAR YOU,' in big headline letters. It was like they were saying, 'Oh, if we'd only known how bad things were! But now we'll fix them.' But that was the last time anybody heard from the administration until the next union drive in 1981. It went back to what I assume business as usual had been like in the preceding three hundred fifty years—you know, ignoring people."

The people who felt most ignored were women, blacks, and staff support workers of all categories. By 1981 Harvard had made some progress in combating sex and race discrimination. According to a university report, 46 percent of administrative and professional jobs were held by women. Critics noted that many of these positions were classified as "administrative assistant," whereas men who held similar posts were called "assistant administrators" and received higher pay. It appeared, though, that women no longer were being confined to clerical positions. Academic posts were another matter. Of 352 tenured members of the Arts and Sciences faculty, only twelve were women in 1980. Major departments, such as history and sociology, had no tenured women; nor did the Harvard Business School and the Kennedy School of Government. Meanwhile, Harvard's first formal case of sex discrimination in faculty promotions was making news in early 1981. Theda R. Skocpol, an associate professor of sociology and recipient of awards for scholarship, refused to accept a decision denying her tenure. Embarrassed by the publicity, Harvard reconsidered her case and eventually granted tenure. It was said to be the first sex discrimination case in Harvard's 345-year history.

The university did poorly at all levels in hiring and promoting blacks and other minorities. One of the problems, a university official told the *Crimson*, was that Harvard's extreme decentralization—so applauded as an academic good—worked against the social good. There was no central hiring office and no easy way to monitor hiring decisions made by scores of department heads throughout the university. The departments tended to hire according to their own needs, paying little attention to the effect on overall statistics. Even the Medical Area schools, although located in a neighborhood with large black and Hispanic populations, hired relatively small numbers of minorities. The School of Public Health employed only thirty-four blacks and six Hispanics in 364 support staff jobs. Minority workers constituted only 4.2 percent of the supervisory staff.

Richard Pendleton, an Afro-American who had worked at Countway Library since 1967, said that discrimination on the job did not produce an unusual number of complaints. "But," he added, "we were so few in number, and Harvard was pretty equal at how they hassled people." Management's condescending attitude toward all workers was, in part, why Pendleton had become a union activist. The administration was not above trying to divide blacks and whites on the union issue, he said. During the 1981 drive, a black attorney who identified himself as a special assistant for minority affairs to Derek Bok, arranged a meeting of all black employees in the Medical Area. "That made me suspicious, but I went to hear what he would say," Pendleton recalled. "This guy said the university was committed to improving the position and working status of black employees, and that they didn't need a third party to intercede for them. He didn't directly allude to the union, but a lot of the antiunion rhetoric took that line, that you didn't need a third party. His intent was pretty clear. It was to divide blacks and whites. I made up my mind I wasn't going to go for that. So my question to this guy was, 'Over the years, I've seen Harvard mistreat and abuse so many white people, why should I expect anything better?'"

It is unlikely that Derek Bok would have ordered or supported a plan to create racial divisions. But a person acting for the university did try such a tactic, pointing up one of Harvard's main weaknesses in dealing with a union. The administration spoke out of all sides of several mouths and could not prevent its many appendages from dancing to the conflicting beats of different personnel policies. Even if the university had wanted to address the problems of its female office and lab workers, it would have been hard pressed to adopt an effective university-wide plan.

Economic and social forces at the beginning of the eighties were bearing down heavily on women workers at Harvard and elsewhere. The women's movement's drive for sex equality seemed to have vanished as a national political force. Even Betty Friedan, whose descriptions of women's status in postwar United States did so much to start the movement in the sixties, appeared much less certain where it was headed in the eighties. In *The Second Stage*, a somewhat despairing book published in 1981, she declared that the "movement" phase of women's drive for equality had passed. In this phase, she said, women had aimed for "full participation, power and voice in the mainstream, inside the party, the political process, the professions, the business world." They had made some inroads, but exhilaration had given way to "tiredness."

In a sense, the "easy" part of the revolution, forcing an end to demeaning treatment, had passed into history. New concerns of a more elemental economic nature had come to the fore. Rondeau, who was of the seventies generation of workers, could see a clear demarcation when she looked back from the vantage point of 1994. "In my own generation, a lot of those symbolic things like 'service with a smile' were seen as very sexist, and we were taught to think critically about them. But today's generation of women workers think that being treated in a sexist way is earning a substandard wage. That's a different way of thinking about the problems that women face."

By the early eighties, many women were trying to come to terms with the roles available to them as a result of their unfinished revolution. A married woman had to stand awkwardly divided, one foot in the home and one in the workplace. Many wives had to work because of a decline in men's earning power. Forty-five percent of mothers of children under six were working in 1980, compared with only 10 percent in 1960. Many would-be mothers had put off childbearing because they wanted to work. Society seemed to be saying, "By all means, get out of the home and take a job or start a professional career. You have every right to do this, the law is now on your side." It was like passing a law without appropriating money to enforce it. In the workplace most women still could not advance as far as their talents would allow or even earn as much as men in jobs of comparable complexity. Nor could they easily find a way of responsibly caring for their children.

At Harvard, salaries had not kept pace with inflation in the late 1970s, and Rondeau's union talked of negotiating an annual cost-of-living adjustment. In March 1981, a few weeks before the election, Harvard announced it would raise salaries 9.5 to 15.5 percent. The average clerical salary of about $12,000 may have compared favorably with those paid by other colleges and universities in the region, but it did not compare well at all with the $14,000 estimated to be needed by a family of four in Boston. The university had improved benefits to some degree. But it still did not provide dental insurance, and paid only 40 percent of health care premiums. Working women could not afford the university's day care facilities. There still was no career advancement plan worthy of the name.

Rondeau and her friends had come to believe that a union movement should not confine itself to salaries or to "women's issues" such as child care and comparable pay. They wanted something more. They respected Harvard as an institution and even believed that for all their lowly status they could improve the university. The union women wanted to be a visible part of the scene, but Harvard kept painting them out. They wanted nothing less than what Friedan thought women had started to win in the first stage of the women's movement: "participation, power and voice."

District 65's request for a second election surprised no one in the Harvard administration. Ed Powers considered this almost inevitable given the character of the work force and the nature of laboratory and technical work, which comprised about 40 percent of all Medical Area jobs. Most research assistants had either bachelor or higher degrees and took these entry-level jobs with the hope of advancing to professional scientific research. Frustrated by an inability to make this leap, Powers theorized, the workers turned to unionism.

"No matter what we did," Powers said in 1994, "there would be forty percent of the non-exempt staff who wanted a union." Women with advanced degrees who took research assistant jobs faced two prospects, he said. "They'd either do professional-level research, for which they wouldn't be paid, or they would do nonprofessional work, like washing test tubes, and feel they were being underutilized. Either way, they were mad at Harvard. And that syndrome we never did learn how to deal with. You don't get promoted into professional research by Harvard or any similar institution by being hired as a non-exempt. It just doesn't happen." The labor market was teeming with overqualified people, and Harvard could not expect research leaders *not* to hire them.

University officials took the new union threat even more seriously than in 1977. They had seen Boston University fall to District 65 and undergo shattering strikes. It didn't matter that BU's own actions brought on the strikes. Harvard also still feared that a union success in the Medical Area could lead to Balkanization of the university by several unions. Harvard again questioned the appropriateness of a bargaining unit solely in the Medical Area. But the NLRB regional office rejected the motion because the facts of the situation—the administrative structure of Harvard—remained the same as when the board ruled against the university in 1977. Harvard officials also worried what would happen if the UAW, father-to-be of District 65, threw its very large resources into the fight.

For these reasons, Steiner and Powers prepared and set in motion a more powerful antiunion campaign than their 1977 effort. "The general themes we tried to emphasize," Steiner recalled, "were the strengths of Harvard—showing that we had competitive salaries and that our benefit programs tended to be better. We also tried to mention some of the things that we thought might not be so attractive about unionization. And we tried to correct misstatements that were being made by the union."

Harvard's new campaign would involve, as before, a written attack in letters and memos and meetings with employees. But the meetings would be significantly different in character. In 1977, university officials gathered hundreds of employees together, either as "captive" or "voluntary" audiences, according to rival union and university nomenclature. In 1981, the administration talked to small groups ranging from about a half-dozen to twenty. It was the difference between a colonel addressing an entire battalion over a loudspeaker and appearing in person before each squad and looking each soldier in the face.

The union side, meanwhile, had three paid organizers on a part-time basis, including Rondeau, Sullivan, and a Harvard worker, Johanna Kovitz, who went on the union payroll for three months. This was a small group to cover 800 employees, the ideal ratio being one organizer for each 100 to 125 employees. But District 65, desperately in need of money for all its activities, refused to spend more on Harvard. A new band of activists carried on the person-to-person organizing. The most active included the following.

Martha Robb, thirty-three, was a lab assistant in the medical school and a graduate of Northeastern University. Though only tepidly prounion in 1977, Robb underwent a conversion of sorts when she met Rondeau in 1979. The two eventually became fast friends.

Robert Metcalf worked in Countway Library while studying for a master's in library science at Simmons College. His interest in unionism had been whetted by reading John Steinbeck's *In Dubious Battle*, and he became an activist midway through Rondeau's first talk with him. He felt only scorn for Harvard's personnel policy. "There was no career," he said. "Only once did I hear of a person who got promoted out of the unit and into a professional job. Management was pretty slow-witted and unyielding. Trying to get them to move on a problem was like trying to move the building itself. The complaint system was getting yourself in good with somebody and kissing the right ass." Metcalf became the "morale officer" on the union committee and frequently wrote parodies of Harvard memos.

Marie Manna eventually became second-in-command to Rondeau. She grew up near Providence, Rhode Island, the daughter of New Deal Democrats who strongly supported the civil rights and antiwar movements. She graduated from the University of Rhode Island in 1975. Joining the Vista Volunteers, she spent a year in western New York state, aiding poor people, and then took a course in organizer training. For four years she worked as a community organizer in New Bedford, Massachusetts, and Boston.

This work she found to be ultimately dissatisfying. She wanted to form organizations that would grow and remain dynamic. "When I looked around," Manna said, "I saw that unions made a lot of sense. Unions could have a long-term effect, not just in the workplace, but in broader issues that affect people's lives." She wanted to organize from the inside, as a worker who needed a union, not from the outside as a staff organizer.

Manna heard about the District 65 campaign in the Harvard Medical Area. In September 1980, she applied for and got a job as a clerical assistant in the School of Public Health. She knew no one in District 65 and was not a union "plant." But before two months passed, she had become one of the leading union activists. In 1980, she was a slim, bespectacled twenty-seven-year-old with square, defiant shoulders and a certainty of purpose that rarely retreated.

A few activists remained from 1977, including Pendleton, David Maybury, Jeanne Lafferty, and Kristin Mahon. The two women, close friends, had quit their Harvard jobs after the first election and drifted around Boston as free-lance keypunch operators, or "data bums," as they called themselves. For years the two had searched for an organization on the political left that actually tried to produce change instead of endlessly debating theories and methods. They never found one. But their search gave them a thorough grounding in organizational politics that would turn out to be useful as the Harvard union matured. Both women returned to Harvard in 1981 and got caught up again in committee work.

Many in this group would stay together for several years and form the nucleus of what became perhaps the best team of union organizers (in white-collar workplaces) in the country. Their leader and chief strategist was Kris Rondeau.

A paid organizer theoretically serves as a union liaison to a committee of workers which determines how the union can best serve their interests. Typically, the organizer is an outsider who, after the election, will move on to another town, another campaign. The idea of moving on rarely occurred to Rondeau. She wanted not just to organize Harvard but also to reform Harvard.

By 1981, she had begun to develop strong ideas about organizing. She never tried to instill anger in workers or draw it out of them. She believed that anger was a poor organizing tool in most circumstances. Anger might win a vote (if it peaked at the right time), but it would not construct a union that helped people. Many years later, commenting on what might be called the Rising Gorge Method of Organizing current in some quarters, Rondeau said: "I think anger is the enemy of union organizing. It's the union's responsibility to create an environment in which you can be part of a union and believe in self-representation and worker's voice without being mean, without being aggressive, without being merely oppositional. If you introduce anger into a drive, you can kiss the drive goodbye."

Bob Metcalf remembered Rondeau's way of drawing people in and making them feel part of something important. "When we gathered for committee meetings, Kris often would close the door and look at us and say, 'This is confidential.' Not in a stage whisper but in a very serious, low voice. She would tell us something of strategic importance. You could see everybody in the room sort of lean forward. This was a bunch of people who had never been trusted or taken seriously by Harvard. This was the first time anybody had said to the people in this room, 'This is important, this is confidential, and I want your input on this.' Harvard didn't understand the importance of trusting people and taking them seriously, and Kris did."

Rondeau and her friends put most of their energy into what came to be called one-on-one organizing, or personal contacts with each and every employee who agreed to talk to an organizer (some refused). But "contacts" understates the way Rondeau and her crew went about this. The idea was not just to "make contact with" but to become friendly with each and every worker, to talk with each as often as it took to implant the concept of forming a community of workers.

They worked day and night for three months during the critical part of the campaign. During the day Rondeau usually would stop briefly at the District 65 office on Beacon St. in Kenmore Square, then drive or walk to the medical campus. Every day she would tramp through the corridors of the austere old buildings, moving from office to lab room to cafeteria to office. At noon she would have lunch with one or more workers. Often she met with activists in university conference rooms. The union had an unusual degree of access to this employer's property. But if Harvard would have closed off its conference rooms to the union, a furor over free speech probably would have erupted.

The union committee often worked at night, phoning employees they could not see during the day. Although they had learned from the bitter experience of 1977 not to reply in writing to Harvard's charges, they still put out a newsletter. At eight or nine or ten o'clock they would go home, sometimes stopping for a drink on the way.

Rondeau would return to her apartment in Cambridge late at night. Even in sleep she continued to organize. "I called it 'sleep-think,'" she said. "It's not sleeping like you sleep on vacation. You are still connected to the day." In her dreams she saw not faces or places but names—workers' names, "rolling around in your head." All organizers had the same experience. "And yet," Rondeau said, "we had a good time. We loved our daily lives. If you have something important to do and you do it with your friends and have a sense of humor, it can be a lot of fun as well as work."

Important things were happening elsewhere in the country. In January, Ronald Reagan took office as the 40th President of the United States and unveiled a radically different economic and budget-cutting program.

Rondeau had cast a despairing vote for Jimmy Carter in November. Now, involved in an intensive period of work, she had only "a half awareness of what was going on nationally." The "Reagan Revolution" of early 1981 was like a noisy caravan passing her tent at night. She saw fleeting images on TV. It seemed that a great actor on a white horse stood in his stirrups exhorting the multitude with promises of wealth for all in a place called Supply-Side Economy. The new economic ideology apostheosized the financial marketplace and ratified a code of materialistic individualism that seemed to place American government and unions in the same category as the "evil empire," Reagan's name for the Soviet Union. The political ethos was shifting further away from the concept of unionism as a positive force in American life.

Harvard's antiunion campaign was in tune with the trend.

The small group meetings were the most effective part of Harvard's antiunion effort. Most were held in small conference rooms, with employees sitting around a table and administrators holding forth with charts depicting salaries and benefits. The management presentations were aimed almost entirely at discrediting District 65. Every negative point made in 1977 about the union's constitution and financial structure, and especially about the District 65 Security Plan, was raised again. Employees were encouraged to speak under the guise of carrying on a debate.

In an NLRB brief filed after the election, Harvard said it had allowed union supporters to "use a substantial part of the time making statements, asking questions, challenging the statements of university representatives and engaging in a full discussion of the issues." But in a forum controlled by one side, fair debate was impossible. It was authority versus upstart. The administrators came prepared for statements challenging their version of the facts. If they couldn't refute a questioner, recalled Martha Robb, "they'd turn you into a rabble-rouser and a person of bad taste."

Rondeau and Sullivan counseled the activists to "be nice" in the meetings. Strong-minded activists like Marie Manna had trouble following these instructions. She attended a meeting with about seven other workers. A female personnel officer lectured them on the Security Plan. "All the union wants is money for the Security Plan. That's why they're organizing," she said. "It was so horrible to just sit there and listen," Manna recalled. "So I started arguing with her. I explained that we didn't have to be part of the Security Plan. It was probably the worst thing that I could have done.

It created a lot of tension in the room. I said one thing, and the personnel manager said the opposite. The workers felt like, 'Who do I believe?' That was the level of Harvard's presentations. A barrage of negative, scary information, making people feel like they were joining a shady organization. It did have an effect on people, definitely."

Harvard took care not to make blatantly false statements in these meetings. Every declaration had some basis in fact. The same was true of Harvard's primary piece of campaign literature, a 32-page dossier of selected information about District 65 and the UAW called *Union Election Fact Book*. Written by Ed Powers and issued on March 31, only ten days before the election, the *Fact Book* described the industrial character and teetering finances of 65, cited problems with its constitution (which still contained obsolete provisions), and disclosed disturbing facts about the District 65 Security Plan. Powers depicted 65 as an incompetent union dangerously near ruin. It was an impressionistic sketch, but the organizers recognized features they knew to be true. So true that Leslie Sullivan, tongue-in-cheek, began referring to the *Fact Book* as "the history of District 65."

The most damaging truths related to the Security Plan. Powers quoted from minutes of trustee meetings and an accountant's report. The plan had run up a deficit of more than $4 million during the fiscal year ended January 31, 1981 and appeared unable to pay current claims without extraordinary infusions of money. To meet the shortfall, District 65 negotiated increased employer contributions, probably at the expense of pay increases in some cases. Most troubling was a diversion of pension fund money to the Security Plan. It so happened that the trustees of the Security Plan also served on the 65 pension plan board of trustees, a potentially dangerous commingling of trustees.

If the Security Plan collapsed without paying bills (as it eventually would), workers' life savings would be threatened. Recognizing the peril, the UAW had inserted a clause in the affiliation agreement with 65, absolving itself of financial responsibility for 65's health and pension plans. Rondeau and Sullivan, as employees of the union, had had personal problems with the Security Plan. "Les and I knew the plan was floundering," Rondeau said. "You'd go to the doctor and submit your forms, and the doctor would have to wait twelve months to be paid. It was really awful."

Sullivan, in addition, was involved in administering plan benefits for Boston-area members whom she had organized in the seventies. She regretted having negotiated the plan with their employers. "First, they [Security Plan] never paid their bills, and I had to spend a lot of time trying to get them to do that. Second, they were very vague on what the plan covered. On maternity, they would only pay a small amount. Here we were, organizing women, and one of the worst benefits was maternity."

Harvard's disinformation on the Security Plan consisted of suggesting in the *Fact Book* (and stating baldly in meetings) that by choosing the union, the employees automatically would lose their existing health insurance and pension coverage and be shunted into District 65's sickly plans. While Rondeau and Sullivan refused to respond to the *Fact Book* in writing, they insisted in private conversations that as lead negotiators for the Harvard union they would not make such an irrational decision.

Powers had foreseen this line of argument. "In fact, most employees represented by District 65 have no choice—they are in 65's plans," he says in the *Fact Book*. No matter what the local organizers "may say now," they would have no control in the matter. Powers, however, was quite wrong on this point. In the 1970s, District 65 organizer Bernice Krawczyk recruited white-collar workers in several New York firms and also bargained their contracts. Although the Security Plan was a "Godsend" to blue-collar workers in small shops, she recalled, it would have been foolish for new members to discard existing health plans in favor of the union scheme. "The union tried to pressure us to accept the Security Plan, but I never did," she said. "In all instances where I discussed this with David [Livingston], I convinced him that it would have been harmful to us in the long run to switch to the Security Plan."

But this history was too convoluted to make sense in an organizing campaign. Ed Powers had attached the monkey to their backs, and the organizers couldn't throw it off.

In a post-election legal brief, Harvard said it had conducted fifty meetings at which administrators addressed small groups of workers. But in addition there were perhaps hundreds of smaller, informal sessions. As the campaign neared its end, employees began receiving letters and memos from management on the order of once or twice a week. "There was a cumulative effect from all this going on in the workplace for three months," Manna said. "It got to the point where a lot of workers felt, 'I don't want to hear any more about this from you, I don't want to hear about it from them, I don't want to hear anything about it.' And, of course, that's what they [Harvard] wanted."

But it wasn't over yet. On April 8, the eve of the election, Harvard put out a final memo in response to a prounion column by a free-lance writer in the *Globe*. The writer had suggested that the union would improve the status of women at Harvard. "That's hard to believe," said the Harvard memo, considering that only one of the thirteen top officers of District 65 was a woman; that male staff members earned an average of 48 percent more than women; and that the union's maternity benefits were so poor they violated sex discrimination provisions in federal law. The union had no chance to reply before the election, which might have been just as well because Rondeau had no idea how to object to the truth.

Harvard's campaign etched an unforgettable record in Rondeau's memory. "That's where I learned about life," she said. "I began to think in very simple ethical terms about what's right and what's wrong. And I came to believe that an antiunion campaign is an immoral thing, and that nobody should ever do it. An antiunion campaign is about fear and lack of self-confidence. Destroying someone's self-confidence is easy. What management said to us was, 'The way you see the world is not right, the people you think you can trust, you can't trust, and least of all can you trust yourself. We're Harvard, we're big, and we know all, and we'll get you, and if you think you have a prayer against us, you're wrong.' They increased the tension level so that people would vote 'no' to make the tension go away. Most of the time, unions play into that game. We learned that the hard way."

These conclusions came later. In 1981, Rondeau felt that she and her friends were defenseless and isolated. They had not publicized their campaign, largely for lack of resources. The outside world knew nothing about it. Boston newspapers barely mentioned it before it was over. Even the *Crimson* seemed jaded, carrying fewer stories than it had about the 1977 organizing effort. The UAW, which knew much about publicity, was not involved, and District 65 had little money to spare. Furthermore, 65 had been outside the AFL-CIO for years and had few allies in organized labor. "We had nothing," Rondeau said. "No money, no support of any kind. We were entirely isolated in the labor community as well as the larger community, including all of Harvard outside the Medical Area. No one was watching, and Harvard went wild with its antiunion campaign. I vowed they would never do such a thing again."

Thursday, April 9. In Washington, President Reagan was recuperating from chest wounds suffered a week and a half earlier when an emotionally disturbed man shot him outside a Washington hotel. In Europe, Soviet troops poured into Poland, threatening a political revolt launched by workers rebelling against Communist rule. Lech Walesa, the shipyard electrician who headed the union Solidarity, called off a threatened general strike to avoid provoking the Russians.

In Boston, an unusual and troubling sight greeted Medical Area employees who approached Vanderbilt Hall to vote in the union election. Armed security guards were patrolling the sidewalk in front of the building and adjacent areas. Voters had to pass between them to enter the building. The implication that violence was to be expected, laughable as it was, could not be wiped away. Sullivan and Rondeau were furious. They immediately protested to management, to Harvard lawyers, to the NLRB, and to whomever else they could think of. They got the run-around. Not until after noon did Harvard remove the guards. Half of election day had passed.

It was not a good beginning. The organizers had kept careful count of the potential "yes" and "no" votes and believed that union supporters could carry the day by perhaps a dozen votes. This was before Harvard issued its final memo and before the security guards appeared. Not that these two events alone would decide the election, but they had some effect. Moreover, no one had thought to organize a comprehensive get-out-the-vote campaign on election day. By the end of the afternoon, Sullivan and Rondeau suspected they were in trouble.

Board agents counted the ballots that evening in the Vanderbilt Hall lounge. Union and administration observers watched from close range while scores of people sat in rows of chairs. About 750 workers, more than 90 percent of the work force, had voted.

Jeanne Lafferty, admittedly a pessimist, felt from the moment she walked into the lounge that the count would go against the union. Bob Metcalf had stashed a bottle of champagne and a bottle of Jack Daniels in a rear cloak room. The former was to be drunk if the union won, and the latter in case of a defeat. Long before the count ended, Lafferty and Martha Robb began swigging Jack Daniels in the cloak room.

"Every once in a while we would go into the main room, look at the piles of ballots and try to guess which were the 'yes' and 'no' piles," Robb said. "For a while they were very, very close, but then the 'no's' began gaining. Kris and Leslie looked awful, standing at the counting table. It was so awful. Everybody was trying so hard not to cry."

The final tally disclosed a union loss by 62 votes; 390 workers voted against the union and 328 voted for it.

Rondeau walked out of the hall with her boyfriend. "I had worked like a horse for several months and felt that I had been awake for two years," she recalled. Grief suddenly overwhelmed her, and she collapsed, crying, on the sidewalk.

The union committee gathered later at Robb's house to mourn over drinks. The party ended happily for Robb and Bob Metcalf. They had been dating for some time and now decided to make a permanent commitment. (Metcalf eventually earned a master's degree, left Harvard, and became a computer software salesman for a small firm in Cambridge. He and Robb were married in 1984.)

For Rondeau and Sullivan, however, there was more bad news. David Livingston, who had come to Boston hoping to celebrate a victory over Harvard, showed up at the party. So did E.W. "Ted" Barrett, director of UAW Region 9A, which covered Connecticut and Massachusetts. Although Harvard was in his territory, District 65 had controlled the organizing campaign because of Livingston's complicated arrangement with the national UAW. The two men did not like each other. At Robb's home, however, they met privately and then called Rondeau into the hallway to talk.

They startled her with news that she would be transferred from District 65 to Barrett's staff in the UAW. Barrett told her to wind up her affairs in Boston and go to New Haven, where the UAW had begun organizing clerical and technical workers at Yale University. It was like being traded from one baseball team to another without knowing why. She later learned that Livingston also traded Leslie Sullivan to Barrett, and the latter assigned her to head up a UAW drive at Massachusetts General Hospital in Boston. The punishment for losing at Harvard was banishment to what Rondeau called "our two Siberias."

Rondeau and her committee did a postmortem election analysis. "We learned that a lot of people who would have voted for the union stayed home," she said. "We counted seventy people who didn't vote. That was the power of the antiunion campaign."

No amount of analysis could salve the wounds of defeat. One weekend shortly after the election, she drove to Cape Cod with her boyfriend. "We walked in the woods and on the beach. He said something, an entirely innocent thing, and I did something I had never done in my life. I turned around and screamed at him. I realized as it came out of my mouth that my anger had nothing to do with him. That's when I decided it was important to go through something and lose."

*W*hat happened to Rondeau in August 1981 at Yale evoked a vivid memory of her job at the wighead plant in Manchaug nearly a decade earlier. Toward the end of August that year, she was assigned to an area of the plant where they sprayed paint, or flocking, on the wigheads in small, enclosed rooms like shower stalls. The older women who did this work wore flimsy face masks to keep out the paint fumes. Nonetheless, they would come out of the booths coughing and sweating and complaining of lightheadedness.

"One day, like a fool," Rondeau said, "I went to personnel and said, 'I don't know if you know, but those paint stalls are really hot.' I believed that if I went there and told them, they were going to say, 'Thank you so much for telling us.' This woman said to me, 'Kristine, we don't need you anymore. You can go now if you would like to.' It was the end of August, and I wanted to leave anyway. It wasn't until years later that I realized I had been fired."

That was a decade ago in Manchaug. Now she was at Yale, and history seemed to be repeating itself. When she arrived in May, both the UAW and the Hotel Employees & Restaurant Employees (HERE) were trying to organize the university's white-collar staff. Rondeau went out and talked to workers and discovered a rather amazing thing. Nobody was for the UAW. "They basically said to me, 'The UAW has no right here, they're screwing up our union drive.'" She concluded that the Auto Workers could not possibly win at Yale—and for a very good reason. HERE Local 35 had represented Yale's dining hall and maintenance workers for many years. In 1980 the business manager of Local 35, John Wilhelm, convinced his members that they could shore up their own bargaining strength by helping to unionize the support staff. He set out to organize white-collar workers into newly created Local 34.

Wilhelm and the members of Local 35 formed alliances with clerks and technical workers all over campus. Their campaign proceeded rapidly. They knew a great deal more about Yale and its organizational strengths and weaknesses than did the UAW outsiders. By the time Rondeau tested sentiments, "the people who were against us were really against us. It wasn't as if they didn't know the difference between the two unions. There was a very strong anti-UAW feeling."

Rondeau voiced her concerns to UAW officials. They took her frankness as a sign of disloyalty. "I was probably stupid to tell them, but I thought they would go, 'Oh, my God! Thank you so much for telling us. We will check it out and get back to you.'"

Through June and July she continued her work but felt under suspicion. On the 10th of August, a call came for her at the UAW office. It was Jerry Rocker, subregional director of UAW Region 9A under Ted Barrett. He told her that Barrett was letting her go. Rondeau interpreted this to mean that she was being fired. "I was actually happy about it," she said, "because I was having such a miserable time."

She walked a few blocks to her apartment and prepared to leave New Haven. She wondered if her organizing career had come to an end. Before she finished packing, she received a call from David Livingston's office in New York. That very morning, Rondeau was told, the NLRB had issued a preliminary ruling against Harvard relating to the April election. An NLRB hearing officer, finding Harvard guilty of improper conduct, recommended that the election be set aside. Livingston ordered Rondeau to return to Harvard immediately and prepare for another election. She was employed again!

By evening she was back in Boston and attending a Harvard committee meeting. Her friend Marie Manna, now a District 65 staff member, had kept the committee intact while the NLRB held post-election hearings in the summer of '81. When Rondeau later talked with Livingston himself, she sensed his annoyance. "I think David hated having to take me back." She was certain that she had been fired by the UAW and re-employed by District 65 all within a half-hour period.

Many years later, former UAW officials questioned Rondeau's version of events. In 1995, Jerry Rocker, the former subregional director of Region 9A, acknowledged that he would have been the one to give the news to Rondeau. But his memory of that period was blurred. "I remember her as being a very talented, very competent woman," he said, "but I don't remember why she left the staff." He had a faint recollection of her being in trouble with Barrett. "Maybe it was disenchantment with her lack of enthusiasm, something like that. She was an extremely honest person."

"She had enthusiasm," Barrett recalled, with acerbity, "but it wasn't enthusiasm for the Yale drive. She had enthusiasm for getting back to Harvard." Barrett did not like Rondeau's independence of mind or her ideas about organizing. But the circumstances under which she left Yale and returned to Harvard had slipped his mind by 1995. He could not remember firing her, *this time*. What happened later was another matter. When reminded of the NLRB ruling on Harvard, he said it was possible that he had transferred her back to Livingston.

Rondeau had a strong memory of being fired. However the events of August 10, 1981 transpired, it was a "there-is-a-God kind of day," she said. As it turned out, her assessment of Yale organizing had been correct. The UAW halted its campaign in January 1982, and the Hotel Employees went on to win a critical election in 1983, one that would have considerable impact on Harvard over the years.

The legal warfare that had erupted sporadically since 1975 between Harvard and District 65 now entered a new phase. The NLRB hearing officer found that in two instances during the '81 campaign Harvard employees with supervisory power made remarks to workers that came under the heading of illegal threats to chill union activity. Harvard disagreed strongly with this ruling and filed an appeal.

Only a few months after losing a second election at Harvard, a core of workers in the Medical Area began a third campaign, expecting that the NLRB would shortly hold a new election. On October 29, however, a decision by the NLRB's regional director dashed this optimistic schedule. Robert Fuchs, who was becoming something of a nemesis for the Harvard union, overruled the hearing officer's recommendation to set aside the April election.

Fuchs didn't think the comments by the two supervisors, even if correctly characterized as "threats," could have affected the outcome of the election. A total of only ten to fifteen workers heard the comments, and the union lost by sixty-two votes. District 65 lawyers disagreed with this analysis, but not until February 1982 did the NLRB's Washington office agree to review the case. Harvard lawyers, meanwhile, saw this as an opportunity to reopen the record on the "unit question." The university asked the board, now controlled by Reagan appointees, to reverse the 1977 decision allowing an election in the Medical Area only. To nudge the NLRB in this direction, Harvard changed the factual underpinning of the old ruling. The Medical Area constituted a separate community of interest, the 1977 board had said, partly because it had its own personnel office. In early 1982, Harvard removed all important personnel functions from that office and transferred them to Cambridge.

It was a clever legal move to take advantage of the new political reality, which was rooted in the political weakness of the NLRB system. Since the late 1940s, prevailing views on the politically appointed board had shifted from prounion to promanagement or vice-versa with each change from Democratic to Republican inhabitant of the White House. In a 1995 book, *Broken Promise*, James A. Gross of Cornell University traced this development to a policy conflict in the law itself. The National Labor Relations Act (NLRA), when passed in 1935, had the single purpose of promoting collective bargaining and the right of workers to join unions. In 1947, Congressional Republicans moved to cut back organized labor's power by amending the NLRA. The Taft–Hartley Act added a new policy goal, to protect employee free choice and the right of employers to avoid collective bargaining. Ever since then, boards appointed by Democratic Presidents tended to interpret the law as promoting the right of workers to join unions and Republican boards favored the right of employers to avoid unions. In the eighties, there would be a more pronounced shift toward the right than usual, in decisions emanating from a board controlled by Reagan appointees.

One did not have to be a unionist to deplore this politicization of national labor policy. "It's not a happy situation," Dan Steiner observed in 1995, referring to the NLRB shifts, "where people think their fortunes are going to turn basically on the political perspective of whatever party's in power." But Harvard could not ignore reality. The current party in power favored employer interests over worker interests, and so did the Reagan board.

Labor law sat down to feast on another Harvard case. The Reagan board focused initially on the question of whether the 1981 election should be overturned. If it ordered another election, the board then would have to reassess "the unit question." Labor law could be at this double banquet a minimum of two years—unless, of course, Kris Rondeau and her committee tired of the bureaucratic repast and went off to do other things with their lives. More than a few times over the years, Harvard officials expected the union campaign to fade away in this fashion. But the women of the Harvard union were inexplicably persistent.

It would be a strange and wearying period, two and a half years of waiting for another legal decision. The election rerun case was not a strong one. Rondeau thought the board would throw it out. But she and her followers had to maintain support in the Medical Area as if the board *might* order a new election. She thought it more and more likely that eventually they would have to organize the entire university. Everything hinged on the resolution of a legal abstraction known as "the unit question." At every committee meeting, someone inevitably brought up "the unit question." The phrase sounded pretentious and silly, and one of the women invented a euphonious substitute, "the eunuch question," which seemed more appropriate to the situation. Before long everyone was talking about "the eunuch question." They stated it in debate form: "Should eunuchs be allowed to vote?"

District 65 stood by the Harvard women during this period and bore the expense of the continuing legal fight. The Harvard organizing unit now was called "District 65-UAW," indicating the Auto Workers' increasing involvement. From their position down in the trenches, however, Rondeau, Sullivan, Manna, and other employees of 65 realized that relations between the two unions were not good. They could hear echoes of a battle taking place in higher echelons, and they knew it mainly had to do with tugging and pulling between Livingston and Ted Barrett.

Livingston had not moved toward completing his union's integration into the UAW. His feud with Barrett arose from the fact that a large portion of District 65, including all of its constituent parts in New York and New England, existed within Region 9A of the UAW. Technically, as director of 9A, Barrett commanded every local in his region, including Amalgamated Local 65. Politically, Livingston controlled 65 down to the last man and woman at the bottom of his staff. The clash between the two men was one of personality as well as politics. Livingston was used to doing things his way, and Barrett was used to telling people what to do. A former auto worker and UAW shop chairman at the General Motors plant in Framingham, Massachusetts, he was elected regional director in 1980. Like an Irish ward politician, he served up a strong mixture of wit, bluster, and bossiness. UAW people who worked over him, and under him, described

Barrett as an autocrat. "That's probably true," Barrett responded to this criticism. "Like the turtle, you can't make forward progress if you don't stick your neck out."

District 65 still had charge of the Harvard drive, but Barrett and UAW organizing officials in Detroit had to be kept informed of developments. Rondeau felt as if she had bosses in three different organizations. Her relations with male supervisors in 65 had not improved over the years. Livingston, despite his prowomen stance as a union leader, was as paternalistic and condescending as any Harvard dean. Rondeau remembered the time in 1982 or 1983 when she, Marie Manna, and another woman staff member were called to a meeting with Livingston in his New York office. "He started being a jerk," Rondeau said. "He was basically telling us, 'It's your fault for losing Harvard.'"

Livingston made a particularly condescending remark to Manna, who replied, "I am not a child, and you can't talk to me like that."

Livingston appeared stunned. Then, Manna recalled, "He had a fit and started yelling at us. He was lecturing us on how to organize. You weren't supposed to have a brain, you know. You were supposed to sit there and listen to him because he was the president. I just didn't feel like doing that that day. I said, 'I feel like I'm being scolded like a child and I don't like that at all.'"

The women's relationship with District 65 reminded Rondeau of the abused women she had known while working at the women's shelter in Cambridge. At one and the same time they wanted to escape a violent husband or boyfriend but also felt compelled to stay. Similarly, in District 65, Rondeau said, "We hated it, but there were complicated psychological variables that were holding us in. We were taught that it was the only politically pure union, you know, the diamond in the rough in the labor movement. Everything else was right wing. A long time later I realized this wasn't true. But it had a real hold on us while we were in it."

Rondeau and Sullivan occasionally attended UAW conferences. "Everywhere we went, we were told, 'Oh, it's wonderful that you gals are here, and we've got to organize those women.' But I don't think anybody ever thought at that time about what it meant if we actually won." A local composed largely of women in white-collar jobs, Rondeau thought, could not be wedged into a slot at the bottom of the UAW, male-controlled hierarchy like the typical factory local. It would have to be able to organize its own internal affairs and to negotiate its own contract. The men who ran unions didn't understand what kind of union women would want. Rondeau wasn't quite sure herself, but she knew it would be different from the typical male-dominated union.

❧ ❧

On the morning of March 2, 1982, James S. Braude had reason to think well of himself. At the age of thirty-two, he was president of a 3,000-member union that he himself had founded. Nature had graced him with a quick mind and physical stature that attracted notice. He made a handsome salary and by all appearances had a bright future as a union executive.

On that morning, Braude flew out of New York on an early morning shuttle to Boston. He planned to spend the day in meetings and fly back in the evening. His union, a local of District 65, had members in several cities, and Braude traveled frequently. Arriving in Boston, he went to a downtown office building for a day-long contract negotiating session. He had no foreboding of anything unusual happening, but he scoffed at premonitions in any case.

Born and raised in Philadelphia of German-Jewish parents, Braude had received a law degree at New York University. He immediately went to work in the South Bronx for an agency of the National Legal Services Corp., an organization created in 1974 by Congress to provide legal services for the poor. Representing poor people with housing problems, he had to appear in court his first day on the job—and countless days after that for seven years. "I got to know in a visceral way what life was like at the bottom, representing people with incredible odds against them," Braude said. "I learned how to fight from people I was allegedly fighting for."

He joined a fledgling union of lawyers in his agency, became its president in 1977, and started organizing a national union at the more than three hundred not-for-profit legal services units around the country. With the help of people like Regina Little, a legal services attorney in New Jersey, he formed the independent National Organization of Legal Services Workers. In 1981, when the Reagan administration threatened to dismantle Legal Services, Braude and his co-workers decided to affiliate with a larger union. They chose District 65, partly because of its liberal stance on social issues but also because Livingston granted Braude's local a free hand to run its own affairs. His legal services division became a leading example of 65's growth in the white-collar professional area. Indeed, it was the only segment of 65 that did grow. By 1982 there was talk of Braude becoming the next president of District 65—whenever Livingston decided that he had reigned long enough.

On March 2, after finishing his meeting, Braude phoned the District 65 office in Boston and said he'd like to drop by in late afternoon and meet the staff before returning to New York. But immediately he immersed himself in more union business on the telephone. By the time he finished, everyone else had left for the day. The elevator had stopped working, and he had to walk down several flights of stairs to the lobby. There he found the front door locked. He was trapped inside the building. After a long period of tramping up and down stairs and "hello'ing" for help, he finally came across a maintenance worker who unlocked the front door for him.

Although it was already eight o'clock, Braude took a taxi to the District 65 office. If no one was there, he would slip a note of apology under the door. He felt foolish enough without gaining a reputation as a New York big shot who stood up staff members in Boston. To his surprise, someone opened the door when he knocked—a young, intense-looking woman with short blonde hair. Braude was, using an expression he'd thought he would never use, "smitten at first glance." Now he began to see the purposefulness of fate, the intervention of which had delayed him downtown until everyone had gone home except this one person. She introduced herself as Kris Rondeau.

They began chatting about union affairs. Soon they were quarreling over internal union issues. She seemed less than awed by him and less than worshipful of District 65. Intending to set her straight, he invited her to dinner. They continued the argument at a steak house on Mass Ave. Rondeau was extraordinarily candid in her criticism of 65 leadership, though he was a stranger who could possibly do her harm in the union. She spoke with a "brutal honesty" that many people would not appreciate, he thought. Later, as he came to know her better, Braude understood why she always seemed to be in trouble with her union superiors. "She told the truth which not only is not popular in parts of the labor movement but is not tolerated in much of the labor movement," he said.

Braude was astonished. In his two years with District 65, he had never heard mention of this preposterous woman. No one in New York headquarters spoke of her. Yet she headed one of the most important organizing campaigns in the union. She knew something of his "special deal" with Livingston, which gave Braude resources for organizing and administration not accorded other sections of the union. Why, she asked, should there be such a large disparity in their salaries when both essentially were organizers? She barely topped $11,000 a year, while he made $35,000.

The union had a policy of hiring organizers at the salary they were paid on their previous job. This may have made sense as a hiring policy, but it also produced ludicrous inequities on the District 65 staff that made the union's demand for equal pay at the bargaining table hypocritical at best.

"The basic difference was," Rondeau recalled, "he was a white man coming from a white man's shop and I was a white woman coming from a white woman's shop, and I thought it was highly discriminatory." She did not begrudge him his salary but argued that the union should raise the pay of women like her and Sullivan closer to his level.

Rondeau told him bluntly that she thought of him as "the fair-haired boy who reached that position because of uncritical, blind, loyal devotion to leadership," he said. "She thought I was in the tank to the guys at the top." He remembered pounding the table with a fist and protesting, "No! No! It isn't true!"

He stayed at the airport motel that night and took the first shuttle to New York next morning. "When I got to the office, it was not a question of *whether* I would phone her," Braude said. "It was how fast could I get to a phone and find the number. I called every day after that."

Rondeau hadn't felt the same excitement, but when he called, "I always came to the phone," she said. "I thought he was a little brainwashed, but I also liked him. We found out pretty quickly we had greatly overlapping world views. The more I talked to him the more I liked him."

They talked every day after that by one means or another, on the phone or in person. She had unorthodox views on how a union should be formed and what it should be for its members and how it should negotiate with the employer. Braude felt that he was a pretty good organizer himself. While expanding his local of lawyers and paralegals, he had never lost a representation election, though the units usually contained only twenty-five to fifty workers. Since his members were advocates by training, his local saved time and money by teaching them how to negotiate contracts and handle their own grievances. Rondeau, he learned, urged workers to join the union *in order to represent themselves*. "We both thought workers should stand up for themselves," Braude said. "I saw it that way mainly out of necessity. With me, philosophy came second. With Kris, the philosophy came first."

He only partially accepted her criticism of District 65, and they continued arguing. "We started fighting about these issues on March 2nd, 1982 and really haven't stopped," Braude said ten years later. "Every once in a while I'm right, but not often."

Rondeau and Braude were married in Boston in December 1982. Every March 2nd after that, they had dinner in the steak house on Mass Ave. . . . and argued.

Braude moved into her apartment in Cambridge and commuted to his office in New York. There was never any question of doing it the other way round. She was determined to organize Harvard and intended to keep trying for as long as it took. People had to accept this about her. Braude did more than accept it; he encouraged her to keep at it. He wouldn't present himself as a selfless, self-sacrificing husband without ambitions of his own, but Braude did believe that his wife's career was as important as his. It never occurred to him that this belief would be tested—though not for some time.

Braude always laughed at the mere notion that he could, even if he wanted to, tell Rondeau how to do her job. Although they often talked about her union business, and though Braude did not hesitate to give his opinions, there was never any question that the final decision was hers. She frequently rejected his advice. "I talk to him as somebody who is experienced in organizations," she said in 1995. "He gives his view and I argue mine, and that's useful." Braude remained Livingston's "fair-haired boy" but didn't attempt to intercede for his wife. She didn't marry him in order to advance herself in the union.

There was no question that having a husband who took an interest in her work helped Rondeau get through some dark periods in those years. She had her small circle of friends and co-workers at Harvard, and now she had a supportive husband. She needed persistence to keep going at Harvard. Through most of 1982 the campaign could go nowhere because of legal circumstances.

Despite her growing contempt for union politics, she had to give credit to District 65 and the UAW for sticking it out. Instead of abandoning Harvard as a lost cause, they hung on through the long waiting period and paid their lawyers to continue the legal fight. Meanwhile, the battle for control between Livingston and Barrett generated a dynamic of its own in Boston. For more than a year, there had been a nasty struggle between UAW and District 65 partisans in 65's Boston local, which included representatives from Boston University, Harvard, and the several smaller employers under District 65 contract. The pro-UAW group, led by Sullivan, Rondeau, and Manna, wanted the parent union to take over Boston operations, including the Harvard campaign, while the other faction favored District 65. Despite her dislike of Barrett, Rondeau considered the UAW the more principled and competent union. Control of the Harvard campaign, because of its size and importance, became a key issue in this fight.

Jim Braude did not knowingly get involved in his wife's union affairs. But one day, by chance, he learned that Livingston intended to remove her from the Harvard campaign and install in her place a woman in the pro-65 Boston faction. Braude called Rondeau and warned her. She acted quickly, enlisting the aid of Leslie Sullivan. The two obtained a meeting with Barrett. He was not overly fond of either woman, but he disliked Livingston even more. Sullivan told Barrett that his nemesis in 65 was laying plans to "snooker" him, and she urged him to keep Rondeau in charge. With the support of other UAW officials, Barrett agreed that Harvard would stay under Rondeau. Harvard remained a District 65 campaign, but the UAW intended to have a stronger voice than before.

Out of this murky period of internecine battling came a bitterness that never fully abated. Rondeau had learned to play the in-fighting game, using back channels to win organizational battles, and in this case gained a number of enemies among other union women while doing so. Of course, they were playing the game, too. They lost and she won, and they would never forget it. But she had survived this attempt to oust her. Now she had to resolve a rebellion within her own committee.

Through seven years of nearly continuous activity, the Harvard organizing committee had remained remarkably free of inner turmoil. The early women leaders had set it on a simple course that aimed straight for union recognition, avoiding ideological hurdles, political detours, and factional divisions. It is hard to conceive of a similar committee dominated by men that would last so long without finding a reason to indulge in a power struggle or two. In 1981, however, an internal rift developed among the women on the Harvard committee and over two years widened into an unbridgeable gap. Finding a path around the gap provided a political education for Rondeau and her group and, more importantly, deepened their understanding of how people can best be organized.

The split began during the 1981 Harvard campaign. A few members disagreed with Rondeau's strategy on such matters as refusing to reply in writing to Harvard propaganda. After the election, the critics coalesced into an opposition group with a core of four to five committee members. The most active members were Donna Spiegelman, Debbie Katz, and Lisa Galatin, all articulate, highly motivated women. They contended that Rondeau and her supporters excluded them from secret meetings where most decisions were made. "Things would get decided by Kris and unknown others in advance of meetings, and then be presented to the group, supposedly for discussion," Spiegelman charged. "We would make suggestions, and they would be knocked down by Kris and her plants on the committee."

Rondeau had developed an informal style of leadership. When she chaired a committee meeting, she didn't ask all heads to nod with approval but more or less divined the consensus of the group from the tenor of remarks. She and the veteran committee members had been together so long, they communicated in a form of verbal shorthand which could well mystify new committee members. The veterans were good friends who formed a close-knit social group. They worked hard but they also liked to laugh and fool around. These included Manna, Robb, Metcalf, Lafferty, Mahon, David Maybury, and a few others.

The opposition group disapproved of the tomfoolery and preferred more formal procedures. They would vote on all matters before the committee, organize workers on an issue-by-issue basis, and challenge management the same way. They wanted things neatly divided and categorized, union on one side and management on the other, a "yes" or "no" vote on everything. The Rondeauites called them the "Purity Caucus" and viewed the split between them as based mainly on philosophy and work methods.

The other group saw more insidious divisions. Spiegelman, in particular, felt that she and her allies were excluded because some were Jewish and some gay. The suggestion of bias on Rondeau's part could not hold up in light of two things: she married a Jewish man and later, when authorized to hire organizers, put some gay men and women on her staff.

For nearly two years the two groups battled within the Harvard organizing committee. On some matters they worked together, for both sides wanted to bring a union to Harvard. The sharpest disagreement involved organizing strategy and methods. Rondeau's group concentrated on "one-on-one organizing," or building relationships with each worker, a comprehensive but time-consuming approach. The Purity Caucus women wanted to devote more time and energy to "issues organizing." The committee should arouse worker interest by engaging management on specific issues, such as health problems on the job. In this approach, organizers would select an issue, do research, elicit employee attitudes through surveys, and organize seminars or "speak out" meetings. The workers who showed up would be signed up and, the theory was, instantly galvanized by their interest in the subject to work for the union.

The debate between the two concepts was not irrelevant either at Harvard or more generally in modern society. How *do* you convince people to come out of themselves, join with others, take certain risks (in the case of work, incurring the boss's displeasure), and work toward an objective that will benefit all? Rondeau's instincts told her that rallying people on a single issue was too narrow an approach. This was intuition; her analysis came much later. "In community organizing," she said in 1996, "you can organize around issues like better housing. But in the workplace you have to organize around power and sharing it." Marie Manna put it this way: "It's not the issue that's going to bring people together. It's people that are going to bring people together."

Despite bad feelings between the two groups, the committee stayed intact. The in-group did not try to eject their opponents, and the out-group did not undermine the committee by attacking it in public. The women leaders on both sides kept making accommodations. Watching the process unfold week after week, with no resolution, some men on the committee grew impatient. Bob Metcalf did not have a high opinion of the Purity Caucus members. "I thought they were spoiled brats who didn't want to do the hard work of actually talking to workers," he said. But he lost patience with women on both sides. "I can vividly remember being in an explosive rage as I walked back from a committee meeting at Countway Library. I was furious at the way the Purity Caucus was behaving, and I was amazed that Kris and Marie could be so patient. My reaction was, why didn't we steamroller them and go back to work?"

Eventually, the situation resolved itself. With the concurrence of Rondeau and her allies, the Purity Caucus women concentrated on exposing the health-related problems of new office technology. In those years, computer terminals were replacing typewriters at a rapid rate in most offices. Questions were raised about the unknown health effects of working many hours each day in front of video display terminals, or VDTs, as they were called. Through newsletter articles and talks by outside experts, the Purity Caucus put on a comprehensive education campaign. They understood the issues. Spiegelman later became an assistant professor of epidemiology in the Harvard School of Public Health, and Lisa Galatin later founded a research organization on office technology.

Toward the end of 1982, buoyed by a good response to a survey of workers, the Purity Caucus group set up what was to be a major event, a "speak out" for all Medical Area employees on the VDT issue. After all this preparation, only a handful of workers showed up. A week or so later, the Purity Caucus leaders resigned in a group from the committee. There were no recriminations or bitter words. They simply left.

Writing a report to the UAW a short time later, Rondeau referred to "problems that arose out of a divided organizing committee," and concluded that "those problems are behind us."

Issues-organizing versus one-on-one organizing would seem to be the stuff of esoteric sociological debate. And yet, could there have been something infectious in the Boston air? Leslie Sullivan had gotten entangled in a similar clash of methodologies when she started a UAW organizing drive at Massachusetts General Hospital in the summer of 1981.

Mass General, as most people called the hospital, was located in downtown Boston and employed about ten thousand union-eligible workers. Sullivan began her new job with much excitement. She was glad to be a part of the UAW, which seemed to treat its employees and members with more respect than District 65.

She quickly saw, however, that the hospital posed almost insuperable problems for an organizer. As a result of earlier union efforts, the NLRB had defined a bargaining unit as consisting of all nonmanagerial employees except nurses. This meant that the UAW would have to organize secretaries, research assistants, technicians, several maintenance crafts, cooks, orderlies, nurse's assistants, and so on, all in one unit. Yet the work force was highly stratified, with occupational groups socially isolated from one another. A large organizing committee with members in all groups might have been able to straddle these boundaries.

But here lay the final barrier. A committee of activists already existed when Sullivan arrived at the hospital. Formed during a previous organizing drive by another union, it consisted almost entirely of political idealogues ranging from mildly leftist to ultra-leftist. Their idea of organizing was to rally workers around external political issues, such as U.S. foreign policy, revolutions abroad, racial inequities at home.

"They wanted to run a very political campaign," Sullivan said. "They would hold meetings and discuss external issues like the revolution in Nicaragua. The ultra-leftists believed in Maoist self-criticism. People were supposed to get up and do a self-criticism on not living up to their ideals. I didn't allow that in committee, and I wasn't into political organizing. So we were at odds from the beginning."

These ideas had been planted in the committee members' heads, and Sullivan couldn't get them out. "I wanted people to do nuts and bolts organizing, talk to workers one-on-one," she said. "But the politicos on the committee preferred leafletting outside the hospital. I just couldn't break through that barrier."

Hospital managers didn't have to lift a finger. The "politicos" on the committee defeated the union for them. The Mass General drive never really got started, and in late 1982 the UAW shut it down. Sullivan had foreseen this decision and, perhaps not so coincidentally, became pregnant with her first child. She and John Rees got married in January 1983. The baby was due in July.

Rondeau watched her friend Leslie tossing about in an agony of joy and bewilderment, joy at the thought of having her first child, bewilderment at what was happening to her at work. After halting the hospital campaign, the UAW didn't give Sullivan much to do. By the following June, she was wandering around the District 65 office, her eyes fixed on a distant point but the rest of her trying to find a place in the here and now. There seemed to be no such place. She had been involved in two losing campaigns, Harvard and Mass General (though neither loss was her fault), and she had differed with Ted Barrett over organizing strategy. It almost did not matter how loyal you were. You also had to be pliant, and Sullivan was never pliant.

"Leslie was always the most loyal of us all," Rondeau said. "She was the hardest worker, the most committed to the union, first District 65 and then the UAW." Rondeau remembered a time, a few years before, when the two of them worked as partners. "This day she and I were on a picket line," Rondeau said, smiling at the recollection. "I turned to her and said, 'Les, let's just quit and have babies.' She looked startled and said, 'What would you do with a baby?'"

By 1983 Sullivan had changed her mind. She wanted to be a mother. Now she had to confront the ageless problem of women who want to achieve things outside the home and bring up children at the same time. In those final months, she was at loose ends. Not much organizing was going on. The New England economy was inching out of the deep recession of 1981–82. Workers were scared. Although the UAW had promised to launch major drives to sign up white-collar office workers, this had not materialized. One day, she recalled, "they [the UAW] just dropped me. Dumped me back into 65. Nobody ever told me directly, I found out through the back door."

The shock was profound. Suddenly, it appeared that her career as a lead organizer was over. This was the woman who had led District 65 into white-collar organizing in the Boston area almost ten years before. For three or four years she *was* the union in Boston. She had laid a foundation in retail stores, day care agencies, and universities that District 65 and later the UAW could build on. She had formed a Boston local and handled its administrative work for some years. Most of all, Sullivan had believed in, and worked tirelessly for, "the labor movement," as some still idealistically called it.

Sullivan took maternity leave from District 65 and a few weeks later, in July, gave birth to a son, Patrick. With her singular capacity for concentrating on a project, she was a good mother. She intended to return to the UAW in about six months, though she suspected this would be difficult given the way she had been treated. She didn't understand what she had done wrong, but she knew it had to do with being a woman in what had been thought of as a male occupation.

In 1995, after a series of interviews about her experiences as an organizer, Sullivan recalled that final, bitter period. By then, she had long been disillusioned with District 65, but "I still had a positive attitude about the UAW." She paused to refine this thought. "As an organization for the members, I had a lot of respect for the UAW, although they didn't know a lot about organizing. Ted Barrett sincerely wanted to organize white-collar workers, Harvard, and Mass General. But I don't think he had a clue as to how to do it. He didn't have the patience or confidence to listen to us. He just couldn't break loose and trust that we knew what we were doing. A lot of it was because we were women and didn't come up through the UAW system."

Rondeau felt helpless as she watched her friend withdraw. The two would work together again, briefly, but it would not be the same. "She had been treated very badly by the unions over a long period of time," Rondeau said. "All women experienced this, but it was a hallmark of Leslie's life. She was a smart, competent, articulate person, but she went unheard."

CHAPTER ELEVEN

O ver several years, the Harvard union women developed a singular style of organizing that seemed particularly suited to women office workers. It consisted of innovative techniques, borrowed and invented, intermixed with traditional practices, the whole welded together by hard experience. The ideas did not leap full-blown from anyone's head but crystallized in untraceable fashion over long periods of time. There are a few documents in the union's archives, however, which give tantalizing glimpses of evolution in process.

One is a report written for the UAW, dated April 10, 1983. It consists of eleven pages of ruled notebook paper filled with Rondeau's distinctive handwriting, with vertical strokes and pointed tops on "n's" and "m's." In presenting an honest if depressing picture of the campaign in the Medical Area, Rondeau pours out much of what she and her committee have learned about organizing during six years of struggle and repeated blows on the head. She and her friends have contended with incessant legal delays, battles with union bureaucracy, the internal challenge of the Purity Caucus, two election defeats, and the lingering trauma of the very tough antiunion campaign waged by Harvard in 1981.

As of April 1983, she writes, her committee is "not capable of winning, or carrying out an election." She continues, "The feeling is of tiredness, defeat and discouragement. The committee and the workers are completely worn out with union organizing. . . . The workers do not feel oppressed. Some might like to have it better, but *most are satisfied* [emphasis in original] in particular with wages and benefits. . . . This is not ever going to be a sure thing because the workers don't know that they need the union, and there is no guarantee that we can convince them as a matter of faith that they do."

A startling admission. Why organize if the employees don't think that they need a union? The answer came from Rondeau's own experience as a woman worker at Harvard. She believed that women workers in particular wanted to be part of something more intimate, more *human*, than Harvard management was willing to provide. Women were isolated by occupation (technical and clerical), by geography (workplaces in a dozen different buildings, in three separate schools), and by gender (confined to lower-level jobs under male supervisors). One thing that a union could do—and that management was *not* doing—was create a *community*. Women workers could feel safe and gain strength and confidence in themselves if they belonged to a union community. They might not know this because they had never experienced it: American life tends to separate people rather than join them.

Rondeau also was beginning to perceive another unspoken yearning felt by most workers but especially evident among a "young, conservative" group of employees, as she categorizes them in the report. They were not "conservative" in a political sense; rather, they spurned unionism (or what they thought unionism consisted of) in favor of professionalism. "Not only this group, but most workers, are concerned w/professionalism and academia," Rondeau writes. "They don't want to be appealed to on the basis of self-interest, but can sometimes become interested in the union because of newer issues such as 'making science better, being more professional, etc.'"

Rondeau does not pursue this notion further in the 1983 report. But it was one in a series of insights that eventually would lead to an unconventional organizing philosophy. Up to this point her group had emphasized the economic benefits of unionism, enabling management to run free with its charge that unions would ruin Harvard. Looking back on the 1981 election in a 1995 interview, she said, "A lot of our people were thinking, 'I wish they would just recognize that we care about this place, that they would see us for what we are.' There were hundreds if not thousands of people wishing that. The fact that we wanted to represent ourselves was not a threat to Harvard University." In short, workers might respond to the idea of joining a union not just out of self-interest but also as a means of participating in decisions to improve the institution.

Rondeau didn't come to this conclusion in 1983. She did, however, recommend what she terms a "radical" change in fundamental organizing methods. The Harvard organizers had spent much of their time getting

workers to sign authorization cards. This was the traditional way of determining how much support the union had and also of marking out a
union's designs on a certain group of workers. Rondeau called it "peeing in
a big circle around ourselves." Of 740 employees in early 1983, about 42
percent had signed cards. But signing a card did not commit a worker to
vote for the union. Moreover, she writes, "this particular group [at Har-
vard], both committee and workers, have been signing cards for 9 years.
We have signed, re-signed when cards were too old, re-signed when we
joined the UAW, re-signed when we lost the election, re-signed when the
board accepted our ULP [unfair labor practice] case and re-signed when
the UAW assumed supervision of the drive. The card push is more than
wearisome. . . . We must take a new approach. . . ."

The report proposes a moratorium on card-signing so her staff could
concentrate on *one-on-one* organizing. She acknowledges that this "flies in
the face of everything we know about union organizing." In many unions,
organizing was, by definition, persuading workers to sign cards. Rondeau
thought that signing a card should climax a process of individual development and signal a commitment to the union that could not be shaken. The
Harvard union, in fact, had emphasized the one-on-one principle from the
beginning. But the long internal conflict over tactics and methods had provoked Rondeau and her committee to make an even deeper commitment
to the concept. It became not just *a way* of organizing but *the way* of organizing a union and of making it live and do the bidding of its members. It
became the philosophical cornerstone of a different kind of unionism.

The Harvard union did not invent something new. As long as there
have been unions, organizers have employed one-on-one tactics at some
level of intensity. But during organized labor's period of greatest organizing
success, from the 1930s to the 1950s, external events swept huge numbers
of workers into new industrial unions like the Auto Workers and Steelworkers. Large parts of the auto and steel industries were organized on a
regional, even a national, basis rather than one shop or plant at a time, and
thousands of workers became members without ever meeting an organizer. But even then, some organizers in some plants conducted intimate,
worker-to-worker campaigns on the shop floor. The United Electrical
Workers (UE), in particular, believed that strong rank-and-file unionism
could not survive if workers were merely persuaded or coerced into
checking the "yes" box on the union election ballot. Long before an election occurred, the UE would form an organization of committed rank-
and-file workers, and this could be done only through what later became
known as one-on-one organizing.

The term *one-on-one* means different things to different people. It sometimes refers to nothing more elaborate than a "phone tree": one person phones another person who phones a third, and so on. Some unions equate face-to-face meetings with one-on-one. In this version, an organizer visits workers in their homes, talks about the benefits of joining a union, and asks them to sign cards. The organizer assesses the attitude of each worker, for or against the union, based on a few such meetings. Much of the organizing work is accomplished, by necessity, in general meetings or through leaflets, handbills, newsletters. There isn't enough time to do much else.

The Harvard women carried the one-on-one concept much further. For one thing, most initial meetings took place on the job, since the organizers consisted either of sister workers or union staff members such as Rondeau and Manna who, in the university setting, could come and go freely in the buildings. It was a very rare event when one-on-one consisted only of one meeting. In many cases, scores of individual meetings were involved, ranging from quick chats at the water cooler to lunch discussions to an after-work drink or even dinner. In advertising jargon, the Harvard organizers did a "soft sell." They avoided anything that might be construed as pressure to join and, in fact, might talk to an employee for weeks or even months without specifically asking her to sign a card.

The objective of one-on-one organizing was to establish a personal relationship with each worker and to introduce him or her to other workers through union activities, so that in the end a very large number of workers were "connected" to one another in a complex web of relationships. An organizer did not offer intimate friendship to each of scores of workers, though close friendships did occur. Rather, the organizer offered "connectedness," as Rondeau and her friends called it, to a community of others in the workplace. Unknown to them, a new body of feminist theory, just then emerging in scholarly papers and books, explained why women seemed to be more interested in community than men. Existing theory had it that people developed psychologically through increasing levels of separation and independence into "the separate self." Carol Gilligan of Harvard, Jean Baker Miller of the Stone Center at Wellesley College, and other researchers were proposing theories of "relational growth." Biological and social factors ("socialization" in society) contributed to a peculiarly female tendency to perceive other people as members of a network of relationships. Men, according to these theories, tended to view others as opponents in a contest of one kind or another.

Rondeau and other women on the Harvard organizing committee were aware only vaguely, if at all, of these ideas at the time. Their organizing principles evolved out of a natural inclination to be together and work together. From this experience, over several years, Rondeau put together the elements of a rough general theory of organizing. She outlined it in a 1992 interview, starting with a description of conventional methods. For many unions the first step is conducting an opinion survey of a target group of workers. "They figure out who's prounion to begin with and who's antiunion, and then go for the middle. We don't do that. We think that people who are prounion have a set of ideas about unions that probably isn't correct. They need to be organized as much as the antiunion people and people in the middle." Instead of focusing on certain people in the work force, Rondeau said,

> we create a relationship with every single person. One-to-one is probably as oldfashioned as any organizing gets. Once a person is connected to the organization, whether they are prounion or not, they're always connected. Every single person is connected to somebody else. There is no such thing in modern life as an isolated person voting 'yes.' It just doesn't happen. There's no such thing in the private sector as an employer not conducting an antiunion campaign. And in order to withstand that campaign, you must be connected. It's as simple as that. It could be Che Guevara or Eleanor Smeal who is voting. If they're isolated they'll vote 'no.' That's why we build an internal structure of personal connections, so that no one is isolated, no one is left out.

Organizing women white-collar workers, Rondeau believed, had to do only peripherally with emphasizing issues like maternity benefits and day care programs. It had much more to do with connecting women to other women so that they, together, might decide what they wanted and fight for it as a group. She also rejected the notion that the most oppressed workers are easiest to organize. "The people who are miserable and disaffected, who hate their supervisor, are not the people who become the most committed or active in the union. What we found is, the more freedom and respect a person has on the job, the easier it is for her to get involved in the union. The people who are the most scared are the last to come forward." Rondeau's organizers first seek out people who are "the happiest at work and the most independent." They are encouraged to "create the environment and the culture in which the people who are badly treated can come forward."

Many unions use a rating system to assess workers' attitudes toward the union, and by the early eighties the Harvard group had developed its own system. The organizers periodically would review a list of all employees in a workplace and assign a number to each. The highest rating was a "1," given only to a worker so committed to the union that she could withstand the strongest antiunion campaign. A "2" was prounion but still vulnerable to employer pressure. A person classified as a "3" straddled the fence between prounion and antiunion. A "4" leaned strongly against the union. A "5" was definitely antiunion (Rondeau later dropped this category on grounds that it acted as an artificial mechanism to divide workers). Finally, a "0" was a worker as yet unknown to organizers, and "breaking eggs" meant meeting "0's."

(Comprehensive one-on-one organizing was employed by relatively few unions in the 1980s. A decade later, the efficacy of this approach became better known through studies by labor academics such as Kate Bronfenbrenner of Cornell and Tom Juravich of the University of Massachusetts. In a 1996 study of 165 NLRB election campaigns, Bronfenbrenner and Juravich found that where unions were built from the bottom up, like the Harvard union, win rates were 10 to 30 percent higher than in traditional campaigns.)

In April 1983, when Rondeau wrote the status report, her ideas had not yet coalesced into a doctrine. Her committee had shrunk to only eight worker activists. Very little was happening. A few months before, the NLRB in Washington had issued its final decision on the 1981 election, absolving Harvard of wrongdoing. A third election at Harvard could come about only if the union started the process afresh and petitioned for another vote. But the committee had been struggling with its own internal conflict. "The feeling [on the committee]," Rondeau writes, "is of tiredness, defeat and discouragement."

This period suddenly came to an end with the resignation of the Purity Caucus members, and Rondeau made a move. In May, with the concurrence of District 65 and the UAW, she filed a request for another election in the Medical Area. She didn't really want a vote at this time. But she expected that Harvard again would ask the NLRB to redefine the bargaining unit in its favor. Knowledgeable people on both sides believed that with the Reagan NLRB tilted to management's side, Harvard would finally win its fight for a university-wide election. It was better to have this decision sooner rather than later.

Harvard lawyers did as expected. The case went immediately to Washington, where the board members agreed to make a decision in the first instance. But this would take most of another year. In the meantime, Rondeau began rebuilding her committee.

&

She had not had good relations with male union leaders, but there was one whom she respected above all others. Doug Fraser, the UAW president, had taken a personal interest in the Harvard organizing. Twice during the 1980–81 drive he had talked to Medical Area employees while visiting Boston, and now he agreed to help Rondeau rejuvenate her campaign. Fraser had a personal association with Harvard which revealed its ambivalent attitude toward organized labor. Under Derek Bok, the university attempted to play a mediating role in the great American game of conflicting economic and social interests, and in so doing it now and then invited "respectable" labor leaders to sit on boards and committees or serve as guest lecturers. Fraser was a Harvard favorite in this respect. He was the academic's delight: a shop-molded trade unionist and militant labor leader who spoke frankly and honestly about union–management relations. In 1980, even as Harvard prepared to launch an antiunion campaign against Rondeau's group, Bok asked Fraser to serve on the Visiting Committee (board of trustees) of the School of Public Health. In 1983 Fraser held a temporary appointment as visiting lecturer at the Kennedy School's Institute of Politics. At Rondeau's request, he had dinner with about twenty workers at an activist's home in suburban Newton. Within a few months he would retire after six years as head of the Auto Workers. In the last half of his term, Fraser had been confronted by an upheaval in manufacturing economics, the Japanese invasion of the U.S. auto market, and a huge decline in UAW membership. To help make the U.S. companies more competitive, he led the UAW into cooperative arrangements based on worker involvement in plant-level decision-making. In the long run, this probably kept some plants open and saved some jobs, but it also angered leftist factions in and around the UAW.

At the dinner in Newton, Fraser talked about these developments and other labor issues in his usual candid way. The workers, mainly young women and men from middle-class families, came to the dinner wary and suspicious of blue-collar unions and labor leaders. But Fraser charmed them with his wit, experience, and evident interest in their campaign. Differences between white- and blue-collar workers seemed to melt away in his presence. Rondeau judged the dinner a big success. She and Fraser did not always see eye-to-eye. He would criticize her behavior in a later dispute with the UAW. She had not been pleased when, in 1981, he provided fodder to Harvard's antiunion campaign by saying publicly that the UAW was organizing at universities, in part, to replenish its shrinking industrial membership. Harvard knew that its employees did not appreciate being valued solely as replacements for auto workers.

But she learned much about leadership from Fraser. She had seen him speak before large audiences and now at a small, informal gathering. She noticed, first, that he did not talk down to people but rather spoke to them as adults who could absorb unpleasant facts. Second, she saw that when he answered questions he did not change his message to fly with each change in the political breeze. "People on the left or the right would accuse him of this or that," Rondeau said. "But it didn't matter which side they were on. He would tell them the truth and not care that it didn't make them feel better. This was one of the most useful things I ever learned."

Fraser retired in June 1983, observing the UAW's 65-age limit for officers. His successor, Owen Bieber, never visited Harvard or spoke to Rondeau, much less any Harvard worker. But Fraser continued to support the Harvard drive after he retired. In another instance of Harvard's ambivalence toward unions, Derek Bok wrote to Fraser in 1983, asking him to recommend candidates to replace a retiring dean at the School of Public Health and to give his "views on problems and opportunities for the future." Yet when Rondeau's organizing committee began handing out pledge cards, the administration urged workers not to sign, declaring that the UAW fostered "a tense 'we-they' atmosphere."

Rondeau and her committee also indulged in excessive rhetoric from time to time. In a 1983 newsletter, they declared that "the power and prestige of the International union [UAW]" was now behind their drive. This was pandering to the old notion that workers wanted a brawny protector to negotiate with the employer for them. Rondeau and her group not only did not believe this but even derided such an idea. But it can be difficult to stop mouthing old propaganda, and they wanted to stay on the UAW's good side.

It was hard not to be amazed by Harvard's blatantly hypocritical positions on the union issue. Another example involved Lech Walesa, the Polish labor leader, who in 1983 was attempting to gain government recognition of his union Solidarity. In recognition of his efforts to bring "free, democratic unionism" to Communist Poland, Derek Bok invited Walesa to speak at Harvard's 1983 commencement exercises. Unable to make the trip, Walesa sent remarks which Bok read at commencement. There was every reason to honor Walesa, a truly heroic man who did as much as any individual to break the Communist grip on Poland. But his success owed everything to his backing by millions of Polish workers who wanted to be represented by the independent Solidarity instead of government-controlled sham unions. If Bok thought unionism was good for Polish workers, why not for American workers? This was the point made in a letter written by Bob Metcalf and published in the *Boston Globe*. ". . . if Pres. Bok feels the need to have a mistreated union represented at commencement next year, he should give us a call," the letter said.

Meanwhile, an event that would have a significant impact on the Harvard-UAW fight took place at Harvard's old academic and sporting rival, Yale. The Hotel Employees and Restaurant Employees (HERE) had been organizing Yale's 2,600 clerical and technical workers since 1980. The chief organizer of clerical workers Local 34, John Wilhelm, ran an innovative campaign. Rondeau was by no means the first organizer to rebel against received lore relating to union cards. Wilhelm avoided card-signing for more than a year while building a solid base of committed activists. On May 18, 1983, the workers voted in favor of union representation by the narrowest of margins, 39 votes out of 2,505 cast. It was only the second instance, after Boston University, of white-collar unionization in a large, private university. The election was just the beginning of a protracted battle for a union contract that would divide the Yale community even further and erupt in a ten-week strike in the fall of 1984.

And so passed 1983. Still waiting for an NLRB decision, the women unionists continued to organize new employees. But as the new year started, few people realized that a union "drive" still existed. To the degree that Harvard administrators thought of them at all, it was as a twice-defeated, small band of female malcontents which would soon vanish.

Finally, almost mercifully, the NLRB gave the union that long-sought (by Harvard) nudge into oblivion. On March 30, 1984, the board declared that a separate Medical Area unit was not appropriate; the union must organize the entire university. A four-member panel of the board voted 3–1 to reverse the 1977 decision under which two representation elections already had been held. Chairman Donald Dotson and two other Reagan appointees were in the majority, and the dissenting vote was cast by a holdover from the Carter Administration. Under Dotson, the Reagan board had set about boldly to overturn, on ideological grounds, precedents established during Democratic administrations when boards had a more liberal view of workers' rights. The Harvard case was just another in this series.

Dotson and his allies did not attempt to justify their decision with fancy legal arguments. The board majority simply adopted the reasoning of two promanagement dissenters in the 1977 case, who in turn had ratified the interpretation originally advanced in 1975 by Robert Fuchs, the regional director in Boston. In a legal sense, the situation was back where it started seven years before.

Rondeau was relieved to have it over; now she could proceed. Ted Barrett, meanwhile, finally prevailed in his long feud with David Livingston. Backed by the UAW leadership in Detroit, he pushed District 65 completely out of the Harvard picture, transferring Rondeau and Manna to the UAW payroll. The organizing unit was renamed "Harvard-UAW." The Auto Workers intended to launch a major campaign in every part of Harvard, and it sent Rondeau and her little party to begin the job in Cambridge.

There was no need to cross the Charles River in the dead of night with muffled oars. Harvard administrators didn't care whether they came or not, for it was assumed that the union could not succeed. It would be practically impossible, university officials thought, to organize clerical and technical workers throughout the university.

Landing in Cambridge, the organizers arrived in an old world milieu. If the Medical Area represented modern science, Harvard–Cambridge resonated with a classical humanist tradition which originated in the universities of medieval France, emigrated to England's Cambridge University, and traveled to America in the hearts and souls of Puritan colonists. Each scholar had his servant in medieval universities, and this master–servant relationship also took root in old Harvard College. The servant's duties, personal and clerical in nature at first, expanded into a myriad of general administrative tasks that kept a huge university functioning. Instead of working in labs jammed with scientific paraphernalia, the clerks of Cambridge labored at computer terminals in accounting offices or waited upon scholars in quaint academic nooks with creaking wooden floors. By the 1980s, only about 5 percent of jobs on the Cambridge campus were classified as technical, compared with 40 percent in the Medical Area.

The structures of Harvard–Cambridge seemed more human in proportion and function than the great laboratories hovering over the white quadrangle in Boston. Old Harvard's architecture symbolized not the technological confidence of modern science but eccentricity and individualism and yearning for esthetic beauty. Harvard Yard's twenty-nine buildings ranged in style from Colonial (Massachusetts Hall, 1720) to modern with prefabricated concrete slabs (Canaday Hall, 1974). In these buildings and many others scattered through Cambridge, some of the most famous scholars, scientists, writers, artists, and statesmen in American history lived and studied. "Cambridge at any time is full of ghosts," wrote Ralph Waldo Emerson, himself a Harvard graduate, in 1836.

There was tension between master and servant from the beginning. When it opened with a class of thirty-one students in 1638, Harvard College consisted of two or three houses located near what is now the south side of the Yard along Mass Ave. Stretching northward were fenced-in rows of "cowyards" where cows were pastured overnight for protection from wolves. One of these became known as "College Yard," which later expanded into Harvard Yard. In 1984, one could stand at the north end of Harvard Yard and imagine what it would have been like, in 1638, to gaze across pastures dotted with glutinous cow pies to that thin line of houses in the distance. All would be quiet except for a murmur of young men reciting Greek before open windows, or the faint shouts of boatmen carried up from the Charles River a half mile to the south.

It was in one of those houses, at the beginning of the second academic year in August 1639, that the master of Harvard College, Nathaniel Eaton, precipitated a crisis in employee relations. The eminent Harvard historian Samuel Eliot Morison describes the event as follows, quoting a contemporary source. Eaton, he writes, "made the mistake of beating his assistant so briskly with a walnut-tree cudgel, 'big enough to have killed a horse,' that a Thomas Shepard rushed in from the parsonage next door to save the poor man's life." From this account, it appears that the very first person who occupied a position something like "support staff" at Harvard was beaten half to death by the very first faculty member.

The concept of professorial tenure not having been introduced by 1639, Master Eaton was found guilty of 'cruell and barbaros beating' and removed from office. Relations with staff apparently improved thereafter, for Morison has little to say about staff assistants elsewhere in his history of Harvard's first three centuries. But one may conjecture about the duties and treatment of nontutorial staff. Privies seem to have played a large role in college life. Morison notes that by the 1760s, College Yard had become "an unseemly clutter of outhouses," which obviously required attending to by persons other than tutors and students. For many years, each faculty member had "his" freshman who performed clerical work and ran errands in return for a lower tuition fee. The beginnings of nonprofessorial administrative work may date to 1849 when the Harvard president delegated clerical duties to the office of regent.

Harvard started as a divinity school. But with the decline of religious influence in the early nineteenth century, Harvard and other universities reoriented themselves to the pursuit of knowledge instead of service to God. Professors became elite persons of eminence and influence who were thought to seek truth for the sake of truth. Their acolytes or assistants were assumed to exist on a permanently lower level, unable to rise to a higher calling but expected to emulate their masters in putting aside thoughts of social and material gain. There is reason and social purpose in a university elitism directed at maintaining high standards of scholarship. At most universities, however, academic elitism also perpetuated the tradition of inferiority of other groups, especially support staff.

In recent decades, some faculty members decried this attitude. At Harvard, Brendan Maher, a psychology professor and dean of the Graduate School of Arts and Sciences in the early 1990s, even lectured his colleagues on the issue. "At the heart of the matter," he wrote in a school newsletter, "is the tacit belief on the part of many faculty and many students that while they have, or soon will have, 'careers,' other members of the University community have 'jobs.'" He pointed out the important role that support staff can play. "In every department and in every doctoral program there are to be found one or more staff members, most often women, who from sharp intelligence, sound common sense and long experience at the University are able to provide real continuity and stability to programs that are too often only nominally directed by the faculty member designated to do so."

In 1984, when Harvard-UAW arrived in Cambridge, clerical workers were widely viewed as unimportant. Harvard was highly stratified to begin with, ranging in the academic area from tenured professors at the top of the hierarchy to assistant professors, down to lowly graduate-student lecturers. On the administrative side, there were vice presidents, administrative department chiefs, supervisors, a very large number of nonsupervisory employees thought to be ineligible for unionization, and at the bottom—the least connected people of all—were the support staff. Psychologically they were ready for some force to bind them together.

Rondeau, Manna, and their staff moved into a new office off Central Square about a half-mile from Harvard Yard. Martha Robb had joined the staff as a full-time organizer along with a young Afro-American man, Anthony Sutton, a former Medical School worker. Leslie Sullivan returned from maternity leave as a part-time organizer. One morning, this group went out to selected university buildings and distributed leaflets to kick off a new, university-wide campaign. "If Susan B. Anthony were alive today, she'd join our union," the leaflet said.

They had an enormous job ahead of them. Thirty-five hundred employees worked in four hundred separate buildings. Some buildings, with only one or two workers, were so isolated that few people in the administration knew of their existence. Others contained dozens, even hundreds of employees. More than five hundred worked in Holyoke Center, a six-story building just off Harvard Square that contained the university's central financial and administrative offices. The organizers had one natural advantage. They were relatively free to come and go. Harvard couldn't fence itself off from the surrounding community like a steel plant. The iron paling enclosing Harvard Yard was not meant to keep people out.

The organizers began meeting people. They were surprised to find that many employees already knew about union efforts in the Medical Area. "They would say, 'Where have you been? We've been waiting for you,'" Rondeau said. "We'd thought all the progressive people worked in the Medical School. But we saw that the Medical Area was a cold place compared to Cambridge."

Over the next six months, the organizers made slow but steady progress. "We didn't follow the things we had been taught about organizing," Rondeau said. "We started to do everything differently, and we loved it." Traditional methods included passing out flyers and setting up large meetings to see how many would show up. The Harvard organizers gradually did away with leaflets and only now and then held a rally. They concentrated on developing activist leaders through long, quiet, one-on-one discussions. It was the antithesis of noisy, flashy campaigns that make headlines one day and disappear the next.

"When we realized how natural it felt, we started getting interested in gender issues," Rondeau said. "The first thing we thought was, 'This is about us doing something we're comfortable with, in our own style, in our own way, with our own values.'" Their style was low-key. Their values included treating people with kindness and respect. Harvard was not an enemy to be beaten down but an institution to be improved. Rondeau had put it this way in a report to her UAW superiors in January: "We like Harvard. In fact, we like it enough to want to make it better, and the Union is the best way an employee can make Harvard better, and the UAW is the best union for us."

These were some of the ways that Harvard-UAW began to allow its natural feminism to emerge and influence organizing methods. Although the women were not theoretically inclined, they eagerly read one book published in the early eighties, *In a Different Voice,* by Carol Gilligan, a Harvard education professor, whose research seemed to show that men and women developed different approaches to moral reasoning from childhood on. "That was a hugely liberating idea to us," Rondeau said. "We had always felt inferior to men organizers because they supposedly knew how to do it. You're supposed to leaflet, and you're supposed to talk about issues, and you're supposed to hold meetings. We always thought the guys were right and we weren't. The idea that we could be different was liberating."

They exulted in their exceptionalism, because it felt so right to them and they knew it was working. But progress was slow and unquantifiable in a time when unions needed speed and measurable progress. Trouble was inevitable.

It was getting to be very hard to form a union anywhere. There were many reasons for this, but one in particular seemed to be gaining ground. Workers were coming to believe that a union could not do very much for them and especially could not protect them from bosses who did not want them to join a union. An influential book by two Harvard professors, James L. Medoff and Richard Freeman, told a grim story. *What Do Unions Do?,* published in 1984, smashed many of the stereotyped notions about the supposed adverse economic impact of unions, but it also painted a bleak picture of the future. Only about 16 percent of all workers in private industry belonged to unions in 1984, down from more than 20 percent in the early 1950s. Freeman and Medoff projected a decline to less then 10 percent by the end of the century.

Many unions had all but stopped organizing decades before this. Others, like the UAW, had continued organizing but with fewer successes. As employment dropped in manufacturing industries, the UAW and other unions stepped up recruitment efforts in unfamiliar territory, such as universities and white-collar service areas. Racing against time and that steep downward plunge in membership, the unions experimented with techniques like employee attitude surveys to select targets that gave most hope of success—rapid success. They wanted and needed a quick return on investment.

Ted Barrett and officials in the UAW's Detroit headquarters began putting pressure on Rondeau, starting in the fall of 1984. The UAW assigned a couple of men to Rondeau's staff apparently to monitor the campaign. Organizers were ordered to take the newcomers on their rounds and introduce them to Harvard employees. "That kind of threw us," Anthony Sutton recalled. "When it came to handling a work force that was predominantly female, the men had a tough time. I remember taking one gentleman around with me. People would say, 'Who is this guy? He doesn't look like he belongs on this campus.' It was obvious they were clamming up. They looked at us as if we had betrayed them."

Sometimes the UAW men took notes when organizers talked to groups of workers. Rondeau began to sense that union officials suspected her of disloyalty because she didn't talk the typical union line. The UAW instructed its organizers to wax poetic over the union, to make much of its size and power and ability to negotiate for and protect workers against most of the vicissitudes of working life. But she thought the union should not be introduced as Big Daddy or Big Brother to a predominantly female work force. She had learned this lesson years before while organizing a Cambridge bookstore for District 65.

In that campaign, she had signed up all fifteen employees except one, Florence (fictitious name), a sixty-five-year-old woman. One evening Rondeau and two workers took Florence to dinner. Never comfortable with "hard sell" tactics, Rondeau didn't mention the union during the meal, and Florence didn't ask about it. They had a pleasant conversation, but by the end of dinner Rondeau thought that Florence would have to be written off. As they put on their coats, "Florence came over and thanked me for not pushing her. She said, 'I grew up in my father's house and did what he told me to do. I got married and did what my husband told me to do. I got a job and did what my boss told me to do. When I sign this card, it will be the first time I've done something for myself.'" Florence signed a card, and the bookstore employees voted unanimously for the union.

"Women don't respond to the-union-is-going-to-take-care-of-you stuff," Rondeau said. Consciously or not, the UAW still was promoting paternalism, she thought. This would not work with Harvard support staff. "I was very loyal to the UAW. But I told workers they should never think of it as being perfect. And they should never think of it as being like an insurance agency that is going to do something for them."

The UAW ordered Rondeau to produce additional reports and provide information about activists she had recruited. She eventually supplied some material. But she strenuously resisted a demand for a list of Harvard employees' names and addresses to be used in a telephone survey. She and Manna passionately opposed polling workers during a campaign. Polling might be marginally useful as a pre-campaign tactic, they thought, but to have telephone pollsters call workers in the middle of a drive would be "intrusive" and would present a ready-made issue to management. "The workers already have been told that the organizers are outsiders with an outside agenda," Rondeau said. "Then you as a worker get a phone call at home from an anonymous person, a third party, asking you a lot of questions. It's out of sync with the internal consistency we had been developing. They also asked the wrong questions. 'Are you miserable? Are you disaffected? Do you hate your boss? Is your supervisor rotten? Do you need more money?' If the answer is, 'Yeah, the workers are miserable,' then the union makes a decision to organize that workplace. But we women don't like to admit we're miserable when we are. Those questions don't indicate the organizability of any particular workplace."

This issue came to a head in autumn 1984, when Auto Workers' officials called Rondeau and Manna to a meeting in Hyannis, Massachusetts, where the former were attending a conference. Present were Barrett and Ben Perkins, who supervised UAW organizing activities as administrative assistant to Vice-President Steven Yokich. Perkins wanted to know why the women had not furnished twelve hundred names and addresses as requested. Rondeau and Manna replied that they didn't have twelve hundred names and that it would take months to accumulate that many. Perkins had a suggestion: women organizers could stand in Harvard Square and give out pantyhose to passersby in return for their names and phone numbers.

Rondeau was appalled. She knew that Manna had a low tolerance for foolish ideas and worried how she might react. But Manna restrained herself. "They were outrageous suggestions," she recalled. "We were supposed to stand in the middle of Harvard Square and give out samples of pantyhose, with a card. It was so insulting."

Recounting his part in this meeting years later, Perkins acknowledged that he had suggested handing out pantyhose but only because Rondeau and Manna said they had no way of getting twelve hundred names. He told them that the UAW had successfuly obtained names for a poll in other campaigns by handing out free products. The union had certain ways of doing things, and, in his view, the Harvard women had no right to resist tried and true methods.

Eventually, Rondeau provided some names and addresses, but not twelve hundred. In the early months of 1985, she and her organizers felt increasing pressure, especially from Barrett. Other organizers continued to show up. After leading the Harvard effort for more than four years, she felt more than a little possessive about it and perceived the UAW as moving in to seize control. Her staff felt the same way. "I felt like our drive was being taken away from us," Sutton said. "When we told union leaders things looked good, that was their clue to move in. It became like a parent–child relationship." Marie Manna had much the same reaction. "It was as if the UAW said to us, 'Okay, you girls did a good job up till now. But now it's getting serious and we will have to take over.'"

When spring came, the UAW sent an experienced organizer, Barbara Rahke, to evaluate the Harvard situation. Rahke had helped organize Boston University in 1978 and joined District 65's Boston staff. She worked occasionally with Rondeau and Sullivan but tended to get along better than they with union superiors. Transferring to the UAW, Rahke went to Cornell and played a leading role in forming a union of maintenance workers in 1980. The school defeated a parallel effort to unionize white-collar workers. She later moved to Detroit and worked in the UAW's Technical, Office & Professional Department, which organized white-collar workers.

In 1995, long after the event, neither Rahke nor Rondeau wanted to talk for the record about personality clashes. But there was tension between them from the beginning. They had different beliefs about unionism and different notions about how best to serve the union. Rahke spent four days at Harvard in April and wrote a report for Steve Yokich. In a 1995 interview, angry about the way the events of 1985 at Harvard had been portrayed in the press, Rahke said she had found the campaign at "a low ebb" and not progressing fast enough. She was not this negative in her 1985 report, in which she described her overall impression as "positive." She pointed out several problems, however. She found in particular that Rondeau and her staff "relate much more to being 'Harvard' organizers than UAW organizers." She recommended that the union send in regular UAW organizers and that Rondeau and her staff "be brought to Detroit for several days of UAW orientation and training."

Rondeau and Manna were not told of Rahke's recommendations. They were aware that the UAW was dissatisfied with what it considered to be slow headway at Harvard. Said Manna, "We were making progress in the way that we make progress in this kind of organizing. It's not by leaps and bounds, it's in small increments. We were getting to know people. They weren't prounion yet. The UAW wanted to see people becoming prounion at a faster clip, and that doesn't happen in this kind of organizing."

After Rahke's visit, things slackened off a little as the summer break started. Rondeau didn't think the UAW was giving up, but she and Braude decided to go ahead with a long-planned vacation in Europe. In July they departed on a three-week trip to France and Italy.

CHAPTER TWELVE

*B*raude thought no one knew where they were staying in Rome because they had switched hotels. Nonetheless, Rondeau received an overseas call from Martha Robb on the penultimate day of their trip. When she got off the phone and looked at him, Braude knew the vacation was over, and perhaps much more.

It was the first time that either of them had traveled outside the United States. They had spent a week or so in Paris and another several days in Marseilles. They drove in a rented car through southern France and into Italy. Arriving in Rome, they discovered they had been booked into what Braude described as "a horrible dump" in the suburbs. Its one amenity was an outdoor pool, which—Rondeau blushed in recalling—was one of the requirements she gave to the travel agent who scheduled their trip. She thought it would be like driving across Ohio: a motel with pool every thirty miles or so. Whitinsville girl goes abroad.

Without unpacking they escaped Horrible Dump and found an elegant little hotel on the edge of a park in the city. When the call came from Robb, Braude was mystified, learning only much later that Rondeau had phoned the union office and left a message. Robb now told her that additional UAW organizers had arrived at the Cambridge office and that Barrett had ordered Manna and Rondeau to go to Detroit for another assignment. Rondeau thought she understood what was happening. The UAW appeared to be taking over the Harvard drive. She remembered feeling very dark and saying to her husband, "That's it. It's over."

They flew home a day earlier than planned, landing at Logan Airport on Monday morning, August 12. Rondeau phoned Barrett's office from the airport. An assistant talked to her. Yes, she had to go to Detroit on Tuesday to help in an organizing drive in Michigan. Why? Because, she was told, both she and Manna needed orientation in UAW organizing methods. She said, incredulously, "I've worked as an organizer for eight years, and I need orientation?"

She went directly to her office in Cambridge and tried again in vain to reach Barrett. On her desk was a one-way plane ticket to Detroit provided by the UAW. Manna already had decided to fly to Detroit that night, hoping that this would demonstrate that she and Rondeau were willing to compromise. They agreed that Rondeau would keep trying to find out what the UAW intended to do at Harvard. The women felt that if both left Cambridge immediately, the Harvard campaign would slip out of their grasp.

Rondeau called Barrett's office again and again. She told them she had her bag packed and would go as ordered, if only she could have a five-minute conversation with the regional director. Barrett refused to talk to her. A subregional director told her that she must follow orders without question. "And then," she recalled, "I got all that sexist bullshit: 'Oh, honey, you're a smart girl. Why don't you just go to Detroit.'"

Barrett's refusal to talk, the arrival of outside organizers, and other signs of UAW intervention in recent months, led Rondeau and Manna to conclude that they were being pushed out of the way. They suspected that Detroit union officials wanted to assert more control over the drive, but Barrett's peremptory behavior focused their suspicion on him. "None of us was stupid enough to think that this was just a shifting around of organizers," Manna said. "It was clearly a move to get rid of me and Kris, so they [UAW] could take it over. You don't have to be a genius to see that. With Barrett, it was really about control more than anything else."

What Rondeau and Manna did not know on August 12th was that the reassignment orders had come from Ben Perkins in Detroit. The UAW was engaged in one of the largest organizing campaigns in its history, involving twenty-two thousand state employees in Michigan. The union was pulling in organizers from around the country to help in the drive's final stages before an election in September. Rondeau and Manna were among several organizers summoned from Barrett's region. "We did not have an ulterior motive in calling them to Detroit," Perkins maintained in a 1996 interview. "We had a hundred staff people on this drive, and we especially wanted organizers who could assimilate with white-collar workers." An additional reason for calling in the Harvard women was that Barbara Rahke had recommended that they be "oriented" in UAW procedures.

Rondeau and Manna were to spend two weeks in Michigan, Perkins said, after which they would return to Cambridge and resume their campaign.

The orders that came from Barrett's office, however, did not specify how long the women would be in Michigan. Manna was told something of the project but not its duration. Rondeau recalled, "I kept asking them, 'How long will I be gone, how much should I pack?' But all they said was, 'Just go!'"

On Tuesday, when Manna arrived in Michigan, she was sent to Lansing to organize state clerical employees. Rondeau was supposed to fly to Detroit on a 2 P.M. plane but stayed at home and continued placing calls to Barrett. If he had answered only a few questions, she probably would have given in. This is how she remembered it. She did not feel heroic. She wanted to find a way out of this mess. But Barrett refused to talk to her. His position was, as an employee she must follow direction or suffer the consequences. "Kris had decided she would be an independent entity all by herself," he said later. "If you work for an organization, you have to take orders."

At 2 P.M., a Barrett assistant called Rondeau's office and found that she had not departed. Barrett obviously regarded the flight time as a deadline, but did not notify her that she was fired. She still hoped there was a way to pull back from the brink. Several things remained unresolved, including the status of the rest of her staff. Five were at work that day: Martha Robb, Anthony Sutton, Kerry Dolan, and two part-timers, Ned Young and Christina Knapp, all former Harvard employees hired by Rondeau. Leslie Sullivan, also a part-time organizer, was on maternity leave, pregnant with her second child. The five requested a meeting with Barrett, and he agreed to see them the following morning.

Barrett showed up at the Central Square office with four or five men. He was blunt. Rondeau had disobeyed orders, he said, and the organizing drive would continue without her. "What I remember," Sutton recalled in 1995, "is the dark suits and the authority that was being put around. 'We want you to put out cards,' Barrett said. He talked about outside organizers coming onto campus. I felt like I was being held captive in there and intimidated. The cordiality was totally gone. It was as if we were kids and Ted was the dad and the rest of the guys were uncles. 'This is what you're gonna do, and don't talk back.'"

Martha Robb recalled the climax of the meeting. "Barrett finally said, 'You have to decide, do you work for me or Kris?'" Sutton also remembered Barrett putting it this way, indicating that Rondeau might already have been fired. He gave them twenty-four hours to think it over.

The staff members followed their normal routines the rest of the day. At 5 P.M. they returned to the office for a previously scheduled rehearsal of a singing group. Unexpectedly, they couldn't unlock the office door. One after another they tried their keys, to no avail. They realized that the lock had been changed. "We let out a sigh," Sutton said, "and sort of slid down the wall with our backs and sat in the hallway, looking at each other. People started to cry. There was fear in the air. Someone said, 'We've been locked out.'" They thought this meant they had been fired.

When Rondeau heard of the changed lock, she felt an overwhelming sense of finality. "Now I knew for sure," she said. It appeared that Barrett (probably in league with others at the UAW) was taking the campaign away from her and her staff. She called Manna in Michigan and filled her in. Manna agreed with her reading of the situation and decided to fly home that night. Now both were disobeying orders.

By the end of the week, unknown men were answering the phone at the Cambridge union office, and employee activists realized that some kind of shakeup was occurring within the organizing staff. Feeling that they owed the workers an explanation, Rondeau and Manna called a meeting for Sunday and spent a few anxious days worrying about what to say. It was the worst of circumstances for a union drive: a fight for control among the organizers themselves. The women assumed they had been fired, or at the very least had been relieved of command at Harvard. How would they present this to workers already suspicious of big unions, and what would they propose to do about it?

On Sunday afternoon, between fifty and a hundred workers gathered in the basement of the Old Cambridge Baptist Church. Rondeau and her staff described as honestly as they could—though obviously from their point of view—the events of the past week, climaxed by the "lockout," as they termed it. The UAW actions, Rondeau said, constituted an intolerable interference in what the union had promised would be a locally run campaign. This being the case, she could no longer endorse the Auto Workers as the union for Harvard workers. But she didn't propose a rival movement, thinking it would be wrong to encourage belief in an enterprise that would have little chance of succeeding. If they were to continue the fight (as she hoped), she wanted the workers to choose this course without her prompting.

One of the leading activists at the meeting was Bill Jaeger, a twenty-four-year-old staff assistant at Harvard. He would remember in particular that Rondeau did not denounce the Auto Workers as a "bad" union from top to bottom. She accused some UAW officials of making "wrongheaded decisions, partly brought about by gender differences," Jaeger said. "They were men in a man's world having trouble getting used to an emerging movement of women."

After the staff spoke, workers asked questions and gave their opinions. Most talked of keeping the drive going as an independent effort. No vote was taken, nor needed to be taken. "The room seemed to feel unanimously that we should continue," Jaeger said. "It felt like a solid base of understanding about the style of organizing that Kris and the others brought to it." Jaeger himself strongly supported the independent effort, despite his own peculiar position. Some weeks before, he had accepted Rondeau's offer to join her staff as a UAW employee and was scheduled to start on Monday, August 17—the day after this suddenly convened meeting in the church. The prospect of receiving a UAW paycheck had vanished, but he stayed with Rondeau's group.

To demonstrate their support, the workers passed a hat and collected eighteen dollars and change. The organizers were touched. Harvard employees did not have a lot of money to hand out. Later that night, Rondeau and Manna talked about the spirit of the meeting and the strong desire to push ahead. "We thought that was a natural response, but the workers didn't know how hard it would be to continue without any resources," Rondeau said. "We thought it would take people three or four weeks to figure out that it was impossible to go forward, and the campaign would die." For the time being, however, Rondeau and Manna would take it one day at a time. "We were pissed," Rondeau said. "I thought, 'The UAW doesn't know how to do it, and they won't do it.' We never made a decision to go forward. We just did it. The UAW was there, and we were going to outlast them. If we were going to build a union, we were going to build it right."

It is a rare occurrence when a local organizing staff breaks away from a large, well-respected national union like the Auto Workers. Within organized labor, it is considered an unthinkable betrayal of such principles as loyalty and solidarity, but to outsiders it may be pictured as a courageous act of defiance in the face of overwhelming bureaucracy. Many stories featuring either of these themes would be told over the next several years about what happened at Harvard in the week of August 12. Both contained misleading elements.

The story told by UAW partisans is that Kris Rondeau seized a sudden opportunity to manipulate a defection, covering her tracks by eliciting public sympathy with contrived accounts of the event. A major feature of this story is the UAW's assertion that Rondeau and her organizers were not forced out of the UAW but rather quit. The union's evidence is a copy of telegrams sent to Rondeau and six other staff members on August 23 after they had applied for unemployment compensation, contending they had been fired. "Your attorney indicated you are not a voluntary quit," said the telegram. "If you are not a voluntary quit, report for work not later than August 27 [August 28 for Rondeau and Manna, who were to report in Detroit]."

The union argued that the organizers had not been "locked out" of the office, as in "fired." Rather, the lock was changed because Barrett's aides discovered (on the morning that Barrett met with the staff) that a computer disk containing "critical" employee files had been removed from the office. This implied that the Harvard organizers already were planning to defect and stole files in order to sabotage the organizers who would re-place them. Rondeau and her staff vigorously disputed this account on two grounds. First, Barrett's people had never worked with the organizing files and could not have known if anything were missing. Second, the Harvard staff did remove material from the office—but *after* the lock was changed, not before.

On the afternoon they found the lock changed, the staff left the office believing they had been fired. Later, they realized that they had left hand-written lists of workers and other personal files in the office. A few of the organizers returned that night, broke into the office through a drop-ceiling, and retrieved their lists. They may have taken a computer disk, though none of the participants remembered this. Rondeau didn't accom-pany them but knew that what they intended to do was, in fact, burglary. "I justified it to myself on grounds that it was our property as well as theirs [UAW's]," she said. Her organizers had drawn up their own lists, and whatever computer files were taken had been generated in a personal computer owned by one of her staff. Furthermore, she said, paper copies of all computer files were left in the office.

The organizers went to this trouble because they had *not* planned to break away from the UAW and had not anticipated being locked out. Three of the participants later recounted details of this episode. They were Martha Robb, still on Rondeau's staff when interviewed, and two men who left the group in 1985—Anthony Sutton, who became a paralegal in Boston, and Ned Young, who later earned a Ph.D. in evolutionary biology at Cornell and became a researcher. Interviewed separately in 1996, all three gave essentially the same account.

Upon receiving telegrams asking them to return to work, none of the Harvard staff responded, believing that the telegrams were designed to influence the decision of the state agency in denying compensation. "I had no reason to believe those offers were genuine," Rondeau said. Not only that, Manna said, but "we didn't believe we would have been able to work out anything by that point." Staff members Robb, Sutton, and Young had the same feeling. After Barrett told them they had to choose between him and Kris, and after finding themselves locked out of the union office, they believed with dead certainty that they had been fired. "The telegram didn't mean anything," Sutton said. They couldn't disprove the UAW's story, however, and were denied jobless benefits after a hearing before the Massachusetts Division of Employment Security.

The story that Rondeau and Manna pulled out of the UAW and made up a tale of being expelled does not fit the facts. On the other hand, an opposing story that lays all blame on the Auto Workers also has flaws. In September 1985, the UAW dispatched a new team of organizers headed by Barbara Rahke to Harvard. She later would complain, with justification, that the UAW was unfairly tagged in the press as being insensitive to the women workers of Harvard. The story was that the Auto Workers sent in "burly factory men" who clomped clumsily around the university and antagonized the female employees. While some UAW men had shown up on campus before the split occurred and before Rahke took over, she herself brought in a team of women experienced in white-collar organizing. Some journalistic accounts, including a 1993 article by the author of this book, mistakenly collapsed the two episodes into one.

UAW supporters also spread absurd rumors that Rondeau, aided by her husband in some versions, planted patently untrue stories about the union in the press. More likely, the exaggerated references to UAW incompetence resulted from journalists' infinite capacity to infer more than is stated. But Rondeau did not repudiate stories with misleading statements favorable to her side (few people do), and confusion about the events of August 1985 persisted.

Did Rondeau and Manna do the right thing? The answer from inside organized labor is a decisive "no!" People like Barbara Rahke, Ted Barrett, and Doug Fraser had different perspectives on many issues but not about organizational loyalty. You must support the union and follow its procedures and rules in all circumstances, excepting only those that require explicitly immoral or unlawful actions. The UAW was funding the Harvard drive and had a right to determine strategy and tactics. Fraser, who appreciated Rondeau's abilities, said flatly of her split with the UAW, "Kris was wrong."

There is no doubt that Perkins called Rondeau and Manna to Michigan, at least in part, to help with the UAW's public employee drive. (The union ultimately won elections involving twenty-two thousand state workers.) But Perkins and Rahke also were dissatisfied with the progress of the Harvard drive and thought it needed an infusion of UAW values. Barrett, as regional director, had yet another objective. He wanted more control over an organizing effort that could turn into one of the largest local unions in his region, and he regarded Rondeau as a "prima donna." Moreover, the conflicts over strategy and tactics were real. "Her whole concept of organizing was different," Barrett said. "In the UAW, we'd convene a meeting in a hall and tell people why they ought to join the union. At Harvard they'd go to someone's house and have coffee and talk about it. It was the whole social thing."

Although Rondeau's organizers rarely went to a worker's home, they did emphasize one-on-one organizing, or the "social thing." This is the nub of the conflict. The Harvard women's organizing methods and concept of unionism differed sharply from that of the UAW officials. Having organized at Harvard for several years, Rondeau and Manna quite naturally thought of it as *their* campaign and did not want to cede control to anybody. But more than instinctual territoriality was involved. The organizers felt morally obligated to the Harvard workers they had recruited, and they believed the campaign would fail if run by the UAW in a traditional way. Rondeau and Manna had been talking to the workers about forming one kind of union, and the Auto Workers would introduce a different kind.

The UAW was a very large union with a tradition, largely successful in the past, of imposing patterns and systems on processes such as collective bargaining and organizing. A leader of another union, who knew Rondeau and was familiar with her work, thought the UAW was too rigid. "Kris is almost anti-organizational, but she is a person of extraordinary talent who was suited by her understanding of the environment to run the campaign," he said. "For the labor movement to grow, we've got to have people like that. We should let them take the bit in their teeth and run with it."

"We tried for over a year, that whole year from the middle of eighty-four to eighty-five, to do what they [UAW] asked us to do," Manna said. "It got to a point where, for our own integrity, we could no longer do the things they asked us to do. To me, the idea of being loyal is not going along with whatever the boss says to do but trying to make the organization work as best as it can."

"I felt that what happened with us was more about gender than anything else," Rondeau said. "It was also about individuals like Ted Barrett. If he had been just an iota less rigid, I don't think any of this would have happened. I have a great, deep respect for the UAW and for many of the people who are part of it. I just had a bad experience."

Rondeau's split with the Auto Workers put Jim Braude in an awkward position. As an officer of the UAW-affiliated District 65 (one of several vice-presidents), he was obligated in some sense to the parent organization. Yet he felt his wife was a victim of "outrageous" treatment. During August, he flew home from New York every evening to be with her. He accompanied her to the crucial meeting with Harvard activists and pulled his chair up close behind her as she sat in the circle. He knew that she didn't need his advice but couldn't restrain himself. Every time she made a point that he thought might have been phrased better, he leaned over her shoulder and exhaled with a sharp "Ohhhh!" Finally, she turned to him and said, "Why don't you relax and let me handle this?" Braude later enjoyed telling this story on himself.

Rondeau remembered asking him repeatedly during this period, "Am I doing the right thing? He said 'yes.'" Braude remembered it somewhat differently. "Her position was that it was irreconcilable. I was trying to convince her there must be a way to fix this." But that way would have to lead through Barrett, who wouldn't talk.

When it became clear some weeks later that the break was final, he resigned his District 65 post. He was still Livingston's "fair-haired boy," but he had lost his ambition to rise in the union. "I couldn't see what was done to Kris and still feel good about going to work," he said. "For me, there had been a souring process [with the union] that began to build after my first meeting with Kris. For all those years, she and her folks had to wade through shit for no reason, except that they were women. The process came to a head for me with the return from Italy."

Braude took a job in Boston handling press relations for the Hotel Employees and Restaurant Employees. In 1987, he was named executive director of the Tax Equity Alliance for Massachusetts (TEAM), a liberal advocacy group funded largely by unions.

And so was born an independent union on the Harvard campus in August 1985. Its prognosis was grim, its future measured in days. The union consisted of a handful of experienced but unpaid organizers and perhaps a couple hundred devoted followers in the work force. It had no money, no office, no equipment, no standing, no recognition in the "labor movement," no affiliation with any larger organization, and no name.

The first thing they needed was a name. The staff began discussing possibilities, trying to combine words that would describe the union and also provide a catchy acronym. The name-inventing sessions might have been titled "Acronym in Search of an Antecedent," a process that proved to be more difficult than expected. One day a number of people were sitting around Martha Robb's kitchen table alternately joking and throwing out ideas. Someone suggested "HELLO," which caused momentary excitement. It started out very well indeed with "Harvard" and "Employees," but no one could figure out what "LLO" might stand for.

Leave it to practical-minded Manna. "Why don't we call it exactly what it is?" she said. "The Harvard Union of Clerical and Technical Workers."

Someone spelled out the acronym, "H-U-C-T-W." How would you pronounce *that?* Impossible! Well, someone said, the Amalgamated Clothing & Textile Workers Union (ACTWU) frequently was called "ACT-TU," so what about "HUC-TU?"

"No," Manna said. She detested this striving for vocal comfort. "We'll call it 'the H-U-C-T-W.'"

There were skeptical faces around the table. Bill Jaeger was one of the first to support the "awkward but accurate" approach. When he sided with Manna, others took notice. A recent graduate of Yale, he worked in Harvard's Russian Research Center. He had sung in the Yale Glee Club, had studied the politics of Eastern Europe, and spoke a little Russian. His knowledge of semantics, politics, and what makes music to the ear, seemed to qualify him to know about acronyms. HUCTW they became. The staff avoided the pronunciation problem for some years, referring to themselves as "the union." Later, Manna-like, they took to spelling it out, "the H-U-C-T-W." Finally, casting aside linguistic purity, even Bill Jaeger began to call it "HUTCH," as did most staff members. But not Manna. "I think that's stupid," she said in 1996.

In the early days, Rondeau, Manna, Robb, and the others tried not to think about the enormousness of the job they had set for themselves. They had their own ideas of what a union should be, and they had a set of values worked out over a long period of time, and they had one another. "We just knew that we really wanted to do it," Rondeau said, "and so we kept moving ahead."

The key to operating independently was to have a staff that worked for nothing. If they managed to raise any money, it would go first to pay for office space and phone service. The senior members of the staff, Rondeau, Manna, and Robb, decided that they could get along, for a while, without a salary. Each had a working husband and a family health insurance policy—and a good thing this was for Robb, who was five months pregnant. She would give birth to a son in December and return to work in January. The three husbands, Jim Braude, Mac McCreight, and Bob Metcalf, along with a few women, formed the HUCTW Ladies' Auxiliary, which supported the organizers in many ways, though the men drew the line at marching under that banner in Memorial Day parades.

For the younger, single members of the staff, working without pay was all but impossible. Three organizers (Knapp, Sutton, and Young) resigned within a few weeks. It was an agonizing but necessary decision for each. When Leslie Sullivan returned from maternity leave at the end of August, she also resigned, though not because of anxieties over money. The split with the UAW merely gave her a reason to take an action she had been contemplating for some time. Her relations with Rondeau had changed from the days when *she* (Sullivan) was the leader. She didn't criticize Rondeau's handling of the UAW problem, though she probably would have acted differently. But it didn't seem to matter any more. Her heart had gone out of the game. She put unionism behind her and concentrated on raising a family.

Bill Jaeger decided to stay—or rather to start on the job—without pay. Rondeau could promise him nothing, but he thought he could make do. He lived with his girlfriend Susan, a graduate student, and he would receive a $1,000 stipend as a graduate student himself for one semester. He worked part-time for the union until January and then went full-time.

Jaeger ("J" pronounced "Y") was brought up near St. Louis, the son of an accountant and manager at McDonnell Douglas. He received a B.A. at Yale in 1984, and got a job at Harvard because his girlfriend went there for postgraduate study. Jaeger liked his work and co-workers, but quickly perceived them to be frustrated because Harvard bosses allowed them almost no control over their jobs. "It took heroic individual efforts to make small changes in any work procedure," Jaeger recalled. He met Rondeau and other organizers and liked what they had to say about seeking power for workers. "I respected the way they were organizing," he said. "There was critical analysis of Harvard but no effort to breed or encourage hostility. Nobody tried to make me feel angry at Harvard, which was good because I didn't feel angry."

Jaeger was just the kind of activist that Rondeau and her group were looking for. They had learned that angry workers rarely made good organizers. They looked for people with a "cheerful" disposition, which was not to be confused with shallow. Jaeger had a sharp wit, an optimistic outlook, and a good head for economics and organizational politics. Working with women and accepting their leadership did not bother him. He later would rise to the top staff position in the Harvard union.

The independent union began business with a five-member organizing staff: Rondeau, Manna, Robb, Jaeger, and Dolan (who quit several months later). Amazingly, the staff actually grew during the independent period, despite payless paydays. Three other Harvard workers would join the group in 1986, *knowng that they would not be paid.* They were Stephanie Tournas, a library assistant and 1981 graduate of Wellesley College; Joie Gelband, a Vassar graduate who worked in the Harvard Divinity School while pursuing an advanced degree; and Ralph Vetters, who had graduated from Harvard in 1985 and gone to work there.

For the first month or two, the staff scraped together enough money from their own pockets and from members' contributions to rent a room in a church near Harvard Square. Rondeau, meanwhile, tried to raise money. "We didn't know anything about fundraising," Robb recalled, "but Kris attacked this problem with the same ferocity she had used in forming the union. She went out to convince everybody [that we could win]." Rondeau, however, learned that fundraising was a tricky business. "I was pretty good about describing the organization and the cause. But saying, 'I need your money'—I had trouble getting this out of my mouth." Nonetheless, she managed to borrow a total of about $30,000 from acquaintances (eventually all repaid) to meet major expenses like office rent and telephone service.

In October, the group moved into a basement office in an old building on Winthrop St. which had been vacated by an architectural firm. It was a long, narrow room divided by shoulder-high partitions, and it had three niches in the east wall that appeared to have been recently excavated from a vein of gray shale. The staff used one niche as a conference room; a second accommodated three desks and a couple of personal computers, and the third was just big enough for an old refrigerator (if you opened the door only halfway) that someone had donated. Along the north wall was another niche, about ten feet long and three feet wide which Rondeau used as an office. She could entertain one guest in here, though she had to back out of the office to allow him or her in. The staff brought in lawn chairs and other cast-off furniture. Rondeau paid $1,000 a month for this shabbiest of dens, a relatively low rent for high-priced Harvard Square. At first the union sublet the office from the architectural firm but later became a tenant, ironically, of Harvard Real Estate, a money-making venture of Harvard University.

They may not have had much, but they kept a sense of humor, even laughing at their own predicament in a proud sort of way. In the fall of 1985, one of the women coined a new slogan, "Too dumb to quit." They didn't have money to have buttons made, but they printed "Too Dumb to Quit" on index cards which they taped to their sweaters and jackets and wore around for a few days.

They experimented with other methods of raising money. Joie Gelband and Ralph Vetters designed a payroll deduction system in which workers could direct contributions to the union through electronic funds transfer. Over the course of eighteen months, the union held several flea markets on church grounds and Cambridge Commons, selling donated furniture, knick-knacks, and clothing. Every couple of months they staged a "New Talent Night" in the back room of Charlie's Tap, a tavern near Central Square. The owners, sympathetic to the union, allowed them to keep collections from a $5 admission fee paid by thirty to fifty patrons who jammed into a small room to watch Harvard workers, talent or no talent, dancing and singing. Actually, there were some quite good performers by all accounts since the union itself had some talented amateurs. Jaeger, who had studied classical piano as a boy and later picked up jazz and pop, frequently played the piano and sang duets with Gelband. A singing group called the Pipets, formed some years before by union enthusiasts in the Medical Area, often performed at Charlie's, singing pop numbers or popular melodies with satirical lyrics jabbing at Harvard. New Talent Night was a lot of fun—until the new talent became distinctly mediocre, and then the staff members began to grumble about spending yet another weekend night at "Charlie's Trap."

Through borrowing and soliciting contributions and selling old goods and "new talent," the union raised close to $50,000 over a period of eighteen months. Toward the end, money was only dribbling in. Rondeau knew that they couldn't possibly carry the campaign to successful conclusion without a major infusion of funds. Eventually, somehow, HUCTW would have to find a sponsor in what Rondeau began referring to as "the mainstream labor movement." This worried her. "I thought to myself, 'It'll be like putting a noose around our neck.'"

The independent period lasted through 1986. Despite constant money worries, it was an idyllic time of rapid growth. The group had always had to learn organizing on their own. Neither District 65 nor the UAW inhibited them in developing their own style, with the exception of the last few months of UAW intervention. Now they were really alone, castoffs, and they were forced to do for themselves and learn from their mistakes.

"We were living on the edge and we learned so much," Rondeau said of that period. "Being out of the mainstream labor movement caused something to happen within us and we changed. It was rapid, and it was thorough, and it felt great to be doing what our guts told us to."

Poverty forced them to do without "literature" as it is called in the trade. Since the early eighties, Rondeau and her group had been cutting back on newsletters, leaflets, flyers, "Dear Employee" letters, and so forth, partly out of weariness and partly out of a growing belief that workers paid little attention to words on paper. Now they learned that HERE Local 34 at Yale had made a strategic decision to approach workers in person rather than through written communication. After the UAW split, Rondeau talked a few times with John Wilhelm, the chief Yale organizer, who advised her against running a "paper campaign." A group of Yale activists who visited Harvard in the fall of 1985 told Rondeau and her staff that eliminating literature had given management fewer targets to shoot at.

It was easy for the Harvard union to take this advice, for it had no paper and no access to photocopying machines and certainly no money to pay a printer. The staff discovered rather quickly that "literature put a barrier between us and the people we were trying to organize," Manna said. No longer could a prounion worker become an activist merely by handing out pieces of paper. Now she or he had to talk to people. "The most important thing we learned about not having literature," Rondeau said, "is that our employee organizers became much more skillful. It was amazing to see people learn organizing in a deeper, better way. We had never realized how much activism is defined as handing out paper. We had always told organizers, 'This is just a piece of paper to get you in the door.' The whole labor movement says this. But we don't really mean it until we have no paper to give out."

Rondeau also came to see that union handouts connect workers to a campaign only "in a very passive way." A worker may feel he has fulfilled an obligation to himself merely by scanning a union leaflet. After reading a few sentences, he concludes that he can reject the union without feeling guilty and throws the leaflet away. "We didn't give out anything, and people eventually would have to ask an organizer, 'So what's going on with that union drive?' Once they asked that question, we could start building a relationship."

One of the union's best slogans came out of the seemingly paradoxical position that Harvard needed a union even though it was a "good" employer. Massachusetts Congressman Barney Frank actually coined the slogan in a speech at a Christmas party in 1985. A liberal Democrat with strong ties to organized labor, Frank had addressed several Harvard union rallies since the early eighties. It took some political courage on his part to continue supporting the independent union despite the presence of the politically powerful UAW on campus. On the day of the party, Rondeau briefed Frank about the basic themes of the campaign. When he spoke, she didn't hear anything special; her mind was wandering. But the next day an activist named Richard Brennan called the union office. He said he'd taken notes during Frank's speech and wanted to make a poster using what he thought was an excellent quote, "It's not anti-Harvard to be prounion."

Brennan produced a handsome poster and had several copies made. When the union presented them for sale at a flea market in the spring, several were snapped up at $5 apiece. A short time later, when a secretary tacked her poster on a bulletin board, a personnel officer found it objectionable and told her to remove it. "We knew then," Rondeau said, "we had found a slogan that resonated with workers and management." She and Manna decided to hold it in reserve for a more strategic time. When they began using the slogan in late 1986, it proved highly popular with workers. Later it was put on t-shirts and made into bumper stickers. The message, "It's Not Anti-Harvard to Be Prounion," would make workers "feel safe" when Harvard unleashed its antiunion campaign, Rondeau said.

The UAW, meanwhile, did not slink off without a fight. The Auto Workers had plenty of resources, and it put out leaflets and letters and held smokers and parties. It had to start from scratch since all employee activists followed Rondeau out of the UAW and few, if any, returned. It was embarrassing for one of the country's premier unions to be out-organized by a ragtag band of female rebels. Rahke later would accuse Rondeau's group of organizing against her union as much as against Harvard. "Emotion is what organizes people, and anger is the strongest emotion," she said in 1995. The workers were not angry at Harvard, and so Rondeau's group incited anger at the rival union. "Their campaign was geared toward hating the UAW."

There exists little written evidence of what Rondeau's organizers told workers. But the UAW is mentioned in two surviving letters to employees.

The first, dated August 20, 1985 and signed by the staff of the new independent union (not yet named HUCTW) and ninety-five workers, gives a brief explanation of the split. "Recent developments have raised serious doubts about the UAW's commitment to preserving our role in making decisions that affect our drive," the letter says. "The organizing staff's loyalty to this principle has resulted in their being dismissed by the UAW." A second letter makes essentially the same argument, which may be self-serving but not hate-provoking.

Organizers undoubtedly used more vigorous language in talking with workers, but Rondeau did not believe in negative campaigning. She described the break with the UAW as she saw it. "We basically told people," she said, "that the UAW had in fact acted like a [intervening] third party. That's a worker's greatest fear, and it's the one that management picks up on the most in an antiunion campaign. We couldn't lie about it. It happened."

"I remember feeling animosity toward the UAW people," said Bill Jaeger. "There was some poking of fun and laughing at the haplessness of the UAW organizers. But we had a philosophy with a central tenet that although people get angry about things, it was wrong to build an organization on anger or resentment. We didn't foster hatred of the UAW in meetings. That wouldn't have worked. We might have got a large group of people hating the UAW, but not people who would have voted for our union."

By the summer of 1986, the interunion rivalry remained very much alive. Rondeau and the staff decided it was time to show their strength. They collected about eleven hundred signatures of pro-HUCTW workers and incorporated them on a poster with the headline, "WE BELIEVE IN OURSELVES." It was perhaps a feminine version of making a muscle to impress someone or some group. "We had gotten the idea from Yale, where they did one for the boss [the Yale administration]," Rondeau said. "Ours wasn't for the boss. It was for the UAW. The poster said to the UAW, 'We have eleven hundred. How many do you have?' We thought we could count the number of supporters they had on one hand."

CHAPTER THIRTEEN

A union staff man named Robert McGarrah was attending a summer program at Harvard's Kennedy School of Government in July 1986. He had come up from Washington for what he thought would be an uneventful, three-week sojourn in academia, only to stumble across an extraordinary find in the brick labyrinths of Harvard.

McGarrah was director of public policy of the American Federation of State, County & Municipal Employees, which had an unusual financial link with Harvard. By 1986, AFSCME had become the nation's third largest union with more than one million members, the majority of whom were employees of state and local governments. It had grown explosively during the 1970s under an aggressive and intellectually inclined president, Jerry Wurf, who harbored a deep admiration for Harvard University. When he died in 1981, his union gave Harvard a $1 million endowment for labor education. It was under the auspices of the Jerry Wurf Endowment Fund that McGarrah and a few other AFSCME staff members were attending a Kennedy School program for executives of state and local governments.

A thirty-nine-year-old lawyer, McGarrah headed a department that provided policy analysis for AFSCME lobbyists and negotiators. He sometimes referred to himself as an "issues man," for he spent most of his time dealing with broad subjects like health care reform and supply-side vs. Keynesian economics. At the Kennedy School, he found the courses useful but less than inspiring. One morning, walking through the basement of the Kennedy School, McGarrah was drawn to a large, tan-colored poster on a bulletin board. A headline at the top said, "WE BELIEVE IN OUR-SELVES." Below the headline were hundreds of signatures and a paragraph of text, which said:

> We, the clerical and technical workers of Harvard University, are joining together to form a strong union. We are proud that our efforts and abilities are essential to sustaining Harvard's reputation for excellence. Standing together we will be an effective voice for equity and justice within the Harvard community.

McGarrah was astonished. This, clearly, was the voice of a union. But he had never heard of the Harvard Union of Clerical and Technical Workers, or of an organizing drive at Harvard. Judging by the number of signatures (eleven hundred, he later learned), the union had substantial support and yet appeared to be an independent. McGarrah decided to find out more about it.

He and two associates later visited the union office. "It was like we had been fishing and got a bite," Rondeau said. She was excited but also careful not to yank too hard on the line. When McGarrah invited her to bring one of her staff to dinner, her first thought was, "Who needs a free meal most?" Her unpaid organizers were getting poorer and thinner by the day. The hungry ones usually could be seen hovering over the office vat of peanut butter. In the end, though, Rondeau chose Marie Manna because she valued her judgment.

Rondeau and McGarrah liked each other from the start. He found her to be "a charismatic individual with a very keen sense of community which is critical to union organizing." She was open to the idea of affiliating with a large union, but only under certain circumstances. "She and her members did not want to be taken over," McGarrah said. "They had to run their own campaign and control their union themselves."

Returning to Washington, McGarrah wrote a memo to AFSCME President Gerald McEntee, describing the Harvard campaign as "a vibrant organizing drive." McGarrah also informed McEntee's chief of staff, Ernest Rewolinski, a former head of organizing for AFSCME who invited Rondeau to Washington. "I knew from that first meeting with Kris that she had the support at Harvard, and the UAW didn't," Rewolinski later said. "I liked her approach because it involves touching the flesh, getting people committed and involved as activists." Rewolinski and McGarrah set about trying to convince McEntee that the Harvard union would be a good investment. They also enlisted Joseph Bonavita, director of District Council 93, headquartered in Boston.

Rondeau traveled to Washington a couple of times that summer for interviews with McEntee and Rewolinski. She learned enough about their union to think that her members would be comfortable with it. AFSCME had a comparatively high proportion of women members, a little over 50 percent. Although the top-level officers were men, four or five women sat on the executive board and most administrative departments had female staff members. McEntee did not seem disturbed when she asked for "complete autonomy" and a guarantee that the parent union would hire her current organizers. For other reasons, though, he seemed less than enthusiastic about taking in Rondeau's group. Harvard already had defeated two union drives, and it looked bigger and more powerful than ever. If the Auto Workers remained in the race, Harvard would benefit from a split vote. McEntee also had to calculate how vulnerable his union would be to UAW retaliation elsewhere if he intervened as a rival at Harvard.

Several months passed. During this time Rondeau also talked with John Wilhelm about possible affiliation with the Hotel Employees. He and the Yale unionists had given generously of advice to Rondeau and her staff, and they in turn had supported Local 34 in its 1984 strike at Yale. Viewed from the outside, the two unions seemed a natural match, and Wilhelm had high regard for Rondeau's organizing talents. When they talked about affiliation, Rondeau sensed that the Hotel Employees would not be inclined to grant the measure of autonomy she wanted, and Wilhelm felt that a merger was not realistic. The Hotel Employees union was not actively seeking white-collar university employees. It had organized clerical and technical workers at Yale only because it already represented dining hall workers there. "I would have loved to have them [HUCTW]," Wilhelm said in 1996, "but it wasn't logical. To the average Harvard employee, the notion of affiliating with us would have seemed odd."

Rondeau continued to build her union's strength with little resistance from a serenely confident Harvard and no real contest by the UAW. But by late autumn, Rondeau was running out of money to meet essential expenses. In Washington, Rewolinski and McGarrah came up with a proposal intended to kindle McEntee's interest in the Harvard union. They suggested polling the workers to get an idea of how HUCTW would fare against the Auto Workers in an election. The only trouble was, the plan proposed by Rondeau's two strongest backers in AFSCME entailed use of a technique that she despised. When McEntee asked her to cooperate with a polling firm, Rondeau argued that whatever prounion sentiment the poll uncovered would be "meaningless" because workers had not yet been exposed to an antiunion campaign. But McEntee was adamant. She saw that she must either bend or write off affiliation. She talked it over with her staff. After all that they had been through, and with hundreds of activists committed to the union, it didn't make much sense to jeopardize everything for the sake of a strategic principle. "In the end there wasn't much to think about even though it hurt to make the decision," she said. "I knew that I had to give him [McEntee] a reason to say 'yes' to us."

The survey was conducted on November 24 and 25 by a Boston polling firm which called 250 Harvard employees from a list of about 3,000. With the help of Rondeau's staff, the firm weighted the sample to ensure that prounion activists were not disproportionally represented. The results were pretty much as Rondeau had predicted. In a three-way election, her union would receive 59 percent of the vote, "no union" 26 percent, and the UAW only 4 percent.

McEntee liked the poll results and agreed to a trial run. He gave Rondeau an advance of $2,100, which she parceled out to hard-pressed staff members to pay bills. Rewolinski went to Harvard, observed her staff at work, and concluded that with proper funding, they could win an election. On this basis, McEntee decided to take in the smaller union on Rondeau's terms. On January 29, 1987, he and Rondeau signed an affiliation agreement. AFSCME agreed to finance the organizing drive and provide whatever legal assistance might be needed. As to Rondeau's demand for independence, the agreement stated that "HUCTW shall retain its identity and shall have full autonomy in the conduct of HUCTW business and affairs without intervention or interference by AFSCME."

McEntee immediately made good on financial assistance, beginning monthly payments that would total $300,000 in 1987. Rondeau expanded her staff, eventually hiring about fifteen additional organizers, full- and part-time, mostly Harvard workers who "came out," as the expression went. The organizers received annual salaries of $17,000 and Rondeau $22,000. "They didn't ask for a lot of money," Rewolinski said. "They kind of helped each other. They made great sacrifices, probably greater sacrifices than I've seen in my thirty years in this union. This was dedication and commitment to trade unionism that's hard to find today."

Nor was $300,000 by any means an exorbitant amount to organize an employer with more than 3,500 employees. By contrast, in 1990 AFSCME would pour at least $15 million into an effort to unionize Indiana state employees. It emerged with 8,000 new members and a soiled reputation. This campaign, which involved a vicious, wasteful battle among AFSCME, the Auto Workers, and the American Federation of Teachers, generated an enormous amount of bad publicity for the labor movement. All three unions promoted themselves in costly TV and radio commercials. At Harvard, Rondeau spent nary a penny on broadcast advertising. Her only mailing and printing expenses involved letters sent to faculty, alumni, and community leaders. The Harvard union developed a strong following in the best of all ways, through personal contact with workers.

As cheap as Harvard was, few other national unions would have handed over $300,000 *carte blanche* to a cast-off group of female organizers. Years later Doug Fraser shook his head at the recollection that McEntee did not insist on running the campaign. "Gerry gave them a budget, whatever it was, saying, 'This is your budget.' We [the UAW] just would not hand over to *anyone* the finances of the union." The arrangement was not that unusual for AFSCME, however. The union had a history of granting local control when it acquired long-existing employee associations in state governments. "McEntee did a very brave thing," Rondeau said, "especially with the UAW screaming in his ear about us. He and his staff figured out that we knew a lot about organizing. In the end he convinced me this was what he was buying."

In 1992, McEntee himself explained why he allowed the Harvard union so much freedom. "It seemed to us that one of the reasons the other organizing drive [the UAW's] failed was that the people on site didn't have the independence to make their own decisions. They [HUCTW] had a different organizing model. I and others were convinced that the way to go was to let them do it. We wanted them [HUCTW] to remain an independent entity so the boss would have difficulty painting them as this big union from Washington."

With an expanded staff, the Harvard union could develop one-on-one relationships fairly rapidly with hundreds more employees. The percentage of workers either definitely for, or leaning toward, the union jumped from less than 30 percent at the end of 1986 to nearly 49 percent in December 1987, according to Rondeau's calculations. The union reached its goal of developing 120 top-flight activists, defined as people with the ability to do "cold organizing." An additional 350 activists performed less demanding tasks, such as putting up posters and phoning people.

The UAW, meanwhile, remained at Harvard through most of 1987. Organizers for the two unions occasionally would meet by chance and glower at one another. When UAW organizers held meetings, HUCTW activists counted the number of employees who turned out. They never saw more than twenty or thirty. Rondeau felt the Auto Workers had no chance whatsoever with Harvard workers, but she couldn't afford to dismiss it.

❧ ☙

When two unions go after the same group of workers, organized labor's image usually suffers and the workers often wind up as battle casualties. To prevent this from happening at Harvard, Ernie Rewolinski discussed the situation in early 1987 with the UAW's Stephen Yokich. It was then clear that Rondeau's union had a commanding lead but that if the two unions competed for votes, Harvard most likely would win. "Yokich felt it was better that some union win than no union win," Rewolinski recalled of their meeting. But the UAW was reluctant to abandon the fight after investing so much time and money. The situation had not improved for the UAW by the time of the AFL-CIO convention in mid-October, and Rewolinski and Gerry McEntee met with Yokich and UAW President Owen Bieber to settle the issue. The UAW officials agreed to pull out of Harvard. There was conciliatory talk of the two unions forming coalitions to organize public employees in some states, but within a few years they would be battling one another in Indiana.

At the end of October, the UAW staff at Harvard issued a letter announcing the end of its campaign and endorsing Rondeau's union. Now Rondeau could seek an election with the near certainty that no other union would be on the ballot. On December 1, she and her staff began asking workers to sign authorization cards, a necessary step but a very public one. Employees responded immediately, and so, too, did Harvard management. For the third time in eleven years, Harvard launched an aggressive campaign to prevent its (mainly) female white-collar workers from forming a union. This time the university put a woman in charge. It would be female vs. female, or which version of a female theory of work life will you vote for?

If Harvard management had learned one thing in eleven years, it was that "forming the union was a gender issue," as Rondeau said. "We had made it clear that the highly-paid men who ran the university should not tell us what was in our best interest. They would not be credible." She didn't mean to imply that a female recruited from management ranks would be any more credible. In her view, no matter who made the argument against the union, "it was a bad argument." The university leaders, of course, thought they had a good argument and now, after watching this sassy band of women unionists disappearing and reappearing with disturbing regularity, they decided they could make it disappear for good by having a woman lead their charge.

Ed Powers, the man who did much to defeat the union drives of 1977 and 1981, had resigned in early 1987 to set up a consulting firm. By chance, his leaving coincided with the retirement of Harvard's director of personnel, Daniel Cantor. Efforts to replace these key people, while at the same time reorganizing the management structure, led to a series of missteps which would leave the university rudderless in the field of personnel and labor relations for some years to come. (Six different persons would serve as director of personnel, renamed human resources, in the first nine years after Cantor retired.) In the reorganization, the personnel function was taken out of Dan Steiner's office of general counsel and transferred to an administrative vice president, Robert Scott. He was primarily a financial executive with no experience in the labor field.

These changes occurred within a few months, at a time when the white-collar union drive did not occupy a prominent place in the thoughts of university officials. David Kuechle, a professor in the School of Education, in 1990 prepared a copyrighted case study of the campaign which made this observation: "In early 1987, Harvard was ill-equipped to deal with an organizing drive, a condition caused, in part, by the belief that HUCTW did not represent a serious challenge and that any union drive, even if heavily financed, would almost certainly fail due to the considerable diversity of the proposed bargaining unit and the geographical vastness of the properties where the members worked."

In filling managerial positions, Harvard had a way of moving people from slot to slot with little more than surface logic, as if one-Harvard-administrator fit all. To replace Powers, Scott chose Anne E. Taylor, a lawyer on Dan Steiner's staff in the general counsel's office since 1983. Before that, she had dealt with employment discrimination for government agencies and commissions and had served briefly as a staff attorney with the NLRB. Under Scott, she was to handle labor relations and personnel on an interim basis. When the union affiliated with AFSCME, Taylor also agreed to take on the antiunion responsibility. This made a Harvard kind of sense. She *was* an energetic lawyer, and she *was* a woman, and Harvard wanted to defeat a union organizing women. Her first project, in early 1987, was a series of meetings in which she explained labor law to supervisors.

Powers, still working for Harvard on retainer, observed Taylor's activities at close range. She was an "excellent lawyer," he said, but out of place as head of an antiunion campaign. "I remember Bob [Scott] saying to me how wonderful it was to have a woman doing it this time. But the bottom line was that she had never practiced labor relations. When she met with supervisors, it was to tell them about the law, rather than about how could we keep the union out. That was a fatal mistake."

Taylor was given the mission of defeating the union without tearing apart the university community. This meant paying scrupulous attention to legality while using polite but firm language—appropriate to the academic concern for freedom of expression—in what the union regarded as intimidating settings. When organizers began passing out cards at the end of 1987, Taylor initiated a two-pronged attack on the union. She prepared and distributed a 104-page manual for supervisors called the *Briefing Book*, as well as a series of booklets on various money and benefit issues. But the literature was only academic-looking window-dressing for the main portion of the campaign which consisted of meetings with small groups of workers and supervisors at the departmental level. In the last few months before the election, Taylor and four other women administrators conducted hundreds of these meetings throughout the university.

The meetings, in particular, would test Rondeau's theory of how to beat an antiunion campaign. The 1981 experience had taught her that small group meetings led by managers and supervisors can have a powerful effect on individual workers. To soften this impact, she started an anti-antiunion campaign in the fall of 1987 with a day-long meeting of about 120 activists. Organizers told them how to anticipate each argument and communications technique that Harvard would employ. The centerpiece of the sessions was a simulated "captive audience meeting" (the union still used this term, though it overstated the "captive" aspect: in 1988 some workers did not attend and were not disciplined.) A tall, lawyerly appearing man strode into the room and took over the meeting. For a half-hour, he lectured the audience on the well-known negative sides of "Big Labor"—corruption, lack of democracy, bureaucratic rule-making, exorbitant dues, strike-prone behavior, and so forth. He told them why they should vote against the union. By turns he was ingratiating, condescending, friendly, authoritative, sarcastic, and just plain mean. Most of the audience had never seen him before, but they could picture him as a management lawyer. Actually it was Jim Braude, acting out a play script written by his wife. Other unions had used the mock-meeting technique, but only rarely and probably not as extensively as the Harvard union. It required time, imagination, and no little amount of courage to criticize unionism as ruthlessly as management would. The union staff recorded Braude's performance on videotape and replayed it many times before other groups of workers.

Rondeau had always believed that Harvard defeated the union in 1981 partly because it waged its antiunion campaign in isolation. There had been little press coverage and little interest expressed in the wider community. She was determined to change this in 1988. Union organizers handed out "Dear Friend" letters door to door and in supermarket parking lots in Cambridge. It sent open letters to prominent civic leaders, Harvard alumni, faculty members, students, and supervisors. The letters were models of decorum, void of hostility to Harvard and full of praise for its leadership in education and research. The university could be even better, the union contended, if the workers were allowed a collective voice.

When it came time to ask the NLRB for an election, Rondeau made certain the event would not go unnoticed. On March 14, 1988, during noon break, she took two busloads of Harvard workers to the Tip O'Neill Building in downtown Boston. They sang and waved placards and balloons and followed Rondeau to the sixth floor, riding elevators in shifts. She filed an election petition along with signed authorization cards representing about 60 percent of eligible workers at the office of Regional Director Robert Fuchs (who in the past had issued critical decisions against the union). When he appeared in the hallway, the crowd cheered. It was a day of celebration, not a day of protest. Not wanting to make too much noise, the workers hummed "Solidarity Forever," linking arms and swaying to the rhythm—*humming* with such religious passion that they could have passed for a choir humming "The Battle Hymn of the Republic." The Harvard union women had a facility for organizing demonstrations so silly as to be almost self-parodying but also hilarious and also somehow moving. Their members appeared to love it. But any self-respecting male union leader would have been embarrassed.

Beneath the gaiety, however, Rondeau was worried. Although her organizers had urged workers to sign cards only if they intended to vote for the union, she knew that the 60 percent showing overstated actual union strength. Her rating system, a more accurate barometer, told her that only about half of the eligible employees really would vote "yes" at the time of filing. She had rushed the decision for several reasons. AFSCME leaders, eager for internal political reasons to obtain a quick victory at Harvard, were applying pressure. Moreover, it was important to have an election before the annual summer turnover of employees began. To obtain an election by the end of May, she had to file the petition in March. She also realized that personal pride may have played a role. She wanted to demonstrate to skeptics in AFSCME, the Auto Workers, and the rest of the labor movement how brilliantly she and her organizers could perform.

Rondeau was annoyed with herself. To go to election with "about half" of the workers committed was engaging in a "crapshoot," as she later called it. Crapshooters figure they have as much chance of winning as losing, and since it is a game of risk to begin with, "What the hell, throw the dice." But when a union organizer walks away from a losing crapshoot, she leaves behind hundreds or thousands of profoundly demoralized workers. "I don't think I did the right thing," she said in 1996, looking back. "Winning a union election is so hard these days that there should be a moratorium on rolling the dice. We shouldn't do that to workers anymore. If you're at forty-eight percent, the election shouldn't be tomorrow. It should be two years from now when you're at fifty-eight percent."

Expecting Harvard to engage in stalling tactics, AFSCME lawyers (with Rondeau's approval) took a step that could have turned into a costly error. They served subpoenas on Harvard deans and administrators, demanding disclosure of personnel data on each worker. Anne Taylor disclosed the move in a letter to employees, and the publicity threatened to turn ugly. The union withdrew the subpoenas. "We made a mistake," Rondeau conceded. "It was a legal decision, not an organizational decision, and we really didn't need this stuff." In mid-March, Harvard reluctantly agreed to an election date of May 17.

With two months until the election, Taylor intensified her campaign of small group meetings. Rondeau had taught workers that the most damaging thing about an antiunion meeting was the "tension level," not the information imparted by management. The psychological power of the meeting derives from the exercise of managerial authority in a closed setting. Most workers did not want to be there in the first place, and if conflict occurred, they blamed it on the union. Rondeau urged that activists not allow themselves to be provoked into heated arguments.

Many activists had experiences like Donene Williams, who attended five or six "captive audience" meetings. Later she would become a union officer, but in 1988 she was a twenty-five year-old staff assistant in the Law School with less than a year on the job. "I was still scared, even though I'd seen Jim Braude perform in the mock meeting," Williams recalled in 1993. She and her activist friends wore their "We Can't Eat Prestige" buttons to the meetings, not without some concern. "At one meeting," she said, "a personnel officer was handing out name tags. When I got to the door, wearing my button, she said, 'Oh, hello, Donene,' showing that she knew who I was. They were trying to intimidate us."

The content of the meetings was standard union-busting fare. The administration no longer had District 65 to kick around, but it pictured AFSCME as a huge, strike-prone union that would collect $200 a year in dues from each worker. The parent union knew nothing about bargaining in the private sector and where it did represent university workers, at state-related schools, it insisted on seniority-based rules for transfers, promotions, and job bidding that would reward mediocre workers at the expense of the more qualified. Quoting selective excerpts from union contracts and emphasizing polarization, Taylor and her aides painted an image of unionism that would turn aside employees inclined to believe that they could bargain for themselves without all this conflict. The administrators also used the old debating trick of citing facts and making generalizations that no one in the audience would have enough knowledge to contradict.

Williams recalled a meeting presided over by Anne Taylor. "She said things I couldn't respond to, like ninety-seven percent of union contracts had a seniority clause. How would I know? Suddenly, I would have these feelings, 'Maybe I don't know what I'm getting into.'" In addition to the group meetings, supervisors were required to have one-on-one talks with each of their employees, using a sample conversation from Taylor's *Briefing Book*. "My supervisor, Margaret, was a sweet person," Williams said, "and when she started to read from the book, she began to cry. I said, 'Margaret, it's okay. Just *tell* them you had the conversation with me.' I liked Margaret. She ended up leaving the university."

All in all, Rondeau later said, the small group meetings of 1988 lacked the impact of those organized by Ed Powers in 1981. This was partly because the union had "inoculated" several hundred worker-activists against the technique and partly because Anne Taylor was no Ed Powers. "She didn't embarrass the university," Rondeau said later. Even so, many hundreds of employees were vulnerable. They ranged from "undecideds" and confused to fence-sitters and strongly antiunion. Some of the latter joined a group, the Support Staff Action Committee, which handed out "Vote No" buttons. These were especially visible in administrative offices at Holyoke Center. Seventy employees signed an antiunion letter published in the *Crimson*.

By the end of April, a curious thing was happening. Although the university could easily make the standard arguments against unionism, it was stumped on how to focus an attack on the Harvard union. Taylor couldn't engage her adversaries on a specific issue like salaries or benefits because the union women didn't list priorities or promise anything. When a reporter asked Taylor what issues were involved in the election, she replied, "They're trying to position us as bad guys. Except for that they've got no issues. The rest of it is just feel-good stuff."

This was a profound misreading of the union campaign.

As the election date approached, everybody knew that it would be a critical union vote. The Harvard union seemed to be saying something important about working women, and many observers speculated on what this might be. But practically everyone who watched the campaign unfold—reporters, union officials, labor academics, and most especially Harvard managers—got it wrong. In retrospect, it is evident that HUCTW told the world what kind of union it would be, but few listened.

In December 1987, the union put out an open letter to the Harvard community, listing five guiding principles. The first asserted that workers needed a collective voice. The fourth and fifth principles received most attention because they mentioned specific remedies for sex and age discrimination: pay equity for women, child care and parental leave programs, job flexibility, and a career advancement plan. Principles two and three, however, went to the heart of the union's beliefs and philosophy of unionism. They read as follows:

> Second, we believe in self representation. We are building our union for this reason, and not out of anger or negativity. Responsible, self-respecting adults should represent themselves in important matters affecting their lives. We have until now allowed Harvard to decide everything to do with our work lives. Now we are ready to participate as equals in making those decisions. Third, we believe in the mission of the university. We value our role in its educational and research work . . . But too often our knowledge and expertise are overlooked, rather than [being] treated as resources for overcoming some of Harvard's managerial problems.

Self-representation and participation. These are powerful ideas but so alien to the American concept of unionism that most onlookers—particularly the Harvard officials charged with knowing something about unions—dismissed them out of hand.

The Harvard union had borrowed organizing techniques from other unions, including the Hotel Employees at Yale and even District 65 and the UAW. But Rondeau and her staff developed their own, highly individualized message in a fusing of insights about women in the workplace and Harvard in particular. Out of this evolved a novel emphasis on the concept of *worker participation*. For many decades, the phrase "participate in decisions that affect our members" had been a staple of trade-union rhetoric referring to participation at the bargaining table through representatives. Marie Manna recalled that in 1980–81 the union talked of "participating in decisions that affect work life." By 1988 the union had embraced a broader concept of participation. "It evolved into an idea that you could participate in decisions that weren't thought of traditionally as under the union's banner," Manna said. In addition to negotiating with management over wages, benefits, and general conditions, individual workers should have some ability—never defined in the election campaign—to have a voice in work organization, for example, in their offices and labs. Organizers also talked of "self-representation." Workers with personnel complaints would be encouraged to represent themselves, with union support, in any grievance procedure developed in contract negotiations.

These ideas came from several sources only partly definable. On self-representation, union leaders like Rondeau recognized there had always existed a strong individualistic strain in the Harvard work force, a tendency in particular of educated women to prefer negotiating their own deals with supervisors instead of relying on a union representative. This concept also meshed with the women leaders' concept of unionism. Since the union, as labor leaders from time immemorial had insisted, *was* the members, then logic said that the purpose of the union was to provide collective force to enable its members to act for themselves. If breaking away from centuries of male supremacy and patriarchy meant that women workers did not need male union representatives to handle their problems, then they didn't need female representatives either.

Many strands of social attitudes, beliefs about women workers, and national trends came together in the union's blossoming notions of worker participation, hereafter referred to merely as "participation." From her first days as a lab assistant, Rondeau had felt frustrated by irrelevant work rules and boundaries set by management, as well as by pennywise but dollar-foolish administration decisions. Later, as a union representative, she saw that many co-workers felt the same and tried to speak out only to be ignored by bosses who thought they knew best. She remembered in particular Richard Pendleton, the veteran library worker in the Medical School, who always told stories about the costly errors of administrators who would not listen to workers. The high price of administrative misjudgments rarely came to light because Harvard was not operating on a thin profit margin in competitive trade. Harvard was a huge, wealthy nonprofit institution that monitored the return on its $4 billion endowment with sharp eyes but overlooked the cost of managerial debacles at the department level.

Workers like Pendleton wanted a union that would, among other things, give them the power to help Harvard avoid such missteps. "I have concern for the running of the library," Pendleton said in 1994. "I believe that information should be accessible to people and we should take care of the place and make sure that books and journals and services like copy machines are available when they're needed. Sometimes the administrators made dumb decisions that would cause services to deteriorate. I'd try to point out, 'It's been tried before, didn't work then and won't work now.' But they'd go ahead and do it and it would blow up in their face. They just didn't learn, and they wouldn't listen to us."

Pendleton and others like him wanted to make the institution even better than it was. The union tapped this vein of feeling. It promoted the idea of union not to bring Harvard to its knees but to its senses. It would force the university, for its own good, to listen to workers' ideas. Furthermore, the union knew that workers liked many aspects of their jobs and wanted no part of a union campaign that painted Harvard as an "evil empire," as Manna put it. This is why using the union slogan, "It's Not Anti-Harvard to Be Prounion," was a brilliant stroke.

These ideas on worker voice also were influenced by a national trend in industrial relations. The "discovery" had been spreading since the 1970s that rank-and-file workers held a reservoir of job knowledge that could be used to improve product quality and productivity. The process of tapping this knowledge, allowing workers to use their ingenuity to improve work methods, first occurred in the United States in the 1920s, or earlier, as a short-lived trend toward "industrial democracy." Sweden later refined the ideas, but it was Japanese automakers who popularized their version of the concept starting in the 1970s. Motivated largely by Japan's success, American manufacturers began experimenting with methods of extracting this knowledge and putting it to work. They set up a variety of shop-floor discussion groups, often called "quality circles," to obtain workers' suggestions. All too frequently, management manipulated this process and exploited the employees—to such an extent that terms like "employee involvement," "worker participation," "teamwork," and even "workplace democracy" became tainted in the eyes of militant unionists. But some unions, including the Auto Workers, Steelworkers, and Communications Workers, succeeded in putting their own stamp on the process with controls that prevented management from using workers' ideas to eliminate their jobs or reduce their pay.

This trend was, and still is, highly controversial in organized labor. But by the late eighties, polls showed that a majority of workers wanted more involvement in workplace decisions, not less. Harvard union leaders may have been isolated from the mainstream labor movement, but they were very much aware of this trend. It was in the air. It had not yet found widespread use in white-collar jobs in industries like banking, financial services, and universities. But the notion was not foreign to women office workers. Back in the early seventies, 9to5 founders like Karen Nussbaum and Ellen Cassedy found that women wanted the ability to change the flow and organization of work, to make their jobs more satisfying and more efficient. But it was precisely in this area that employers threw up the highest barriers to change. One fear was that once workers got a foot in this door, they could move into the room where higher level decisions were made—decisions on product quality, deployment of workers, product pricing, location of plants and offices, capital expenditures, investment policy.

(The Harvard union may have been the first to use participation as the major theme in an organizing campaign. Rarely, if ever, did unions adopt the strategy when organizing mostly male workers. In the late 1980s and early 1990s, however, more and more women organizers saw the value of stressing governance issues in female-dominated workplaces. This trend is driven by women's conception of power, speculates Marion Crain, a professor at the University of North Carolina School of Law, who links feminist theory with labor practices in her writings. Women typically do not conceive of power as a patriarchal domination over others, she says in a 1992 article. Women instead focus on "ability, competence, and capacity to influence others." The desire to "empower" union members by gaining a voice in decision making appeals to many women workers. In a later survey of organizers in 44 unions, Crain found that where target work forces are disproportionately female (especially in health care), female organizers ranked "participation in decision making" highest in terms of its importance as an issue in organizing campaigns.)

Rondeau recognized instinctively that Harvard would resist the idea of participation because it would mean giving up power at some level. Yet she had learned from experience with antiunion campaigns that the employer can defeat a unionization attempt emphasizing wages, or health insurance, or any one of many other economic benefits. "The employer can beat you on any issue except power and the right to participate as an equal," she said in a 1992 interview. The employer can grant a salary increase or improve a pension plan or add benefit coverage to a health insurance program. "Power is the one thing they can never turn to the workers and say, 'Okay, I give you power.' Power is not something you can give to somebody else. Power is something you have to take and use wisely."

The union, however, did not frame the issue in terms of power. Nor did it propose a specific mechanism that might give workers a voice in decision making. "You have to introduce the word 'power' slowly in a campaign," Rondeau said, "because people are wary of the term. Right away, when they think of 'power,' they think of corruption. We were always careful to say, 'This is something that can't be described verbally. It's like when a woman tries to describe what childbirth is like. It's indescribable. What we can promise is that you'll recognize power when you have it.'" She thought that the notion of participation had a psychological power for women. "It had been so ingrained in them that workers must be quiet and obedient that the idea of having ideas and using them at work was a liberation. Women of my generation, the first generation of women to be in the work force in large numbers, really want to have something important to do, to have work that is productive and meaningful. I'm sure this is true of younger women, too. I know a man who says, 'I reserve the right to hate my work.' That's okay, but I don't think women are like that."

Rondeau was aware that some unionists rejected any kind of labor–management cooperation on grounds that the employer could not be trusted. To avoid being manipulated, the argument went, a worker should work to rule and let management worry about efficiency and the quality of the product or service. She thought this was unnatural. "The way people treat each other, the product they put out, the reputation of the place—all of this matters a huge amount to most women. People want to be part of healthy organizations and if they're not healthy, to make them healthy. That's what we meant by participation."

These comments, made some years after the 1988 election, characterize the *essence* of what the union was saying to workers rather than what it literally said. Since the union put out no pamphlets or leaflets, the literary framing of the concept is best found in the letter of December 1987. Organizers from that period do not recall workers raising the question, "How?" How would the union ensure worker participation beyond the traditional representation at the bargaining table? If they had asked such questions, Rondeau and her people could not have answered them. "We had no idea what we wanted to do," Rondeau said. "We only knew that we didn't want to be rule-bound. This need was deep inside us."

Harvard couldn't respond to this theme, not even understanding what it was. The university had poured out a torrent of facts, comparative statistics, and negative assessments of unionism in general. What did it receive in return but vague words like "dignity, respect, and participation?" The administration's frustration is indicated by the aggrieved tone in a May 10, 1988 letter written by Taylor in response to Rondeau's challenge to a debate. There was nothing to debate, Taylor said, adding, "There has been no clear statement of union objectives or priorities, much rhetoric and very few facts, and little reliable information for voters to evaluate."

If Harvard management had not decoded the union's message, the student editors of the *Crimson* came close. "Worker empowerment is the central theme of the [HUCTW] campaign," the paper said in an April 18 editorial. In seeking "a role in policymaking," the editorial said, the union had "gone beyond the issues of the day by representing a theme that will serve workers in the future." The paper urged workers to vote for the union on May 17.

⋙ ⋘

May arrived with its springtime scents and colors. Tulip trees, elms, and honey locusts blossomed in Harvard Yard. Boatmen and boatwomen swarmed on the Charles at first light, oars rising and dipping before dawn. As usual, classes were called off for a one-week reading period to allow students time to prepare for exams that would start in mid-May. Many crammed an entire semester's worth of academic work into that one week, while others read by day and played by night. The social swirl thickened in Harvard Square. People dozed in the sun at sidewalk coffeehouses. Business boomed at boutiques and bistros, and street musicians came out on mild May evenings.

Everyone connected with Harvard had reason to take pride in the state of the university in the spring of 1988. In a report on academic accreditation released in March, a team of scholars from other New England schools described Harvard as "a great university effectively meeting its obligations to foster the advancement of knowledge, to develop young scholars, and to educate undergraduates." Barely able to contain its enthusiasm, the team declared, "the students [are] superb, the faculty distinguished, and the resources of the institution enviable."

Chief among the resources was money. An annual financial report had portrayed Harvard's fiscal status as "excellent," with an operating budget "solidly in the black," an endowment of $4 billion, and record giving by alumni. Reflecting this fiscal and academic well-being, other records were being set: a record number of applicants, 14,430, applying for admission in the 1988–89 academic year; of this number Harvard accepted only 1,605, but a record 43 percent of the total were women, 14 percent were Asian-American, and 9 percent Afro-American. Under a "need-blind" admissions policy, two-thirds of the new class would receive some form of financial aid, averaging $12,450 over four years. Meanwhile, Harvard regretfully raised tuition by 5.7 percent. Counting the cost of room and board, a student would need $17,805 to attend Harvard for one academic year—only about $2,000 less than the average annual salary paid to Harvard's clerical and technical employees.

In his annual President's Report to the Board of Overseers, Derek Bok included a lengthy essay on the need for ethical studies in the Harvard curriculum. He made a particularly telling point about the administration's ethical obligations. "Universities," he writes, "periodically encounter moral problems in the course of investing their stock, interacting with the surrounding community, implementing affirmative action, and carrying out other tasks. The way in which they address these issues will not be lost upon their students. Nothing is so likely to produce cynicism . . . as a realization that the very institution that offers such classes shows little concern for living up to its own moral obligations."

A group of about three thousand students, calling Bok to account, issued a call for neutrality in the election campaign. In early May, twenty-seven faculty members followed suit, signing a statement urging university management to "remain scrupulously neutral." The statement did not endorse the union and affirmed the right of the administration to express its views. But it went on to say that "an antiunion campaign conducted with all the means available to a great corporation is nothing to be proud about."

The faculty signers included such well known professors as Derrick Bell, Alan Dershowitz, Susan Estrich, Richard Freeman, Carol Gilligan,

Nathan Glazer, Stephen Jay Gould, David Maybury-Lewis, and Laurence Tribe. But the list of names was just as significant for those who chose not to sign. Numbered among these were faculty members noted for writings on labor law, labor history and economics, and industrial relations.

Bok himself, so long in the background, now became a central figure in the unionization fight. Reporters from all over the country began appearing on campus. Almost invariably, they stressed the ironies evident in the effort of Bok, who had asserted the right of workers to form a union, to beat this particular union. Bok did not waver. In a four-page letter to all employees, he declared, "I have always believed that it is a good thing for America and for working people that employees have the opportunity to vote for a union if they decide that their wages and working conditions will improve as a result."

"However," he added, "I am not at all persuaded in this case that union representation and collective bargaining will improve the working environment at Harvard or help us to sustain the highest quality of education and research." He doubted that a union contract would allow the "individual initiative and flexibility" that is needed in the "academic enterprise."

By the night of May 16, Rondeau had become even more certain that she had prematurely asked for an election. The union's defensive measures had stood up to the test of the antiunion campaign, but prounion workers still constituted only a little more than half of the Harvard work force. The arguments and pressures brought to bear on the "undecideds" in small group meetings definitely had had an effect.

At 10 o'clock that night, Rondeau was sitting in her tiny office, watching her staff making last minute preparations. Many had been on the phone constantly for hours, calling workers thought to be prounion and reminding them to vote. If the organizers discovered that a previous "yes" vote seemed to be weakening, they would cross the name off the master list of prounion voters. It was now down to a little more than 1,700 names of 3,400 eligible voters and dwindling by the hour. She knew the vote would be very, very close, verging on defeat.

Someone told her that Jesse Jackson was on the phone. "I said, 'Oh, sure!', thinking they were playing jokes. But I picked up the phone and there he was, calling to wish us good luck."

Jackson had appeared at a union rally and signed newspaper ads endorsing the union. That spring he was campaigning for the Democratic Presidential nomination, and Rondeau hadn't expected him to remember the date of her union vote. On the contrary, he told her on the phone, he had good reason to remember May 17. He read a telegram which would be sent to the union. It pointed out that the U.S. Supreme Court had issued its *Brown v. Board of Education* decision on May 17, 1954. The last line of the telegram said, "Keep hope alive." The call made her feel better, and she went home to try to rest.

The day of the vote started out with a sense of gaiety suggested by a campus adorned with balloons ("coercive" balloons, Harvard later would charge). By the time the polls closed in late afternoon, Rondeau was reasonably sure the union had lost. She asked her staff not to cry in public when the vote tally was announced. In early evening, she and Manna and their husbands walked to Memorial Hall, just north of the Yard, where the ballots would be counted. She thought of the eleven years during which the fight to organize Harvard had consumed her, and she prepared herself for the likelihood of yet another defeat. She said later, "I thought we had lost and that maybe Harvard was unwinnable after all."

Leslie Sullivan, founder of the Harvard union and an organizer for District 65, pickets a Cambridge store in May, 1980. Credit: Photographer unknown

Kris Rondeau in her Harvard Medical School laboratory, c.1978. Credit: Photographer unknown

David Livingston, president of District 65 (center) and Douglas Fraser, UAW president, appear, at a union meeting in Harvard Medical Area, March 31, 1981, during the second campaign to organize Harvard. Credit: Photographer unknown

Harvard-UAW Organizing Committee, c. 1983. Key organizers and activists include: (bottom row) Bob Metcalf, far left; Marie Manna, second from right; (middle row) Martha Robb, second from left; Anthony Sutton, third from left; Kris Rondeau, second from right; (top row) Richard Pendleton, far right. Credit: Photographer unknown

HUCTW organizers and activists in fall, 1985, when the union was an independent. Rondeau is at top right, with Martha Robb to her right and Marie Manna in front of both. Bill Jaeger is at left and Kerry Dolan in rear. Others are worker-activists and students. Credit: Marilyn Humphries

Rondeau and Gerald McEntee, president of AFSCME, signing affiliation agreement on Jan. 29, 1987. Standing at right rear is Ernest Rewolinski, McEntee's chief of staff. Credit: Rick Stafford

Prounion workers attend a rally in Old Cambridge Baptist Church, February, 1988, during the third campaign to unionize Harvard. Credit: Marilyn Humphries

*M*emorial Hall, "the great bristling brick Valhalla," as Henry James called it, was built in the 1870s to commemorate Harvard graduates killed in the Civil War (but only those who fought on the Union side). The east end of the building contains Sanders Theater with an auditorium that can seat more than 500 people. On the night of May 17, 1988, at least that many gathered there for the vote count. The audience consisted mainly of Harvard workers but also included officials of other local unions, Ernie Rewolinski and Joe Bonavita of AFSCME who sat in a stage right balcony, and Anne Taylor with other administrators sitting in a stage left balcony. Rondeau and Manna sat with their husbands in the front row.

The tallying of votes would take place on stage at a long table on which board agents placed cardboard boxes containing ballots. In the momentary silence before the count began, the near perfect acoustics of Sanders Theater came into play. Down in the audience, people who had been waiting for two hours stopped chattering and gripped each other's hands, forming row-long chains. Some said you could hear small bones snapping. And then, BOOM! BOOM! BOOM! board agents were popping open the sealed boxes with karate chops. They began removing the ballots and placing them into "yes" and "no" piles for each of nine polling places. Management and union observers stood at each location.

All over the theater people watched the growing piles of ballots, trying to judge the outcome. The count took a long time. Toward the end, union observers at two of the counting locations looked down at Rondeau and shook their heads. She tried to ignore their meaning. But Braude sighed and groaned. "It was the single worst feeling I'd ever had," he recalled.

At last it was finished. The chief board agent cleared the stage except for two Harvard lawyers and the union lawyer, Craig Becker, who gestured to Rondeau to join him. The group stood at a grand piano with their backs to the audience, doing the final arithmetic with calculators and legal pads. The audience fell silent. Suddenly, the group broke up, and Rondeau walked down stage. She leaned over, hugged Manna standing in the pit, whispered in her ear, and went back to the piano. Manna began crying and sat with her head down. This confused everybody, not least Braude. He leaned across Rondeau's empty seat and asked her what his wife had said. Manna shook her head. Irritated, Braude said in a loud whisper, "Marie, tell me!"

Manna said nothing, sobbing quietly. "I thought Jim would kill me, but if I told him, everyone would know before they announced it," she said. "You're supposed to go by the rules."

Many others who saw Manna crying, assumed the worst, or the best. Donene Williams remembered thinking, "Kris wants Marie to be the first to hear we'd lost. No, she wants Marie to be the first to hear we'd won. I didn't know what to think."

The audience realized that somebody had won and somebody had lost, but only the people on stage and sobbing Marie knew the result. There seemed to be some confusion about who would make the announcement. Enter stage right an unknown man who turned out to be an official of the U.S. Department of Labor. He walked up to Rondeau and shook her hand. She half-turned to the audience and smiled.

Pandemonium ensued. People were jumping and screaming and hugging. Bill Jaeger, a sports fan, had heard many a loud cheer, but this was different because people were simultaneously crying and screaming. "It was a primal noise of excitement, of joy," he said. Williams recalled: "You'd hug the person next to you and then you'd have to hug somebody else. You had to have a 'moment of realization' with every person you had worked with." Organizer Stephanie Tournas looked at the balcony where Anne Taylor and the management people appeared devastated. "It was satisfying to see them watching us celebrate," Tournas said. "But it was a joyful feeling, not a 'now we've got you' feeling."

It was several minutes before the lead board agent could announce the results. The petitioner (union) had received 1,530 votes and the university, 1,486, a 44-vote difference. There was no need to resolve 41 challenged ballots. Even if HUCTW had lost them all, which was unlikely, it would still win by three votes.

Rondeau was asked to speak. She remembered looking up at Rewolinski and Bonavita. "They were sitting there like two old guys in the Muppets, Statler and Waldorf, and I could see how happy they were," she said. "I remembered they had given me so much room to do it our way." Then she gave her brief speech, the one she had prepared for both contingencies. "We didn't do this to win or lose," she said. "We did it because it was the right thing to do, the way we wanted to live our lives." As her final point, she stressed that the union held no bitterness toward workers who had voted against the union. "We need to make room in our organization for people who voted 'no.'"

Why, after all the years of organizing, did HUCTW win "only" 50.7 percent of the vote? This could be explained partly by Harvard's high turnover rate; nearly 800 workers leave and are replaced each year. But Rondeau thought it had more to do with the antiunion campaign, as low-key as it was in comparison with union-busting efforts that many employers use. Although 89 percent of eligible voters cast ballots, she had expected even more to vote. About 200 supposedly prounion votes did not materialize, and she thought most of these workers did not vote.

"After an antiunion campaign," she said, "a lot of 'yes' votes stay home. And an antiunion campaign can make a lot of prounion people vote 'no.' It may be a soft 'no,' but it's a 'no.' They think, 'I know what we have now. I don't know what we will have when the union gets in.'"

In 1992, when animosities had abated, Anne Taylor offered her analysis of the union victory. "Kris and her folks knew us better than we did. We didn't know our employees in this huge, decentralized place. They organized employees that we didn't know existed." When Rondeau's group split from the UAW, Taylor said, "we thought we wouldn't hear from the unions for years. By the time we were aware something was going on, they were unbeatable. If they had stayed with the UAW, they would have put out a flyer, and we would have put out a flyer, and we would have beaten them. Kris understood intuitively what the people were hungering for and nurtured it. The approach was conflict-averse, a much more typical way for women. They want to be in relationships rather than putting up their dukes."

On the day after the election, however, Taylor wanted to put up *her* dukes. She had been incensed about the balloons and posters that appeared all over campus, and employees now began calling her office with complaints about this "intimidating" atmosphere. Within days the administration formally asked the NLRB to overturn the election. The fight would continue.

~~§ ~~

As she took her seat in the witness box, Rondeau was not unlike an actress grown weary of performing in a long-running play. With not too much exaggeration, she could imagine her professional life since 1980 as participating in a series of back-to-back NLRB proceedings of various kinds. She had prepared data and conferred with lawyers for several sets of hearings, and she had sat through hour upon hour of legal sparring over matters such as "unit scope." But this appearance, on August 16, 1988, was her first as an "adverse witness," called by Harvard University in its attempt to invalidate the 1988 election.

The university had filed "objections" to the vote, charging that HUCTW conduct violated NLRB rules for holding fair elections. There were balloons and posters festooning the "line of march" to the polling places; organizers checking off voters on lists; vans dashing around campus to carry union sympathizers to the polls. All of this activity, Harvard contended, added up to coercion and interference in the right of employees to a free choice. An NLRB administrative law judge, Joel S. Harmatz, had convened hearings on August 15 as a means of investigating the charges.

The lawyer representing Harvard, Nelson Ross of Ropes, Gray, had started off his case in an unusual way. Instead of presenting his own witnesses to describe instances of misconduct that they saw, he subpoenaed several union organizers as "adverse witnesses." He questioned them in some detail about their actions on election day, obviously groping for bits of evidence that he might use to buttress his own case. The more they talked, the more likely it was they might unintentionally state a half-truth that the lawyer later could seize upon. Harmatz, an experienced judge in NLRB cases, warned Ross not to use this "adversary device" as a substitute for presenting first-hand testimony by his own witnesses.

By the time Ross called Rondeau to the stand, the judge several times had admonished the Harvard lawyer for questioning the union reps on matters of which they had no first-hand knowledge. Nonetheless, Ross tried to get Rondeau to blurt out damaging things about the union's Get Out the Vote campaign. The tone of the proceeding is indicated in the following excerpt from the transcript. Ross has asked her if she is aware of complaints made "about union signs and balloons right outside the polling places."

A: The only thing that I'm aware of is—and only just a little bit—is something to do with John Strickland at the Business School [reference to an administrator who complained about balloons in his area] and nothing else.

Q: Are you aware that there were signs right outside the polling place at the Business School?

A: Right outside the polling place . . .

Q: Yes.

A: . . . or outside the building?

Q: Right outside the polling place?

A: No.

Q: You're not? Are you aware of complaints that were made to the . . .

Judge Harmatz (to Ross): What is her idea of outside the polling place may be different from what your idea is. . . . Put it in through your primary witnesses, please. Stop delaying this proceeding. If you want to examine the witness as to matters that are beyond the knowledge of your primary witnesses, proceed. But after warning you over and over again, I can't do anything but assume that you're trying to delay this proceeding.

It went this way with each of several union organizers. When Ross finally introduced what the judge called his "primary" sources—antiunion workers and administrators who actually saw conduct that they thought was illegal—his problem became evident. The university had little first-hand evidence for its allegations. This was at odds with statements made by university officials immediately after the election in what amounted, perhaps inadvertently, to a smear campaign. Officials talked publicly of receiving many calls complaining about union behavior and even sent a questionnaire to all employees, soliciting more examples of wrongdoing. On May 24, when Harvard asked the NLRB to investigate, Vice-President Robert Scott said the administration had received 150 complaints, charging that the union "in a variety of improper ways pressured staff members known to be opposed to the union not to vote."

Taken aback, HUCTW conducted its own investigation to prepare for the NLRB hearings. With so many activists involved on election day, Rondeau acknowledged, "We might have done something that would taint the process. But we couldn't find anything. The only thing we did on election day was be as happy as we could [by floating balloons, etc.], and Harvard seemed to be offended by this."

The 150 complainants of May dwindled to a couple dozen who actually appeared as Harvard witnesses in August. As each began testifying, Rondeau was apprehensive, wondering if Harvard, after all, would come up with evidence of a gross illegality unknown to the union. "I kept thinking that each one would say, 'They did this to me, or that to me.' But within a few minutes, I would feel a flood of relief. All they said was, 'I saw balloons, I saw posters, they asked me if I had voted.' After five or six of these experiences, I realized they had brought us there on a wild goose chase."

Judge Harmatz later counted the number of Harvard witnesses who gave credible testimony on various issues. His arithmetic reduced many of the allegations to practically nothing. One of Harvard's strongest objections involved list-keeping by union organizers. In a 1951 case, the NLRB had declared a ban on keeping and checking off lists of voters by anyone except NLRB agents. Knowing that company or union officials were recording the names of those who voted might "coercively affect the employee's decision to vote." The board applied the ban in several other cases. Citing these precedents, Harvard argued that the ban covered all list-keeping regardless of reason and method.

But HUCTW's attorney, Craig Becker, referring to more recent cases, contended that the original ban was ambiguous and narrow and covered only instances in which list-keepers were stationed at the polls and openly checking off names of *all* who voted. In contrast, Harvard union organizers and employee activists carried lists only of prounion workers. When they checked off names, they were not in the polling places and observing the actual balloting. Rather, they called workers on the phone or went to their offices and asked them if they had voted.

Harvard declared in its closing brief that union reps were "stationed outside polling places openly manifesting lists." But Harmatz later noted that this statement was based on testimony by only one witness, who was not even sure *what* she saw. Moreover, a common element in the early NLRB list-keeping cases was that most workers *knew* that lists were being kept. This was not true at Harvard. Twenty staff organizers and 240 employee-activists (considered "agents" of the union) knew of the lists. But the university presented as witnesses only twelve other workers who became aware of, or suspected, that a count was being recorded, in most cases after they themselves had voted. These twelve, Harmatz said, constituted less than 0.4 percent of 3,400 eligible voters. If voters don't know lists are being kept, they can hardly be described as coerced.

Another misleading assertion involved union phone calls to employees on election day. Union reps conveyed the "impression of surveillance," Ross asserted in his closing brief, by indicating that they knew the workers had not voted. But when Harmatz reviewed the testimony of thirteen university witnesses on this issue, he found that in every instance the union rep had asked if the worker had voted. "There is not a scintilla of evidence to support the employer's factual statement that the union knew they had not voted," Harmatz wrote.

What had happened to all of the people from whom Harvard claimed to have received complaints? The most likely explanation is that many of the complaints came under Harvard's charge of atmospheric intimidation. "Employees encountered a blizzard of campaign propaganda on the 'line of march' to the polls," wrote Nelson Ross in his closing brief. The sight of union decorations very likely irritated employees who abhorred the thought of a union at Harvard. The question was whether the balloons and posters interfered with workers' right of free choice. None of the university's eight witnesses on this issue testified that they saw union propaganda within a "no electioneering" area. On this issue, too, the testimony did not support Harvard's charges.

As the hearings neared an end, Craig Becker was reasonably confident in the union's position. He knew that Harmatz was an experienced judge who had seen real coercion by unions and employers in other cases. "The judge was telling Harvard, 'If workers were coerced, why don't you call them as witnesses?'" Becker said. Almost no credible testimony of this kind was given.

Nonetheless, Harvard still could win the case. If its reading of NLRB case law prevailed, the judge would overturn the election on the basis of the old list-keeping ban of 1951. Furthermore, Harvard had objected to the union providing transportation for prounion voters on grounds that this discriminated against antiunion voters. The union contended this was merely an alternate transportation system since Harvard itself ran shuttle buses and provided taxi vouchers for voters. It remained to be seen how Harmatz would view this issue.

The NLRB hearings consumed eight days and ended in late August. It would take Harmatz more than a month to pore over the testimony and make his decision.

Derek Bok had come under increasing attacks for his stand against the union. In continuing the fight after the union had won, relying almost entirely on unsupported allegations, Harvard seemed to leap from union-avoidance to union-busting. Individuals and organizations that chided Bok before the election now raised the level of rhetoric.

In May the *Globe* reported that national union officials were reevaluating their relationships with Harvard, indicating that "they may withdraw labor support for the Harvard Trade Union Program and could call for a boycott of labor speakers and representatives at Harvard." Gerry McEntee, chairman of the Trade Union Program's labor committee, told the *Globe,* "We don't know who Derek Bok is anymore. In his writings he talked about labor and the AFL-CIO being such a positive force in America. But now he's behaving like any other antiunion boss."

Bok didn't respond publicly to his critics at the time. It was not until 1993, two years after he had retired as president, that he spoke openly about the episode in a one-and-a-half hour, taped interview on February 18 in his office in the Kennedy School. He talked about the difficulties involved in running a huge university with many conflicting constituent groups. When asked to elaborate on his reasons for opposing the union so resolutely in 1988, Bok's demeanor changed abruptly. His voice rose in pitch and his hands chopped the air in sharp, emphatic gestures. He said he had "worked" the labor problem in his mind along several different trajectories. First, he had asked himself, if university employees could organize and bring collective action to bear on their interests, why shouldn't other groups do the same? If this should happen, Bok said, the Harvard system of governance would become a gaggle of interest groups struggling for dominance. Organized groups would demand ever greater income shares on grounds that Harvard's $4 billion endowment ensured financial security into eternity. "It might have been in my interest to spend money in the short run to make my administration look good," he said, still hypothesizing. "But if you really worked the problem as I did, you saw that if you started eating into that $4 billion endowment, as they've been doing in Washington, you're going to get yourself into a lot of trouble."

For this reason alone, Bok thought a white-collar union would not be appropriate for Harvard. While there were an "enormous number of arguments in favor of unionism," Bok said, "we have enough evidence that unions don't always work out." History told him that most likely this union would act in traditional ways, erecting barricades around jobs and complicating a wide range of administrative actions. He worried especially that the union would bring with it the kind of troubles that erupted at Yale during and after its ten-week strike in 1984. This precipitated the resignation of President Bart Giamatti.

Bok summarized the events at Yale as a sort of horror story in higher education. "When you look at Yale and see what it went through, and what that did to the central mission of the university and what it did to the Yale administration—it disrupted an entire year's work, and they lost a president—it seems to me that no president of a university is going to observe that and not be concerned about a risk that goes to the heart of the conduct of the academic and intellectual life of the institution."

The question is, however, whether Bok took the wrong message from the Yale experience. Yale imported a consulting firm specializing in union-busting to run the campaign against white-collar unionization. This action set relations on an inflammatory course at the outset. When HERE Local 34, notwithstanding, won the election, Yale retained a second antiunion firm to negotiate a contract for the university. There followed more than a year of sparring climaxed by the 1984 strike. Regardless of which side made a more reasonable case in negotiations, Yale did much to bring chaos and disruption down around its own head.

The circumstances that produced havoc at Yale did not exist at Harvard. Indeed, Bok remarked pointedly that "*we* didn't hire any high-priced consultants to put on a sophisticated campaign" against the union. This being the case, Bok might well have taken the opposite lesson from what happened at Yale—that, instead of embarking on actions that would inflame union-management relations, Harvard should attempt to find out what kind of union it was picking a fight with.

This formulation may sound naive in the practical world of industrial relations. After all, what *could* a union want except to cause waste and inefficiency and extort exorbitant wages by means of the strike threat? But Harvard was an employer only secondarily. It was, on the first level, a university trying to teach, among other things, the value of seeking out causes in order to make ethical, moral decisions. Neither Bok nor any of his aides made any attempt to find out what Rondeau and her union represented.

In 1974, when a group of women workers started to form a union to fight for equal treatment, the men who led Harvard threw up a wall around themselves and *their* institution without bothering to investigate the intentions of the marauding group of females. Fourteen years later, when essentially the same group of women came knocking at the gate, Harvard leaders followed the model of 1974. Apparently they had learned nothing—and what is worse, had not even tried to learn.

"During the campaign," Anne Taylor conceded in 1992, four years after the fact, "we didn't know anything about this union. We listened to what they said, but we had no basis to believe or disbelieve them. They had no track record. We looked at AFSCME and found it to be a traditional union. If I had been prescient and had known that they [HUCTW] really meant what they said and would pull it off, [things might have been different]."

But it didn't take prescience so much as powwow. An experienced labor negotiator or mediator—and Harvard had several on its faculty—can discern what kind of track a would-be union intends to follow by talking to its leaders. That this could have been done is proved by the fact that it *was* done, though not at the request of university officials. An unofficial mediator *did* emerge from the great pool of talent that was the Harvard faculty and began to talk to Kris Rondeau. Eventually, this effort would enable Harvard to avoid stumbling into the kind of labor debacle that Derek Bok feared. The mediator was John Dunlop.

In the summer of 1987, the Harvard labor economist Richard Freeman happened to see Kris Rondeau walking in Harvard Square. He had met her once or twice, and now he was startled by her appearance. "I thought, 'My God, she looks exhausted, like she had lost weight, like she was struggling,'" Freeman recalled. "I tried to think of some way I could help her."

The best thing he could do, Freeman thought, was introduce her to his former professor, John Dunlop, who had mediated, arbitrated, or negotiated in thousands of labor situations. Dunlop, seventy-three years old and a professor emeritus, was not involved in labor relations or other administrative matters at Harvard. He still had much influence at the university, however. If anyone could work out "a socially desirable solution" in the HUCTW–Harvard fight, Freeman reasoned, Dunlop could. "I was a marriage broker," Freeman said, "but what transpired went way beyond anything I had imagined." At Freeman's suggestion, Rondeau and Dunlop arranged a meeting.

From the time he began teaching economics at Harvard in 1938, Dunlop concentrated on the theory and practice of setting wages. He later held advisory positions on labor–management issues under every U.S. President from Franklin D. Roosevelt to Bill Clinton. He served as chairman or director of several governmental bodies, including the Construction Industry Stabilization Committee (1971–74) and Cost of Living Council (1973–74), and as Secretary of Labor under President Gerald Ford in 1975–76. Dunlop dealt with organized labor as a force to be reckoned and negotiated with, not shoved out the door. He usually searched for a balance of power between labor and management. His primary goal was to make the system work, not to further a revolution of the masses led by militant unions. For this reason, unionists and academics with a leftist perspective thought of Dunlop as a "conservative" supporter of the old industrial relations system.

When Dunlop mediated wage disputes, he was no mere technician who found compromise in the middle. Using his considerable intellect and forceful personality, he would push disputants to develop long-term wage policies that made sense for their company or industry, whether they wanted to or not. Often irascible, he not infrequently acted the intellectual bully. But he brought to every task a compelling sense of duty and service that may have had much to do with his upbringing as the son of a Presbyterian missionary in the Philippines.

Dunlop and Rondeau met one morning at the Wursthaus, a restaurant in Harvard Square where Dunlop had been holding breakfast meetings for decades. It was a getting-to-know-you kind of session, and Rondeau later remembered, in particular, that Dunlop used the "royal we." She recalled him saying, "We wanted to see who we were dealing with." She came to understand that Dunlop tended to talk this way to avoid using the unscholarly "I," and that "we" referred to himself, not to the university. "I left that first meeting realizing I liked him and that he was someone I could talk to about all kinds of issues," she said.

Over the next year, the two met occasionally, always at Rondeau's suggestion. They talked about many things relating to unions, labor–management relations, and Harvard. Dunlop knew a great deal about the university, having served on three different faculties, including the prestigious Faculty of Arts and Sciences (FAS) and faculties at the Business School and Kennedy School of Government. According to a contemporary history of Harvard, Dunlop displayed an authoritarian bent early which earned him the nickname "iron chancellor." It apparently was this quality that convinced the Harvard Corporation to appoint him dean of FAS in 1970. Before this, Harvard officials had either vacillated or overreacted to student revolts of the 1960s. Dunlop brought a military-like toughness to the post, and no serious disturbances occurred during his three years as dean.

It was a curious chemistry that bonded these two, the dean of U.S. industrial relations and the unknown female organizer more than thirty years his junior. Rondeau contributed raw experience and a point of view foreign to Dunlop—that of a young woman critical of the academic and industrial relations structure that he and his male colleagues had built over a half century. Dunlop had met most possible varieties of union leader at least once, and he knew someone different when he saw her. He thought she was a person of ability with interesting ideas. "My motivation [in meeting with her] was not utilitarian," he said in 1996. "I wasn't thinking, 'Ah, this lady is going to win an election, and I want to influence what she does.'"

No one ever had accused Dunlop of being overly sensitive to women's issues, but Rondeau didn't feel that she was being patronized. Indeed, he was the only eminent male personage at Harvard who ever made an effort to understand what she and her union stood for. He could not speak for the university, but she realized that it would take someone of Dunlop's stature and knowledge to negotiate seriously with the union if it won the election. "I found him to be always confident in his own perceptions and abilities," she said later. "Harvard wasn't a confident enough organization to have a healthy relationship with the union without someone like John."

In the summer of 1988, Dunlop came under pressure from union friends like Doug Fraser to push for union recognition. Dunlop, however, did not presume to give unasked-for advice to his friend Derek Bok. When the two talked, Dunlop gave his reading of the situation but refrained from arguing for or against the union.

The issue remained unresolved through September and most of October. Five months had passed since the election, and the NLRB administrative law judge was off someplace working on his decision.

On Monday, October 24, hundreds of people filed into the Sanders Theater auditorium for a political rally featuring the Reverend Jesse Jackson. He had lost his bid to be the Democratic Presidential nominee and now was stumping for the man who beat him, Michael Dukakis. Jackson's ability to dramatize the plight of all poor and downtrodden with inspirational rhetoric had energized liberal Democrats throughout the campaign, and he drew enthusiastic crowds wherever he went. Rondeau and her staff, who would not forget Jackson's support before their election, had set up this rally. It would become, as Jim Braude later described it, "one of the most Hollywood-like events of the entire Harvard union story."

Rondeau was sitting on stage with other speakers. As Jackson began his speech, she was summoned to a stage door in the wings. There she found a staff member who had managed to talk her way through rings of security guards to give an urgent message to Rondeau. "Craig just called, and we won!" she announced breathlessly, referring to the union attorney.

Rondeau returned to her seat, wanting to shout out the news. She tried to pick out her staff members and activists in the balcony but couldn't see clearly through the glare of stage lights. She gave a furtive thumbs up signal in that direction, shielding the thumb with her free hand to avoid distracting the audience. There was no response. Finally, she whispered the news to a Jackson aide who had noticed her distress. The aide passed a note to Jackson as he spoke.

Jackson paused nearly in mid-sentence. He raised his head and said, speaking as one who had seen the Coming, "A ray of hope in Cambridge!" He turned to Rondeau and called her to the podium.

The union organizers and members knew then why she had made that curious gesture with her hands. For the second time that year, Sanders erupted with screams and cheers. Jackson raised Rondeau's hand: the victor. The applause intensified. "We won again," she said when the cheering stopped. "Their unmistakable goal was to beat the union, and they just failed. Now, finally, I hope they can recognize reality."

If there was exultation in the theater, there was lamentation, and no small amount of anger, in the Harvard general counsel's office. The decision written by Judge Harmatz not only dismissed all of the university's objections to the election, it also severely censured Harvard's lawyers. Harmatz repeated his attack on their legal tactics, especially the attempt (unsuccessful, as it turned out) to induce union organizers to convict themselves without offering credible evidence of wrongdoing from university witnesses. In several places he chastised the Harvard lawyers for distorting testimony. "The Employer's brief," he wrote, "is replete with misinterpretations of the record. Indeed, a pattern emerges that transcends what might lightly be dismissed as an aggressive adversarial approach."

The judge agreed with Craig Becker that the old NLRB ban on list-keeping did not apply in this case. He also dismissed Harvard's charges that the union unduly influenced workers by "festooning" walkways with posters and balloons and by offering to transport prounion workers to the polls and provide medical assistance. "Stripped of glossy unconfirmed characterization, the Employer's complaint here addresses a perfectly legitimate, apparently successful, tactical maneuver," Harmatz concluded, referring to HUCTW's Get Out the Vote drive.

From Harvard's point of view, the dismissal of its objections was bad enough. Worse were the unusually harsh reprimands about legal tactics. Dan Steiner said later that Harmatz's comments confirmed Harvard's suspicions of antimanagement bias on his part. Bob Fuchs, the regional NLRB director who twice before had issued critical rulings in Harvard's favor, said he thought Harmatz made "a very good and correct decision." The judge's remarks about the Harvard lawyers, however, were "completely unwarranted," Fuchs said.

Harvard's next move was up to Derek Bok. He had eleven days, until Friday, November 4, to decide whether to recognize and negotiate with the union, or to ask the NLRB to review the case. He sent a copy of Harmatz's decision to Archibald Cox, his former law professor, whose opinion on labor law he valued above all others, and asked Cox to assess Harvard's chances of winning at the board level. Bok also consulted Dunlop.

Although he considered Harvard's election-day complaints trivial, Dunlop left the legal issues to Cox and instead tendered some very practical advice to the president. "I said that in my experience anytime you did something in collective bargaining before you had to do it, even a few minutes early, you might try to get something for it," Dunlop recalled in 1992. If Bok voluntarily recognized the union, Dunlop said, he might ask for a sixty-day "transition period" before contract bargaining began. It was important to purge the atmosphere of the mistrust and bitterness that existed between the university and the union after fourteen years of nearly constant warfare. Moving abruptly from the adversary mode to one of peaceful and constructive negotiation would be difficult. In most cases, employers and unions were unable to jump that gap without falling into deeper trouble. At Yale, for example, the university and Local 34 never declared a truce after the union won its election but plunged into adversary bargaining that culminated in a devastating strike. Harvard could avoid such a fate, Dunlop suggested.

Bok's next move startled Rondeau. He invited her to meet with him at his office in Massachusetts Hall. It was Saturday, and he was alone in the building. He came to the door and escorted her through an elegant hallway which once resounded with the noise of Colonial troops quartered there during the Revolutionary War. When they sat in his office, the president of Harvard University seemed nervous. He was very polite and not condescending, Rondeau remembered. They had met once or twice by accident on campus but never had really talked, and this first official meeting consisted largely of mutual inspection. "Mostly what we did was look at each other," she said. Bok asked what she thought of Dunlop's proposal for a transition period. Rondeau, who already had discussed it with Dunlop, said the union approved of the idea.

On the following day, Bok convened a meeting in his home of about a dozen people, including lawyers, university vice-presidents, a few deans, and John Dunlop. Both the in-house lawyers and the Ropes, Gray attorneys, incensed over the Harmatz ruling, wanted to push ahead with the legal battle, according to Anne Taylor. At the meeting, she presented the arguments for appealing Harmatz's decision. The lawyers felt certain that Harvard would prevail on the legal issues—a certainty that might well have been inflated by desire for personal vindication. Dunlop repeated his suggestion that immediate recognition would give the university leverage to request a peaceful transition period.

Bok didn't make his decision that day but waited for Cox's opinion, which came a day or so later. "It was his judgment," Bok related, "that certainly we had a case. But he didn't think it was strong enough that we would be well advised to go forward." Even after receiving Cox's advice, Bok faced what he called a "wrenching decision." Ending the fight against the union would upset many people at Harvard, including not least the powerful deans who headed Harvard's professional and graduate schools. "There were people I really love within the university who strongly felt that we should go on," he said. "And there was really quite a large group—I don't want to exaggerate—but it was a quite large and quite spontaneously organized group of secretaries who had gotten worked up against having the union and felt that they were in jeopardy and would be let down if we didn't pursue our rights as far as we could go."

Bok pondered his options for a few more days. Rondeau met privately with him a few more times and came to believe that "we could have established an actual working relationship if we had met long before this." She thought Bok wanted to settle the issue without further fighting, but when she talked with him, she "got the impression that all kinds of forces were bearing down on him, powerful forces in the Harvard community."

The university obtained a five-day extension at the NLRB, and when Friday, November 4 arrived, everyone was prepared to wait five more days. Suddenly, however, Bok announced that the university would recognize the union without further ado. In a press release, he said he did not want to risk "a long and fruitless delay" that further NLRB proceedings might entail. He urged everyone to put aside "partisan feelings" in order "to make this relationship as constructive and harmonious as possible." Bok backed up his words. On the same day, according to the *Crimson*, university administrators began distributing buttons which said, "We'll Make It Work."

For the union leaders Bok's decision seemed anticlimactic after victories at the polls and the NLRB. But Rondeau and Manna issued a statement pledging that the union would "try to develop a model of union–management relations based on mutual respect and cooperation."

The *Crimson* quoted some antiunion employees as saying they felt that Bok had betrayed them. But the more important effect of his announcement was to lift the barrier of management opposition to the union. Organizers now found workers eager to sign membership cards. Dozens came voluntarily to the union office and signed up. In a period of a few weeks, membership surged from the 50.7 percent of the work force who voted "yes" on May 17 to about 75 percent. It appeared that a large majority of workers really did want to be represented by the union.

The union had won the ribbon and now it had to collect a prize by converting this support into a contract which would materially improve members' lives and give them some measure of control in the workplace. Rondeau wanted this to be more than a routine commercial transaction. "Organizing had become so satisfying," she said, "that we wanted to build a union that held on to the fun. We had inadvertently built a culture where people were involved in continuous learning in the union. We didn't know what it was called, but we knew we wanted to continue it."

The two sides entered a sixty-day transition period, as proposed by Dunlop, and assembled bargaining teams. In a situation involving a new local, AFSCME typically would send in an experienced negotiator to bargain a typical AFSCME contract. But McEntee knew of HUCTW's strong desire to do it themselves and left bargaining in Rondeau's hands. Her experience had been limited to a few small firms in District 65, but she thought she could learn while doing.

Bok, meanwhile, named Dunlop as chief negotiator for the university. He would report directly to Bok instead of going up an administrative chain of command. The many people at Harvard who suspected that Rondeau influenced this decision were right in a sense. She didn't specifically ask for Dunlop, she later said, but urged Bok to name someone outside the administration, knowing that Dunlop would be a prime candidate. (Anne Taylor was given a role in negotiations, though Dunlop would mostly ignore her. She had been named director of human resources in September, but she soon resigned this position and returned to the legal staff.)

The deans of some of Harvard's graduate and professional schools later would complain about the role played by Dunlop. Yet it is doubtful that any administration official could have guided the university through such a dramatic shift in labor relations. Preoccupied with fighting the union, the deans and administrators had not prepared a contingency plan for negotiating with it. Dunlop filled this void. He designed a negotiating process that would carry Harvard through a difficult period. More importantly, with Bok's approval he formulated a new labor policy to accommodate a new union with boldly different ideas about representing workers.

The university could have continued to frustrate the union by engaging in sham bargaining. Rather than learning how to get along with a newly elected union, many employers in the 1980s were laying plans to get rid of it. Typically, a company would merely go through the motions of negotiating a first contract. By convincing workers that the union caused a bargaining deadlock, the employer could surreptitiously bring about a decertification election (allowed after one year) and bid good riddance to the union. By the late 1980s, one-third of newly certified unions failed to negotiate a first contract.

Bok, however, had concluded that if the university must deal with the union, he wanted to "forge a relationship that would be valuable, interesting, and even new." In deputizing Dunlop, he closed off the sham bargaining aproach: Dunlop was not a man who would pretend to succeed by failing. Moreover, Dunlop himself had undergone something of a conversion. In the early 1980s, when economic events forced a new kind of bargaining in many industries, Dunlop scoffed at suggestions that an erosion of old-style pattern bargaining and the beginning of cooperative employee involvement plans represented a new trend in industrial relations. By 1989, however, he was eager to negotiate an innovative contract at Harvard, one that would reflect HUCTW's ideas of participation and self-representation.

Before confronting this task, the two sides held a series of prenegotiation meetings during the transition period. Each side formed teams of six to nine members which met seven times during December and January. The purpose was to learn something about one another and to measure intentions and trustworthiness. The university disclosed employment data and brought in experts to explain Harvard's complicated system of financial governance. The union, meanwhile, sought to fill a gap in management's knowledge of the work force. "We explained what it means to work at Harvard from a very personal perspective," Rondeau said. Believing in what the Harvard psychologist Robert Coles calls "the moral power of story-telling," she invited individual workers to describe their work and personal lives, showing how they were intertwined. Collective bargaining, she thought, should view a worker as a whole person and family member, not merely a job holder.

Dunlop suggested that a mediator, or facilitator, be used in these talks. His choice, which Rondeau and Bok endorsed, was James J. Healy, seventy-two, emeritus professor of economics and industrial relations at the Harvard Business School and one of the nation's foremost labor mediators and arbitrators. Healy, like Dunlop, had seen every kind of union–management relationship in a career of more than forty years. He had served on many government panels, including a famous Presidential board which in 1963 recommended elimination of the fireman's job on diesel locomotives. He had been the permanent grievance umpire for Ford Motor Co. and the UAW, as well as several other companies. In the transition meetings, and later in bargaining sessions, Jim Healy kept the talks moving and suggested ways of dealing with what appeared to be irresolvable conflicts.

He and Dunlop provided a combination of knowledge and authority that could be found nowhere else in the country. Their involvement in these negotiations held a rare irony. While the women workers had finally forced the men who ran the university to bargain with them, their eventual success would owe much to the collaboration of two patriarchs of U.S. industrial relations. Dunlop and Healy were among the last of the World War II generation of practitioners who created a system of collective bargaining that had governed unionized workplaces since the war. In the 1980s, this system was breaking down under the competitive pressures of global trade, which were undermining American wage patterns and collective bargaining itself as the national standards-setter for most employment terms. But Healy still traveled around the country on mediation/arbitration assignments. In contrast with the impatient, cranky Dunlop, he was exceptionally mild-mannered. Decades of passing judgment on sometimes petty, sometimes significant, conflicting interests had given him an unpretentious Solomonic air. As Kris Rondeau once said of these two old friends, "One is a lot nicer than you think he is, and the other is just as nice as you think he is."

While the transition meetings were going on, Harvard and the union initiated another critical plan. In a work force as large as Harvard's, many personnel problems arise in a period of two months, ranging from disciplinary cases to disputes over layoffs, promotions, and other management decisions. To handle these problems, management and union each designated two people to meet as a problem-solving team. From the union side came Marie Manna and Bill Jaeger. The administration representatives were Vivienne Rubeski, a former personnel officer in the Medical Area who had been named director of labor relations for the university, and Mary Opperman, another personnel officer. This group became known as the Gang of Four. Working in teams of two (management and union), they investigated situations and recommended solutions, a process that served as forerunner of a unique problem-solving provision in the contract.

The transition talks concluded on February 13, 1989 with agreement on an "Understanding." In it, the two sides agree to "work together to advance the long-term role of Harvard University as a premier center of learning, research and teaching." The statement goes on to make a fundamentally important point:

> It is commonly understood that Harvard has come to be governed, in the broadest sense of the term, through a cooperative process among governing boards and administrators, faculty, students and alumni, in which each plays a role. This Understanding welcomes the support staff in libraries, in laboratories, and in academic and administrative offices and centers, represented by HUCTW, as a valued and essential participant in this process.

The Understanding later became the preamble of the union–management contract. For the first time in its history, Harvard acknowledges that support staff should have a role (yet to be defined) in governance. But the time would come when this idea would clash with another principle, also expressed in the Understanding, emphasizing the value of decentralization. Harvard's deans were intent on keeping the old "every tub on its own bottom" philosophy intact. While "some matters affecting the support staff and their work environment need to be consistent across the university," says the agreement, "other questions are better left to joint discussion in the separate and diversified units and departments." If management in some units chose not to engage in "joint discussion," the workers would have no voice.

Negotiations for a contract began in mid-February 1989, and lasted into June. The union's overall approach grew out of ideas that Rondeau, Manna, and others had been developing for years. The leaders also gathered suggestions for wage and benefit improvements in a series of meetings with members. Sixty-five workers, elected to serve on a bargaining committee, were divided among eight separate negotiating "tables," each mandated to discuss categories of issues, such as salaries, pensions, health and dental care, family and dependent care, safety and health, career development, and participation. Instead of requesting the help of AFSCME technicians, HUCTW organizers and workers developed expertise in several areas. Bill Jaeger became the lead salary negotiator along with Rondeau; Donene Williams led the health care team; Bob Mendelson, a lab assistant in engineering, served as team leader on pensions.

About fifty administrators and faculty members, including administrative deans, were distributed among the negotiating tables. Although Dunlop later would be accused of running the talks to suit himself, he actually involved management people at every step of bargaining. He and Rondeau supervised the entire process and gave general directions to the several tables. As each negotiating group reached consensus on assigned issues, they would send draft language to Dunlop and Rondeau who gave tentative approval or asked for changes.

Out of this process came one of the more unique labor agreements in the United States. Unlike the traditional union contract, the Harvard agreement does not carve out areas of management rights and union rights in elaborately detailed rules. In the former, one set of rules usually specifies a precise order in which workers will be promoted, transferred, laid off, or recalled according to seniority. Other rules establish job classifications and spell out duties for each job. A grievance procedure enables workers to appeal management decisions that violate their contractual rights. Traditional grievance procedures usually work very well as a means of adjudicating workers' complaints. But they have disadvantages from Rondeau's point of view. First, a worker depends on the union to "process" her grievance at progressively higher steps, negotiating with management officials. After the first step, the worker has little control or ability to affect the outcome. Second, the procedure often becomes a weapon in an endless adversary game between union and management. Third, workers have no rights beyond those spelled out in the contract.

Rondeau and her staff had decided long ago that Harvard employees—and especially women—did not want a rule-driven approach in which decisions were taken out of the hands of ordinary members. In a traditional union–management relationship, she said, "there's a basic belief that if it's not in the contract, you can't grieve it. We thought this was too limiting. If women see a problem, they want to solve it whether it's written down or not." In saying this, Rondeau wasn't propounding a general theory about women, merely saying what she knew about the women workers of Harvard. She added, "Our goal was to build a process that would support moral reasoning in problem-solving and to leave people free to ask the question, 'What is the right thing to do?'"

With these ideas in mind, negotiators produced an agreement consisting mainly of philosophical statements and general guidelines rather than detailed rules and delineation of management and union rights. They also rewrote a Harvard personnel manual which is incorporated by reference in the main agreement. The manual contains rules that neither side could do without, relating to hours of work, holidays and vacations, sick pay, leaves of absence, and prohibition of sexual harassment, among others. But there are no ironbound job classifications and descriptions (a secretary would be allowed to change a light bulb) and not a word about "seniority." One section provides guidelines covering layoffs but no provision to ensure that longer-service employees would be the last laid off and the first recalled. This omission would draw criticism from traditional unionists, for whom a contract is an instrument to prevent management from playing favorites. Although layoffs occurred all the time at Harvard as government grants ran out, affected workers usually could find jobs elsewhere in the university. It was by no means a perfect system, and the union in later years would address the "work security" issue. But in 1989 the union had too many other priorities.

Instead of a grievance procedure, the agreement contains a "problem-solving" process intended to encourage workers to represent themselves with the union's help. The union also wanted to provide a means for groups of workers to have a voice in decision making. The forum created for this purpose was called Joint Council (JC), a committee of a dozen or so union and management representatives to be set up in each school or administrative department.

The problem-solving and Joint Council provisions were central to the union's philosophy of unionism. Other issues were important, including the always nagging problem of "union security." For many unionists, accepting anything less than *union shop* (employees must join the union as a condition of continued employment) would be contrary to trade union principles. Union leaders, however, recognized that the Harvard work force probably always would contain a goodly number of people who objected strenuously to being required to join a union, and Derek Bok himself insisted on an *agency shop* provision (workers do not have to join the union but are required to pay an "agency fee" for representation services).

In the area of family benefits, the university granted a 13-week paid leave for birth mothers with assurance of return to the same job; a 1-week leave for fathers; and a small day care program which the union would expand in later negotiations. On health insurance, Harvard agreed to raise its contribution to premium payments from 70 percent to 85 percent and added a short-term disability plan. On pensions, the agreement not only raised the monthly stipend but also added an annual cost-of-living adjustment (a relatively rare feature of pension plans). These and other pension improvements were part of a two-pronged effort to correct what the union viewed as Harvard's neglect of older employees. The other part involved salary policy, and it was here that the innovative bargaining process experienced difficult going.

Although the union did not organize on promises of big money gains, Rondeau thought it vital for the strength of the union to win a large salary increase. The average annual salary of full-time Harvard workers in 1989 was about $20,000, nearly $7,000 less than average pay of all workers in the Boston metropolitan area. The historical reason for this had much to do with female workers being paid less than men in comparable jobs. But union negotiators chose not to base salary demands on the comparable worth concept, as a women's union might have been expected to do. The leaders thought they could make a better case for the argument that all members, men and women, deserved more for their contributions to Harvard. The union also wanted to give workers incentive to make a career of their Harvard jobs. Heretofore, long-service workers suffered under an old practice that kept them static at the same salary level (in real dollars) for years while newer employees came in at nearly the same rate. And finally, Rondeau intended to exact a price—"war reparations," she termed it—for Harvard's long fight against the union. Rondeau explained: "We said to Harvard, 'We've watched you spend millions to defeat the union, and now that you've got the union you have to continue to spend millions.'"

To deal with the salary problems of older workers, Bill Jaeger developed an annual "progression" increase. At the same time, the university agreed to de-emphasize the principle of merit pay—which enabled supervisors so inclined to play favorites in handing out pay increases—in favor of fixed percentage salary hikes for all workers. Starting on July 1, 1989, Harvard would grant across-the-board raises totaling 16 percent over three years (7, 5, and 4), plus merit raises averaging 2 percent of payroll each year. The total effect of the three elements of a salary package—progression, across-the-board and merit raises—was to increase salaries by an average of nearly 25 percent during a three-year agreement. This was an exceptional gain for an era of relatively low price inflation. When Rondeau presented the proposal to her bargaining committee, she was greeted by enthusiastic applause. No one even suggested that a vote be taken.

On the management side, the Council of Deans demanded a renegotiation of the salary package and a few other items. The talks resumed and continued for about two more weeks. This time, Rondeau and Jaeger negotiated salary matters directly with Robert Scott, Harvard's financial vice-president. In the end, the union leaders retreated on salaries but only in a small way. They agreed to reduce the amount that Harvard must contribute in merit raises each year, saving the university roughly $1.2 million. Nonetheless, the final settlement would result in an increase in average salaries for full-time workers from $20,000 in 1989 to $24,000 in 1992. The deans approved the revised package. On the union side, a small group of members campaigned against ratification. But on June 29 the members approved the agreement by a vote of 1,551 to 98.

Derek Bok retired in June 1991 after serving twenty years as president of Harvard. He had fought his share of battles on a wide range of issues with many individuals and groups, including students, faculty members, administrators, and politicians. Few had been as long-lasting or made as deep an impression as the intermittent struggles over a fifteen-year period with a small group of union women. In 1993, looking back at those episodes, Bok did not directly express regrets about his decisions, and yet he wanted the record to reflect how he personally felt. "Nobody was ever *very* angry at anybody," he said. "We had a point of view and tried to get it across, not in a hostile way." When the interviewer pointed out that many in the union would not agree with his characterization, Bok conceded, "It would have been easy for them to be hostile toward us [in the 1989 negotiations] but they weren't."

Bok had greeted the interviewer with a comment about Kris Rondeau that summed up many things. "We almost came in together," he said, smiling. "She has admirable qualities of persistence."

"Her husband says she is absolutely relentless," said the interviewer.

Bok nodded. "Yes, she is. She is the most relentless person I've encountered during my twenty years. She had a fixity of purpose that was. . ." He paused and added with a laugh, "breathtaking."

View of the audience in Sanders Theater, moments after HUCTW has been declared the winner of election to represent Harvard workers, May 17, 1988. Men in the foreground are mainly officials of other unions who (behaving like men) pushed to the front of the auditorium, while the women members of HUCTW were left in the rear. Rondeau's husband, Jim Braude, is the man with clenched fists, wearing a cardigan. Credit: Marilyn Humphries

Jim Braude and Kris Rondeau embracing on election night, May 17, 1988, shortly after vote tally was announced. Credit: Rick Stafford

Jesse Jackson announces that the NLRB has upheld the union's election victory at Harvard. Jackson and Rondeau happened to be attending a political rally on Oct. 24, 1988 when notice of the board ruling came. Credit: David L. Ryan/ Boston Globe

Rondeau and John Dunlop, on the first day of contract negotiations, Feb. 22, 1989. Credit: Joe Wrinn/Harvard University

HUCTW members demonstrate outside the home of Harvard President Derek Bok in fall, 1988, demanding that he negotiate with the union following its election victory. Credit: Rick Stafford

On the first day of contract negotiations, Feb. 22, 1989, Harvard President Derek Bok greets members of the HUCTW negotiating team. To his left is John Dunlop and to his right, Kris Rondeau. Credit: Joe Wrinn/Harvard University

The first executive board of HUCTW, elected in fall of 1989. President: Donene Williams, middle row, second from right; Vice-president: Cory Paulsen, bottom row, far right; Treasurer: Gloria Buffonge, bottom, second from right; Secretary: Randall Kromm, top row, far right. Next to Kromm is Tom Canel, the man who covered himself with Magic Marker reds and blacks while keeping track of election-day vote. Credit: Ellen DeGenova.

*I*t was early January 1992, three and a half years after workers startled Harvard University—and the entire world of labor—by voting in the union. Kris Rondeau ushered a visitor through the union's Winthrop St. office and into a
small, stuffy conference room. If physical space determines
philosophy, one could see from these cramped quarters why the Harvard
union embraced one-on-one organizing. And judging by photographs
crowding the whitewashed brick walls, organizing really was "a lot of fun,"
as Rondeau and her friends always describe it. Every picture showed
laughing staff members gathered for some joyous event. There seemed to
have been many such events in recent HUCTW history.

Rondeau sat on an old couch with cushions bursting at the seams, a
relic of the independent days. As the visitor placed a tape recorder on the
low table between them, she said, "How do you want to start?"

The interviewer pulled out a copy of the Harvard union contract, prepared to ask about various provisions. It was a reflexive act, born of experience as a labor reporter in the not-so-long-ago when all good union
stewards carried a dog-eared copy of the contract in a hip pocket. The
contract ruled the workplace, and union and management alike consulted
it to find the substance and spirit of their relationship.

"Forget the contract," Rondeau said abruptly, waving it aside. "When
we give it to workers, we tell them to read it once and put it away." She
continued: "We don't want our members to think the whole world is in
that booklet. People with ideas are welcome here. We take the position
that anything is possible and anything is negotiable. We want our members to see themselves as being players in the world." Later she expanded

on this idea, quoting the first sentence from her favorite novel, *David Copperfield*. "'Whether I shall turn out to be the hero of my own life, or whether that station will be held by anybody else, these pages must show.' I think," she added, "that people really do want to be heroes in their own lives. That's exactly what we want our members to become." It was an intriguing application of Dickens to the American workplace.

Outside the conference room, nine or ten staff organizers were holed up in various niches and cubicles, typing at computer terminals and working the phones. There were no union contracts bulging in hip pockets, but every shoulder bag carried a Franklin Planner, a thick notebook with colored tabs dividing the owner's life into a time-management system. On the phone, the organizers were chatting with old members, introducing themselves to new workers, taking notes on personnel problems, setting up meetings. Talk and meet, and talk: running a local union in the participatory mode is labor-intensive business. The Harvard union style incorporates many elements; it is romantic but hard-headed, reform-minded, garrulous with a broad satirical edge, often comic—in a word, Dickensian, though in a female way. If this was not a wholly new kind of unionism, it was certainly unusual in the United States.

In American labor, organizing workers into a union came to be thought of as a skill or function preliminary to and quite apart from leading a union. Organizing was "grunt" labor performed by angry militants with a talent for inciting people to rise up against the employment status quo and cast a vote for collective action. While the newly unionized workers settled back to be "serviced" by union executives, the organizer would pack up his tools of trade and, like an itinerant carpenter, go looking for another "hot spot," or workplace vulnerable to unionization. Organizing thus had a one-time purpose and either "took," like a good wood preservative, or didn't take; but if it took, it would never again be needed in the same place.

The women who organized Harvard stayed on and built a unique local union, combining the fast-moving features of an organizing vehicle with the stand-in-place bureaucratic functions of negotiating and administering a contract. The staff and activists never stop organizing. They organize in two different but overlapping spheres. First, they organize continuously among new and old Harvard employees; and second, they mobilize the energies and creativity of workers in carving out enlarged roles for themselves in the life of the university. Success in the second area has been limited by the resistance of top-level Harvard administrators, oddly unreceptive (perhaps *typically* unreceptive, as American managements go) to union involvement in improving the way work is organized and managed and thus the quality of services produced. But there has been progress in some areas of the university where middle-level managers endorsed and invited worker participation.

The union framework enables large numbers of members to take an active role in the local. At the top is a seventeen-member executive board, with four officers elected across the university and thirteen members elected on a regional basis. An experienced, politically stable group, the board in 1996 still consisted mainly of workers who were active in the 1988 election campaign, served as team leaders in the first negotiation, and wrote the local bylaws. A female–male split of twelve to five remained the same. A tiny opposition group within the local has run candidates for various offices without success. The president, Donene Williams, has been re-elected twice since 1989, winning 80 percent of the vote against a challenger in 1995. As a full-time local president, she does a little of everything, from planning strategy and negotiating, to organizing, to helping members resolve workplace and family problems.

There are also 110 "union reps," or about one for each thirty-five employees, elected at the departmental level across the university. Another union body with elected members is the Joint Council (JC), typically composed of five union and five management representatives. By 1992, about thirty-five JCs existed throughout the university with 120 union members. In addition, nineteen Local Problem Solving Teams, each consisting of one union and one management appointee, handle personnel problems. In 1995, union leaders created a new ad hoc body called a "cabinet" consisting of about fifty top-level activists from around the university who meet once every few weeks as an advisory body.

The total of all activists—including appointed and elected reps and volunteers—generally hovers in the area of 300 to 400, 10 percent or more of the entire membership. This is a very high percentage when compared with traditional unions run by a relatively small cadre of elected officers and stewards, often numbering little more than 1 to 2 percent in a 3,000-member local.

Rondeau's staff occupies an unusual position. Consisting mainly of former Harvard workers, many of them veterans of the Harvard organizing campaign, they are employees of AFSCME, not of the local union. On a daily basis, they coordinate the work of elected union reps and report to Bill Jaeger, who holds the appointed post of director. Since 1989, the staff has numbered fifteen to twenty, which by any standard would be a very large staff for a local union. Most staff "organizers," however, have several duties. Working day and night, each organizer covers a major section of the university and also spends the equivalent of about three days a week on AFSCME organizing campaigns. In 1996, four or five worked full-time on other drives. Rondeau divides her time among directing these other campaigns, managing the staff, and (along with Jaeger and Williams) negotiating with Harvard management. She neither has nor wants a formal title, but she is Undisputed Leader.

The paid staff more or less leads the work of the union, but elected executive board members are by no means supernumeraries. The board meets once a week and is consulted on all major decisions. Board and staff roles are mixed and overlapping. Many men would have trouble accepting this lack of hierarchical order. But the genius of the HUCTW arrangement lies in a high degree of involvement of a large number of people. When it moves, it moves more like a cluster or colony than in regimented ranks. In an organization modeled along participatory lines, everyone works hard to keep everyone else informed. Hundreds of activists are drawn into this mesh through meetings of other committees.

Organizing remains the crux of union activities. Because of high worker turnover, there are always new employees to be signed up. But "organizing" is defined in a more inclusive way than normally is the case. It also includes encouraging more activity by existing members, maintaining relations with workers who never join the union, and even "organizing" managers to practice participative management. One part of every staff meeting is set aside for reports on new workers, or old workers, who have just signed membership cards. A burst of applause greets a breathless announcement from an organizer, "I got two cards today." In HUCTW's agency shop arrangement, workers don't have to belong but they must pay fees equivalent to dues, unless they ask to be exempted from a portion used for nonbargaining purposes. This being the case, the local could simply collect the fees and ignore those workers who do not voluntarily sign up.

The leaders believe, however, that the union would become little more than a shell and a dues-collecting body unless it tries to involve every employee in the life of the union. During its first few years as bargaining agent, HUCTW maintained membership at about 75 to 80 percent. Starting in 1995, it increased organizing activity, so that membership shot up to 85 percent. It is hard to do better than this among individualistic American workers.

The emphasis on *continuous organizing* would not count for much unless it enabled the union to improve the lives of members in a variety of ways. In terms of economic benefits, the Harvard union has done very well. In 1996, after three rounds of negotiations, the average yearly salary of full-time workers was $28,000 to $29,000, compared with less than $20,000 before the first negotiation. The union has won significant changes in Harvard's salary policy to reward long-service employees. The university agreed in 1993 to do away with merit raises, formerly the primary basis for salary increases. The merit policy had resulted in large disparities in salaries because wealthier schools, like the Business and Medical Schools, could afford a higher range of merit increases. A progression increase formula encourages workers to make a career at Harvard with a middle-class income. As of 1996, employees who stayed at Harvard for more than twenty years could expect to receive in the high $30,000s or even low $40,000s (in constant dollars).

Harvard negotiators also have made important advances in the noneconomic areas of participation, work security, and the handling of personnel complaints, with most success in the third category. Harvard's "individual problem resolution" eschews the legalism and adversary politics that often mark traditional grievance procedures and relies on moral reasoning. A worker may bring up any problem associated with his or her work and is encouraged to represent herself in working out a solution with supervisors. Frequently, a union rep or staff member will advise the employee on how to present the issue but will intervene with management if necessary.

Most complaints are resolved in this informal way. If not, they can be taken up by a Local Problem Solving Team (LPST), consisting of one union and one management representative who have been trained in handling personnel disputes. The team members act as partners, rather than adversaries, who can use a wide variety of investigative and fact-finding methods to get to the source of a problem and recommend a solution. Because managers become part of the process, it is expected in most instances they will accept the LPST's recommendations. A higher body, the University Problem Solving Team (UPST), consisting of four management and four union representatives, takes up problems not resolved below. The UPST can follow any path it chooses to settle the issue, with an emphasis on whatever works and is fair to all sides.

Few problems go beyond the UPST, but the union agreement contains a mediation/arbitration provision to be used for more intractable problems. A professional arbitrator from the outside (in most cases, this has been Jim Healy) is asked to help find a solution through mediation. If this doesn't work, the neutral can take the case into arbitration and issue a decision which is binding on both sides. The remarkable thing is that in the first seven years of the agreement, not a single case went to the ultimate arbitration step. Indeed, Healy and other "med/arbs" have been called in to work only on seven cases. Six involved employees who were fired and one who charged sexual harassment. In most bargaining units of comparable size, two to three cases a year would have reached the arbitration stage, and in many corporations or government bodies, the union–management relationship is so bad that practically every major case winds up in arbitration, with all the legal panoply of lawyers and briefs and formal hearings.

Under the Harvard system, an employee complaint is viewed as an objective problem to be solved and not an instrument for assessing blame. In many unions, the steward is under political pressure to file a grievance on practically every member complaint, no matter how frivolous. At Harvard, union reps discourage members from pressing minor gripes and encourage them to develop facts and strategy to represent themselves in talks with managers. Joie Gelband, who served as a union member of the UPST, said that in the union's early years, members tended to ask for union help. As the union matured and the self-representation philosophy became understood, more and more members began resolving their own problems. Indeed, the union will drop a complaint, no matter how much merit it has, if the member refuses to be involved in the process. The types of issues most handled by LPSTs are disciplinary cases, complaints about work schedules, the effects of reorganization, harassment by supervisors, and disability claims arising from the job.

For years the university had justified its opposition to the union on the need to avoid rigid personnel rules. But in the end it was the union that took the lead in devising this, rule-free system—and traditional managers have not been entirely happy with the time it takes to resolve problems. Observing this reaction by some managers, Jim Healy said: "The absence of rules means that you deal with situations on an ad hoc basis. You have to be creative and flexible to accommodate the philosophy behind the relationship. A number of administrators would prefer to have set, well-defined rules. This would make their job easier. But the really good administrators enjoy the new challenge of creative problem-solving."

A process that allows for settlement of personnel problems at little cost and that spreads a perception of fairness through a large work force has to be considered a major achievement. "Before the union, I observed a bitterness, a rancor, and people feeling frustrated," Healy said in 1996. "Workers had no way of getting problems resolved. And management often made arbitrary decisions. Now they have a process, and I think it has been very, very meaningful."

Another joint program is aimed at helping laid off workers find other jobs. In a second round of contract negotiations, in 1992–93, the union and university agreed on a "work security" plan administered by a joint committee. If a job is eliminated, displaced staff members are to be given hiring preference for any vacant job for which they are qualified elsewhere in the university. This had been a real problem because workers laid off in one department tended to be viewed as damaged goods by other departments. The committee is empowered to "intervene" in cases where the policy is not being applied fairly, and a worker may receive up to three months of wages and benefits until placed in a job. The union still has no seniority provision. It tries to ensure fair treatment through moral suasion rather than a hard-line contractual approach, which means that it sometimes puts up with managerial behavior that would not be acceptable in other unions. On the other hand, seniority clauses have their own shortcomings as sources of intraunion battles.

In 1989, Rondeau and other union leaders viewed the Joint Council structure as an experiment. The union had no idea whether JCs would afford an important channel for members to influence decisions or whether they would amount to little. But this is the way of participation. The most carefully planned mechanism may turn out a dud if not strategically placed in the institution, or if one side or both choose to ignore it.

By 1996, the union's experience with JCs had been a mixture of excellent, mediocre, and poor. Joint Councils were set up initially in major administrative units and departments. For example, each professional school had at least one JC. There was one representing all libraries on the main campus, one for University Health Services, one for a department dealing with alumni and fundraising, and so on. It turned out that a significant number of managers at the department level believed in a participatory model of work relationships, and in these cases Joint Councils accomplished good things. Some of the best projects involved reorganization of offices, labs, and other work sites—the kind of change that constantly occurs throughout the university. JCs in several departments worked out elaborate plans for shifting work, transferring or creating job duties, rearranging offices, and so forth, to minimize the pain and trouble of dislocation. When Morgan Hall on the Business School campus was remodeled, a joint committee arranged for massive movements of secretaries and staff assistants and professors from site to site with a minimum of trouble.

Other projects included developing departmental snow policies, covering the circumstances under which offices would be closed during bad weather; installing ventilation systems and other comfort items like employee lounges at the request of workers; conducting joint studies of work hours, job duties, work flow, and turnover; establishing rules for performance evaluation; and similar issues. In many places, managers used JCs as sounding boards, getting opinions of the union members about changes in personnel policies. In some cases, special joint committees formulated plans for saving money by shrinking a departmental work force; in one area, the union even agreed to the elimination of a few bargaining unit jobs in order to reduce an operating deficit.

Joint Councils encountered a lack of worker interest in some areas and management disinterest or outright opposition in many areas. Some administration officials were suspicious of the idea from the outset, believing that the union intended to worm its way into "co-management" status through JCs. Marie Manna, who played a big role in negotiating the JC provision in 1989, said the management bargainers "had this idea that we wanted to delve into issues that had nothing to do with us. We did our best to explain we were not talking about curriculum and tenure, but they weren't sure what we were trying to do and didn't trust us. And they were especially flipped out at the idea of a body that would somehow override the dean."

For this reason, the union agreed that a Joint Council could only make recommendations to a chief administrative officer or dean of a school, who would have final say. In a few cases, councils devoted many hours of study to an issue only to have their proposals rejected. Many other unions and corporations had discovered that allowing one or two management officials the power to veto proposals arising from a joint process is a mistake. Obviously, some proposals will be too costly or time-consuming, or ill-directed for other reasons, to carry out. But such a decision is accepted more readily by the workers and managers involved if it is made, say, by a joint steering committee overseeing the entire process.

Some of the problems might have been avoided if the two sides had conducted a joint study of "best practice" examples in U.S. corporations. They didn't do this when negotiating the provision in 1989, partly for lack of time but also for another reason. The women of HUCTW rely on intuition to an extraordinary degree in running their affairs, having learned from experience that trying to duplicate other models of behavior—and most existing ones are built on male values—will lead to failure. The insistence on home grown solutions, however, can lead to self-limiting parochialism. Harvard administrators, meanwhile, seem to have little knowledge of advanced practices in the fields of labor relations and human resources and little disposed to seek it out, even at their own Harvard Business School.

There were plenty of limits on what Joint Councils could do. Quite sensibly, they were prohibited from taking any action that would contravene the union contract. The union recognized it was not competent to be involved in decisions on tenure and curriculum. In practice, the councils never approached a wide range of matters such as financing of university activities, capital spending, tuition, and other major categories of decision making. The Joint Council concept thus had weaknesses from the union point of view, but it was a major achievement in a first contract. And, as Rondeau said in 1994, "This is not the revolution." But participation had changed the lives of many workers.

The psychological rewards for workers who take on more active roles in a union and joint activities can be very large. They become more self-confident and self-possessed. They learn new skills like problem-solving and public speaking that can be used in other parts of their lives. Hundreds of Harvard workers had experiences somewhat like Susan Leavitt. A library assistant, she joined the union effort in 1988. She got involved in contract negotiations, later was elected to a Joint Council, and still later to the executive board. "The union really helped to develop me as a person," she said. "I had to force myself out of being a shy person to being an initiator and talking to all kinds of people. I'm knocking on doors I'd never knocked on previously."

During the first three years under union contract, hundreds of workers like Leavitt began blossoming into leaders in all areas of the university. Workers in each unit had to take the initiative (for the most part, managers did not) in setting up Joint Councils. For the first time they had a source of power enabling them to suggest, propose, even demand changes in the organization of jobs and alignment of duties and to create labor–management groups that could get things done. Some workers took naturally to this effort. One was Jennie Rathbun, a specialist in rare book collections at Harvard's Houghton Library. "I know my job better than my supervisor does, and I want to have a voice in how the work is designed," she said in 1992. "I should be treated as an expert in my work, not as a slack-jawed incompetent who needs heavy supervision." She participated in a Joint Council, was elected to the union executive board, and later became secretary of the local.

Some workers had exceptionally good experiences. "We have wonderful managers on our Joint Council," said Carrie Normand, who worked in the Office of Continuing Education in 1992. "They are high enough to make decisions, and they don't feel like we're seizing power. The areas they manage are more productive and have fewer problems because of the JC. Ours has gone phenomenally well."

The union, perhaps overconfidently, began referring to the budding union–management relationship as "jointness," a term that originated in cooperative efforts between the UAW and General Motors in the 1980s. A few influential Harvard administrators were as enthusiastic as the union. One was the director of labor relations, Vivienne Rubeski, who had undergone a complete change of mind about the union. As a personnel officer in the Medical Area, she had actively opposed the union since it first reared its head in 1974. "I fought the union for fifteen years in every position I had," she said in early 1992. "When they got in, I thought things would be very difficult. But it turned out to be great. The union has had a profound impact on the way in which we solve employee problems. I believe in problem-solving and so does Kris. She believes in 'jointness,' and I believe in 'participation.' But if I ever talked about 'joint management,' the deans would have my head."

It was an exhilarating time for Rondeau. She began to see more clearly why she and her friends had spent so many years knocking on Harvard's door. Now that they had a foot inside, she saw opening before them the possibility of a community of workers being involved in redesigning their workplace, and work life. "We saw early on that the idea of participation was exciting to workers," she said. "Getting management involved could be frustrating, but generally the members were having a good experience."

Other problems would emerge, but HUCTW had made a good beginning in the first three years. It was a very unusual brand of unionism, particularly when viewed from the inside.

Some men attribute a sort of mystical sexual power to groups of women who flourish where men fail, in a man's world. The women's success could not be because they are smart and strong, since men are by nature smarter and stronger. It must have to do, therefore, with a mysterious bonding that converts individually weak females into a group with a potent punch, rather like fruit macerating in a dark cask. This is the psychological viewpoint from which some men sized up Rondeau and her organizers as they began attracting attention in the mid-eighties. She remembered the male organizers of one union who scornfully referred to the Harvard women as "lesbo-cunts." A few years later, she heard men use the word "cult" in describing her staff and other tightly knit and successful groups of female organizers. "I realized it was about being happy," she said. "You don't run into many people in the labor movement who are excited about what they're doing. I recently met some nurses in Kentucky who were like that, excited about organizing. And I heard a union guy saying, 'Oh, yeah, they're a cult, they're always smiling.'"

The manner in which the Harvard union runs its affairs undoubtedly has something to do with a "female way" of thinking and doing. That some men are befuddled by this is normal in a society organized around the male view of social reality. But there is nothing darkly sinister about it or any suggestion of same-sex magical rites being performed. The difference is most apparent in the way the group conducts meetings. Meetings are always going on, meetings of the staff, executive board, Joint Councils, and of many special committees dealing with specific subjects. The process of decision making appears to be very loose and indefinite, but actually there is a structure, held together by the one rigid rule the group has: everyone must treat everyone else with kindness and respect.

What a male outsider notices first is that there is no competing for attention, no interrupting or cutting in, certainly no shouting. The designated leader—usually Jaeger, Williams, or Rondeau—calls on people in turn as they raise their hands. A visitor may think he has wandered into a children's classroom but soon notices that this method of running a meeting produces more opinions more efficiently than the typical male free-for-all where the loudest voices and most forceful personalities prevail. Everyone has a say. There are no sharp disputes that divide people into combative subgroups. When one member disagrees with another, she doesn't challenge the other's logic in disdainful tones. Differences are expressed in subtle ways. An entire meeting represents a sort of color wheel with one hue shading gently into another. Layer upon layer of opinion and fact is laid down, forming a thick carpet that floats the leaders toward a decision. The decision-making moment is not sharply defined. Votes are never taken, but the ultimate policy decision may differ significantly from the original proposition.

On major issues involving two or more sharply differing alternatives for action, one leader may have to draw all strands of thought into a final decision. Depending on the issue, this could be Rondeau, Jaeger, or Williams. Staff and executive board members defer to Rondeau but not in a fawning way or as children before a matriarch. Senior members in particular have no qualms about dissenting from her views, often in private conversations, sometimes in meetings.

The kindness-and-respect rule doesn't mean that a naive faith in the goodness of humanity prevails at all times. The union has to deal with many unfriendly people pursuing policies that can hurt workers in various ways. Anger about officialdom often erupts at union staff meetings. The escape valve is humor, usually expressed in mimicry and ridicule. Upper-level Harvard administrators bear the brunt of the joke, while department-level managers and supervisors are more likely to be complimented for cooperative efforts. There is a fair amount of speculating about the strategy and motives of university officials, a natural outcome of the fact that they rarely condescend to talk to union leaders, thus inviting speculation. Rondeau herself, though an excellent tactician and strategist who rarely makes a wrong move in public, now and then lashes out in closed meetings at perceived enemies. This arises from a natural frankness along with an embattled defensiveness; she sometimes sees others conspiring against her and the union.

In the 1990s, a combined staff and executive board generally totaled about forty people with a strong male minority of nine or ten (30 percent). The men, however, fully accept the leadership of women. They acknowledge, as Rondeau occasionally puts it, that HUCTW exemplifies a "feminine model of trade unionism." She is wary of this description, not wanting to imply that she is a feminist missionary bent on remaking other unions in HUCTW's image, or that the Harvard union is "soft" in the sense of caving in to the employer. "We do win battles and make progress," she adds, "and we believe that our view of unionism came directly from our experience as women organizing women workers."

This model, Bill Jaeger said, "definitely celebrates women's ways of learning and leading, but does that without malice toward men." Nor are men subjected to feminist brainwashing or required to live up to a feminist ideal. Said Bob Rush, a staff organizer since 1987: "I don't feel there's a tape measure which I'm expected to measure up to. There is a feminist component, but the expression is personal and individual."

Both men and women perceived one real difference between male and female behavior in the union—one that has been found in other unions and organizations with mixed membership. Men tended to be more aggressive in large meetings and to speak with more self-confidence. Their interest in being active, however, tended to ebb rather quickly while committed women were more likely to follow through. Rondeau noticed during the organizing campaign that "men expected us to go away and the women didn't."

Over the years, Rondeau has hired a few gays of both sexes as organizers, and some leading activists are openly gay. This reflects to some degree the sexual orientation of the Harvard work force. In 1993, HUCTW played a key role in the university's adoption of a Domestic Partners provision as a health insurance benefit. It extends coverage to the live-in partners of lesbian and homosexual employees. But whatever their private thoughts about feminism and sex, union staff and executive board members do not impose on their colleagues. Sexual politics is not apparent.

HUCTW staff members practice an unorthodox unionism. Having worked with other union groups, they see their system as better than conventional brands. And it is in many respects, especially for women and men workers in a university and, by extension, in many other occupations. But the Harvard women are neither cultists nor elitists. They feel themselves to be part of the labor movement and believe in acting in concert with other unions. As early as 1989, Rondeau's staff began helping AFSCME organizers in other drives, eventually traveling to Connecticut, Maine, Minnesota, Illinois, and California.

At Harvard, meanwhile, HUCTW took the lead in forming a Coalition of Harvard Unions with six other organizations that represent mostly blue-collar employees such as police and building trades workers. The most visible collaboration has involved a united protest against the university's practice of hiring nonunion contractors to perform maintenance work. Although the issue was peripheral to the concerns of women office workers, the clerical union has spoken out strongly in support of construction unions. "Kris has figured out how to fuse a feminine perspective with a class perspective," said Mark Erlich, business manager of Carpenters Local 40. "'Class' is a dirty word in Cambridge, but Kris and her people have invigorated the notion of class from the other side."

The question of social class aside, one particular group within the Harvard administration did not look as admiringly on Rondeau as did Erlich. By late 1991, this cluster of people, consisting of high-level administrators and several academic deans and personnel officers, was acting to slow down the infiltration of union-led participation by workers in university affairs. The effects were felt first on the University Joint Council (UJC). This essentially was a steering committee formed to guide, coordinate, and smooth the way for participation at the local level. Chaired by Rondeau and John Dunlop, the UJC had other leaders from the union and administration, including a university vice-president, Sally Zeckhauser.

The council had made progress since 1989, despite a formidable problem posed by Harvard's decentralized structure. The central administration had no authority over the academic deans of the eleven professional and graduate schools. When a corporation chief executive orders division managers to adopt a participative style, they usually comply to avoid being fired. Harvard was not a corporation. As Dunlop once put it, "Nobody tells a Harvard dean what to do."

The spread of participation was uneven to begin with. Many department-level administrative chiefs, it turned out, were eager to practice participative management and voluntarily got involved in Joint Councils. But many others either rejected the idea or held back, fearful of lending themselves to an insidious "co-management" scheme. This is where, for Rondeau, the value of having a partner like Dunlop became apparent. Operating with the specific approval of Derek Bok, Dunlop pushed administrators to embrace the spirit of the labor agreement.

Then came the summer of 1991. Rondeau was away much of the time, organizing at other universities. But what happened at Harvard was not something she could have changed in any case.

In June 1991, Neil Rudenstine was sworn in as the twenty-sixth president of Harvard University, succeeding the retiring Derek Bok. Shortly before he stepped down, Bok suggested to Dunlop that the new president probably would want to make his own appointment to head the University Joint Council. Dunlop resigned, though with some reluctance. The work of the UJC had just begun, and he would have preferred to see the job through. Neither Dunlop nor Bok would talk publicly about the resignation, except to suggest that any new administration wants to develop its own leaders. But other people close to the situation said it was more a case of a group of Harvard managers who wanted to rid themselves of Dunlop.

Irritated about the outcome of the 1989 negotiations, a number of deans and high-level administrators faulted Dunlop for the way he conducted the talks, and Bok for supporting him. "John was perceived as being extremely close to Derek, and the deans might have questioned whether Derek was being as attentive to them as to Dunlop," said a former faculty colleague. Vice-President Sally Zeckhauser, who replaced Dunlop as UJC co-chair, said that several deans specifically complained about Dunlop's lack of consultation with them. "Dunlop hadn't the buy-in of all the deans on a number of things he negotiated," she said in 1993. "They hadn't been asked, they had been told, and they didn't have a proprietary sense."

On the other hand, Vivienne Rubeski, who was deeply involved in the 1989 talks, said, "Dunlop did a fantastic job. The people who criticize him don't have a leg to stand on." Jim Healy also thought that Dunlop stood wrongly condemned. Each school had had top-level representatives in bargaining who should have been reporting to their deans, he said. Bok pointed out that the deans approved the pact in 1989. Their later complaints, he said in 1993, amounted to "grumbling after the fact."

Rightly or wrongly, Dunlop was in a sense deposed by his colleagues. During the two years of the Bok-Dunlop era, Harvard had pursued a strong central labor policy in relations with HUCTW. But the policy disappeared with the men who conceived it, and the centrality of union relations eroded. Rudenstine, a former provost of Princeton University and scholar of Renaissance languages, was not a man for carrying out unpopular management policies. Deans of the larger schools began setting up separate offices to run their own human resources policies. What was left of the "center" in the Rudenstine administration promulgated a policy not of working with the union but of keeping it in its place.

This was demonstrated repeatedly by Harvard's behavior in the basic area of communicating with the union. In the first five years of Rudenstine's tenure, Rondeau was "allowed" only one brief meeting with the president. It was not as if union relations should rank among his top concerns, such as Harvard's relations with the outside world or the maintenance of academic standards, or perhaps even fund-raising. But an occasional meeting with the person who negotiated for a third of Harvard's employees—and who had demonstrated peaceful intentions—could not be considered knuckling under to a union. Even the chairman of General Motors talks to the president of the United Auto Workers, and GM division managers meet with their UAW counterparts. At Harvard, the rough equivalent of these managers are the academic deans of professional schools. With two or three early exceptions, they also refused audiences to HUCTW leaders. The most absurd example involved a new director of human resources whose jurisdiction is dominated by labor relations, and yet she declined to meet with the union for more than a year following her appointment in 1994.

Harvard's deportment in this respect was reminiscent of corporate behavior during the "union containment" period of labor relations in the 1940s and 1950s. Afraid to grant unions any influence beyond the collective bargaining functions specified by law, U.S. corporate executives rejected the very notion that workers and their unions could be a source of valuable ideas. To refer to a union leader by name or allow him to tramp through executive suites was to confer status and dignity on the "represented group" and foment dangerous egalitarian ideas in the multitude of wage earners. Forty years later, with competitors everywhere breathing down their necks, the corporations were demanding a change in labor law to allow them to form committees of workers (selected by management, of course) who would advise the boss, among other things, on how to produce better products. In the 1990s, Harvard deans had yet to catch up with this development. To talk with the union meant to recognize that it could play a role in improving the institution. The deans were eminent, accomplished men who led what were by current standards "great" schools of medicine, law, sciences, and the humanities. But participitative management was not an element in the deanship ethos.

To the degree that Harvard had a labor policy after 1991 it was in the hands of administrators, as indeed was management of the university. This state of affairs, not apparent to outsiders, had been true for some years. Starting in the early 1970s, the faculty relinquished administrative control to a rapidly growing corps of nonteaching administrators. It is hard to fault professors for wanting to concentrate on research and teaching. Devoting time to administrative duties is not as satisfying and does little to advance professorial careers. As a result of this trend, however, faculty interest and expertise in matters such as labor relations, benefits planning, and a whole gamut of issues that come under the heading of organizational behavior was all but lost to the university. Some faculty members, like Dunlop, deplored the administrators' assumption of control. "Increasingly, this growing bureaucracy would have us believe that they run the university," he said in 1996. "The faculty has always felt in the final analysis it does. And if it comes to a contest on that issue, there is no doubt that the faculty will knock their brains out." This, too, would come to pass but not in a way that would advance union relations.

With Dunlop out of the picture, the University Joint Council began to function less like a university-wide steering group than just another committee. The lesson of fifteen years of restructuring labor–management relationships in the United States is that many midlevel managers will not change management style and many workers will resist changes in their jobs without forceful direction from the top. But no one at a high level in the Harvard administration could fill Dunlop's shoes. When he left, Rondeau had no partner to dance with, and the music of participation began to sound tinny and thin.

The first union contract had a three-year term and was scheduled to expire on June 30, 1992. The only member of the management team with extensive bargaining experience, Vivienne Rubeski, fell ill with cancer in early 1992 and died in June. Sally Zeckhauser, the chief management negotiator, approached her new role with apparent good will toward the union. But she had many other duties as administrative vice-president, did not know much about labor relations to begin with, and had no aptitude for one-on-one deal-making that bargaining usually involves. The entire process became distasteful to her. A group of powerful deans insisted on exercising more control over negotiations. This was quite proper, in Zeckhauser's view, but getting them together for strategy sessions was a daunting logistical exercise. The economic environment also had changed. Harvard faced a decline in revenues from several sources and was determined to hold down employment costs.

These factors stymied bargaining. The two sides extended the contract and finally reached agreement, with the help of two mediators, in January 1993. From the union point of view, it was a good settlement, but the delay had imposed a six-month period of uncertainty on Harvard employees. Although both sides contributed to the delay, it seemed a particularly insensitive way for an employer to manage a relationship with a union that showed no evidence of hostility. "There was an attitude of, 'Let's get Kris Rondeau in line.'" Jim Healy said. "This came from an erroneous interpretation that Kris led John Dunlop around by the nose."

After the 1993 settlement, the pace of joint activities slowed even more. Union leaders had hoped to expand the variety and scope of these activities so that a majority of workers (or all who so desired) could participate in something more meaningful than a 9 to 5 job. But fewer than 300 were involved in labor–management committees and Joint Councils, and many of the latter had become moribund. Yet a large and fertile area for worker participation remained unexplored. The idea of reorganizing office tasks and work flow in order to improve the quality of services was seeping in from private industry, where the trend had been underway for several years. One way of doing this was to redeploy employees into teams which would perform a variety of tasks with little supervision. Harvard was overripe for this kind of reorganization, with more than 4,000 non-union employees in supervisory and administrative staff jobs, a larger segment even than the unionized group. The union saw the possibility of involving large numbers of workers in joint task forces which would redesign the workplace. This had been done successfully in dozens of corporations like Ford, GM, and Corning, where unions became intimately involved in the "change process." At decentralized Harvard, reorganization planning took place at the department level, wherever managers were so inclined, and only rarely involved the workers whose jobs would be affected.

This reorganization was proceeding on a spotty basis, and the union offered to help extend the process. The University Joint Council could be a vehicle for coordinating projects and gathering information about the many initiatives already underway. The union proposed, pleaded, cajoled, and demanded more involvement—but to no avail. The Rudenstine administration was not interested in the kind of partnership that had flourished in the Bok–Dunlop era. Frustrated by management indifference and even hostility, union leaders also made mistakes. During a period in 1995, they were putting out fires elsewhere and not preparing themselves well for UJC meetings. The council declined in importance and eventually stopped meeting.

In late 1993, Harvard made a constructive move in hiring an experienced management negotiator, Timothy Manning, formerly with Raytheon Company, to fill the vacant post of labor relations director. Manning's first three years at Harvard were taken up in bargaining and administering contracts and learning how to deal with the university's numerous management structures. He had little time to work with HUCTW in spreading joint activities, as he eventually hoped to do. His superiors in upper management, meanwhile, gave no sign of supporting this approach. Rondeau was convinced that some of these people wanted to break the union. This may or may not have been true, but the overall labor policy was hostile to cooperative efforts. The question was, why? The union must have transgressed some bounds in order to provoke this reaction. But what bounds? What had the union done wrong?

There are two classic ways in which a union is considered capable of using power wrongly to hurt an employer. One is enforcing a "web of rules" approach that impedes managerial "flexibility," and a second is making "extortionate" wage demands backed up by the threat of a debilitating strike. As to the first possibility, since the contract had no rules, management was not constrained except by moral and ethical considerations. As to the second, by 1996 the union had negotiated with Harvard on three separate occasions, in 1989, 1992–93, and 1995. In none of these rounds did HUCTW even take a strike vote of its members, much less threaten to walk out.

If the union wasn't guilty of these offenses, why did Harvard continue throwing roadblocks in the path of union-led participation? The effect of the policy was to punish employees who wanted to contribute more to their jobs. The union already had improved the institution in many ways. One example was turnover. Continual training of new employees to replace those departing, along with adding each new worker to benefit rolls, can add up to very large costs. In 1996, HUCTW calculated that Harvard's turnover had been reduced from the 30 percent a year in 1988 to about 20 percent. A major incentive for people to stay, the union believed, was a salary-and-benefits program that allowed workers to make a career of what used to be seen as a temporary job. In addition, many joint union–management projects had improved the workplace atmosphere and given some workers a sense of participation. Why would a management not want more of this?

Answers to these questions could not be obtained from Harvard management. Following the 1992–93 bargaining round, the administration rejected requests for interviews with top-level officials. But their attitude about the union may be reflected in remarks by the former Harvard personnel official, Ed Powers. While participation is a good idea, he said, the involvement of a union only mucks it up. "The union brought in a new political structure and interposed it between the employee and the employer," Powers said. "It's just too much discussion, too much time spent talking. Management has to talk forever unless the union says 'yes.'"

The union's attempts to gain a more active role were not seen as good for the university. One reason could be that management did not think that female clerical workers would have much to contribute. While most managers probably would insist on the indispensability of their secretaries, they may privately share Ed Powers's view. "Harvard's primary mission is research and teaching," Powers said. "I think the reality is that the clericals were not and never will be an integral part of the teaching and research function."

According to Powers, support staff are not viewed by many faculty members as being important to their work as scholars and teachers. Professorial indifference probably would be a barrier to the spread of worker participation in any large university, but this is especially true at Harvard. Mark H. Moore, a professor at the Kennedy School, formulated the problem in the following terms. "The way you get to be a professor at Harvard is to have successfully competed in a very demanding national race for individual distinction. You compete and succeed as an individual. In the eyes of many faculty members, the only corporate purpose of a university is to establish an environment in which an elite group of individual scholars can do their work." But this view clashes with the desire of workers to collaborate with faculty in improving the quality of education. "The union challenges the university to become an organization instead of a band of individuals," Moore said. "I think that's an accurate challenge. I need all the help I can get to be a first-rate scholar and teacher. The university should be an organization whose major purpose is to give high quality education to students rather than to enable faculty members to do research that earns them distinguished national reputations."

Moore and like-minded faculty members were in the minority during HUCTW's first years. If a pro-collaboration attitude is to permeate the faculty and senior management, the process will take some years. But hundreds of administrators in middle-management positions willingly collaborated with the union from the beginning. One is Joel Monell, administrative dean of the School of Education, who served on a Joint Council. "I never saw the union concept of jointness as being radical," he said in 1993. "I think a lot of good ideas come from people who are most affected by decisions. Overall, collaboration has been good for the School of Education and good for the university, though not everybody would agree with me on that."

Among those who would not agree were many senior administrators and deans of the graduate and professional schools. In 1996, after seven years of mediating Harvard–HUCTW relations, Jim Healy drew this conclusion: "I don't think they [Harvard management] have enough awareness of what goes on in the world to realize what an extraordinary value they have in a relationship like this. Many in management regard the union as a nuisance. They proceed on the assumption that it's not really strong. I have heard some say that the union wouldn't dare call a strike because they just wouldn't get the support."

The Harvard union, it is true, has gone out of its way to avoid striking. Masculine logic would attribute this behavior to organizational weakness. In traditional unions led by men, the test of the organization's spirit and solidarity—indeed, of its will to exist—is the ability to strike on demand. The members must be lined up in the trenches and prepared to go over the top when the whistle sounds. In some situations, the employer leaves no alternative. But going on strike, or "taking a strike" in management's case, all too often is an automatic response to a disagreement at the bargaining table, especially where there is a history of bitter relations, as at Yale, and reservoirs of pent-up anger from which both sides draw for militancy.

HUCTW has tried to steer around this rock-strewn course, but more out of strength than weakness. Historic and demographic patterns also have exerted a tidal pull away from the strike. The Harvard union did not bring employees together in the first place out of hatred for the university. The continually changing work force always has a large component of new, young, mostly college-educated women and men who know nothing of unionism or the history of the organizing struggle. To "whip up" strike sentiment, as the saying used to go, would take months of pre-bargaining publicity efforts. Members would begin to think of unionism as consisting mainly of preparation for a triennial contract battle. Having to walk around with a fist always raised was not Rondeau's idea of what life in a union should be. Yet the union had to be able to assert its members' economic interests when they diverged from those of the university.

Could the union, without striking or threatening to strike, make its presence felt—that is, inflict just enough pain to force a compromise in its favor? This question has arisen on two separate occasions. The first occurred during the six-month contract extension period in 1992. HUCTW leaders never seriously considered walking out. Rather, the union staged a series of "events." These included noontime rallies in Harvard Yard with trademark balloons, marches through Cambridge, demonstrations at Mass Hall, frequent information meetings for members, and Hollywood-like bus tours of the deans' homes (to contrast the splendor of their personal lives with that of ordinary workers). Some events, in HUCTW fashion, were hilarious. There was the time in 1992, with bargaining in a lull, that the union formed a welcoming committee for Neil Rudenstine and his wife when they returned from a trip abroad. About three dozen union members met them at Logan Airport, playing "Hail to the Chief" on kazoos. The message was, "Welcome home, and please negotiate!"

Whether the events forced management to bargain is uncertain. But they created a sense of momentum. Toward the end of that six-month period, an activist named Emily Scudder, a library assistant in the Graduate School of Design, said: "I think it's pretty impressive that we can keep this up for six months beyond the deadline, all the events, rallies, vigils. The relentlessness of it! I don't think we ever crossed the boundary into being mean-spirited. I think that's why so many support the union. They don't hate Harvard and don't want to be part of a union that hates Harvard." Workers did not lose pay and classes were not disrupted by a work stoppage. The long period of uncertainty probably exacted a psychological toll of some dimension, but the union emerged stronger than before with major advances on economic and other issues. All things considered, the rejection of strike probably demonstrated strength, a feminine kind of strength, rather than weakness as defined by men.

The second occasion posed a more serious challenge to the union. This episode started when a task force appointed by Rudenstine discovered a $52 million deficit in Harvard's employee benefit plans. The group redesigned the health and retirement systems, proposing large increases in employee contributions for health insurance. No one quarreled with the need to revamp the benefit plans, only the means chosen. The task force was made up entirely of administrators; there were no representatives from faculty, unions, or nonunion employees. This provoked an extraordinary faculty revolt against Rudenstine in the fall of 1994. Angered by proposed changes in a pension plan without faculty involvement, professors embarrassed Rudenstine in public debates and forced the administration to set up another committee which eventually (in 1996) partially rescinded the original pension plan changes. As Dunlop said, the faculty "knocked their [administrators'] brains out."

HUCTW agreed that employees had to take on a greater share of health care costs but contended that a task force composed of "top administrators earning over $100,000 . . . could not know enough about our lives, families and needs to shape a fair and compassionate benefits package." The new payment schedule would load a disproportionate burden on low-income and part-time workers, the union said. Lacking the influence of the faculty, HUCTW got nowhere with its complaint.

In 1995 the university began implementing the new health care provisions for nonunion employees and faculty. Benefit changes by law had to be negotiated with union-represented workers, and Harvard induced its smaller unions to accept the entire package in a series of negotiations. By the time bargaining started with HUCTW in the summer, the administration had extended the new plans to all other employees. Harvard thus backed the clerical union into a corner, apparently reasoning that its members could not resist what other employees had been forced to accept.

The administration wanted to bring all employees under a single health care system. Uniformity was a sensible and fair goal, but the strategy for achieving it was needlessly antagonistic. HUCTW, after all, had proved its ability to address difficult issues through joint problem solving. University officials may have had valid reasons for not wanting to engage all employee groups in a time-consuming redesign process. But they could have chosen the next best alternative. After each round of previous negotiations, benefit improvements won by HUCTW were extended to other employees. Following this precedent, the university could have submitted the health care package first to its largest union. If the new provisions were in fact unfair to low-income workers, as the union contended, Harvard could have amended the plan at the beginning of the process. It became clear, however, that the administration intended to take that pattern-setting control away from HUCTW without amending anything. The idea was to meet the legal requirement to negotiate without actually negotiating.

Rondeau and her negotiators resented the all-or-nothing approach. They wanted to modify two items, the most important of which involved part-time workers. For many years Harvard had provided the same medical benefits to part-time and full-time workers. The new health care plan, however, required part-timers who worked less than 28 hours a week to double their health insurance premiums, from 15 to 30 percent. About 500 workers, or 17 percent of union members, fell into this category. An annual premium for a part-timer with family medical coverage would rise from $780 to $1,536, or about 10 percent of the average $15,000 part-time salary. The majority of these people were not working merely to earn pocket money but depended on the job and its benefits. A union survey showed that 25 percent of part-time members wanted, but couldn't get, a full-time Harvard job. Forty percent were in families with less than $20,000 income.

As the contract deadline approached in July 1995, bargaining was stalemated. Harvard refused to modify its plan or consider other ways of cutting health care costs, and the union just as adamantly insisted on amending the plan. To avoid an impasse, Harvard's chief negotiator, Tim Manning, and Jim Healy, who was mediating the dispute, devised a compromise. Harvard's plan would be incorporated in a new agreement with the understanding that it could be modified before various provisions became effective in 1996 and 1997. A Joint Benefits Committee would be created to explore and recommend possible changes. It would have three Harvard administrators (including the directors of labor relations and human resources), two faculty members, and five union representatives.

Harvard, however, would not be formally bound to accept committee recommendations. The union would have to sign a labor agreement containing the new health benefits plan and rely on spoken assurances by Tim Manning that the plan might later be amended (though he could not guarantee that it would be). HUCTW leaders trusted Manning and believed that his superiors were obligated to live up to his word. The committee approach seemed promising for two other reasons. First, the two faculty members, whose influence would be decisive, were approved in advance by the union and were thought to be eminently fair. The union was confident that a neutral study would determine that the benefits plan must be made less onerous for low-income workers. And second, Jim Healy promised to act as the "conscience" of the committee.

Nonetheless, it was a risky approach. The union's eleven-member bargaining team considered the options at some length over several days and for the first time seriously talked of striking. There was a general feeling of wanting to lash out at the administration. Donene Williams recalled, "I would have loved to have gone on strike, and screw 'em [Harvard]. But that was fantasy, a visceral reaction. I don't think our members were ready for that." They were not ready, that is, because union leaders hadn't made provocative speeches or even posed the strike question in a vote. Through information meetings, workers knew of the bargaining stalemate. But they appeared willing to put up with some concessions and to trust their negotiators to find a way to protect low-income workers.

Among the leaders, Bill Jaeger had the most difficulty accepting what he called the "soft" committee approach rather than holding Harvard to a contractual pledge. Men seem to need a leakproof conclusion more than women. "It was really hard for me," Jaeger later acknowledged. "What Harvard attempted to do was offensive and really maddening." Kris Rondeau also was angry. She had no doubt that the union could mount an effective strike. But a temporary display of muscle was less important to her than the future of unionism at Harvard. She believed that walking off the job over an issue that could be settled in committee would be a step backward in the journey toward a collaborative relationship.

The bargaining team, as was its custom, did not vote on which course to take. The members lined up behind Rondeau, ready to follow her down either path—and she took the peaceful one. In the end, as Jaeger put it, the union leaders were guided by "a basic commitment, deeply felt by the members of this local union, that if there is an opportunity for peaceful resolution of a problem we will take it." The compromise on health care was made palatable in part by important advances in other areas, including an expanded child care program, strong salary increases, guidelines for flexible hours, and additional time off for Christmas.

HUCTW ratified and signed the contract in September 1995. The Joint Benefits Committee met frequently over the next year. As the union anticipated, a majority of JBC members favored modifying some of the health care plan's harsher provisions. Harvard officials more or less ignored committee recommendations for several months but finally agreed in August 1996 to grant relief to low-income workers in one area involving co-payment fees for doctor's visits. But the pivotal part-time issue remained unresolved.

In the fall of 1996, the JBC informally proposed a number of ways to modify the part-time premium increase before it became effective on January 1, 1997. Since Harvard's plan was estimated to save about $200,000 a year, the union offered to save an equivalent amount by revising a short-term disability benefit or even by raising the premium $5 a month for all union members. The administration was not moved.

The primary decision for Harvard was in the hands of the provost, Albert Carnesale, a former dean of the Kennedy School who had been assuming more and more administrative power since Rudenstine's fight with the faculty. Like other Harvard officials who became intimately involved in labor policy decisions, Carnesale never talked directly with union leaders and never requested a meeting. (Is it out of fear that male officials, in particular, refuse to expose themselves to the union, as if afraid they might succumb to female "charms" or might meet people who do not fit their stereotype of union leaders?) Over a period of several months, Carnesale refused to approve any of several informal proposals made by the JBC.

HUCTW had given up the right to strike when it signed the contract. But it was not without weapons. Hoping to goad Carnesale or even Rudenstine to action, the union set up picket lines at Mass Hall. Every weekday for nearly three months, a half-dozen to a dozen members, sometimes dressed in lugubrious costumes, marched up and down, carrying signs and chanting. As always, the demonstrations were peaceful, if harassing in a comic manner.

The standoff continued through December and into January 1997, when Harvard finally agreed to cancel the premium increase for part-timers in 1997 and explore ways to avoid it in 1998. The two sides also agreed to add an extra year (with wage increases) to the current contract to provide additional time for peacemaking after the benefits controversy. But the breakthrough came only after an exhausting year-long battle to make Harvard keep its word about a relatively simple committee procedure.

In the end, the union attained most of its goals without going on strike. It had never intended to avoid making any concessions, and, in fact, HUCTW members agreed to pay somewhat more to help Harvard cope with the benefits deficit. But the union protected its most vulnerable members from what would have amounted to a pay cut of up to 10 percent. Another union might have proceeded in a different way, but the peaceful route led the Harvard union where it wanted to go. In the short run, the members had to endure disappointment, uncertainty, and some disillusionment while the administrators fumed and fussed, exhausting their antagonism in shadow boxing with an imaginary enemy.

In the world of work, there is no more precious thing than a collaborative effort in which groups of people overcome adversarial instincts in order to work together. When Derek Bok in 1988 finally agreed to bargain with the Harvard Union of Clerical and Technical Workers, he intended to do much more than set down rules to govern a bureaucratic relationship. He intended, he later said, "to forge some kind of new relationship . . . to try to do something that will be as creative in this area [labor relations] as Harvard tries to be in all it does."

By the beginning of 1997, much of the creativity had been throttled and the "new relationship" that Bok envisioned existed in outline only. Lacking a continuing vision and a guiding intelligence, the many-headed management of Harvard had reduced the relationship to a fragile thing gasping for air. This deterioration was reflected in the written labor agreement. Once a thin document containing a philosophy of participation and a few general principles, it had grown thicker with Latinate legal terms. Seventeen "memoranda of agreement" covering specific practices were included in the 1995 contract. Lamented Bill Jaeger, "We're drifting toward rule-making."

HUCTW leaders still thought it possible to win a participatory role in the university without compromising their ability to fight for members' economic interest. "We have a vibrant union that can take care of itself," Rondeau concluded, "but we've been unsuccessful in finding partners in a decentralized university. It would be better if people at the top embraced these [participatory] concepts, but whether they do or don't, there is still a lot of room for growth, and we won't stop trying."

In the meantime, the union had accomplished quite a lot. It had created a community where none existed. It had advanced the economic well-being of many thousands of employees, union and nonunion alike. By organizing the creative energies of its members, HUCTW had improved the university in countless, immeasurable ways that administrators and faculty could not have managed alone. What remained to be done was something that women in particular and workers in general had been struggling to achieve for more than a hundred years: gaining influence in decision making. With perseverance, that too might come.

In the early 1990s, Rondeau was confronted with a difficult personal decision. She enjoyed her work at Harvard, trying to reform an institution that resisted reform. She also wanted to put her organizing theories to work on a larger scale, in other institutions and industries that employed women in service occupations. And she wanted to be a mother and have a family life. Could she do all these things and if not, what should be sacrificed?

Her union's well-publicized success in organizing Harvard brought calls from many groups of workers asking for similar help. In 1989, HUCTW reps had helped AFSCME win an election covering 1,200 nurses in Connecticut hospitals. Rondeau and her staff later launched campaigns of their own at Middlebury College in Vermont and Tufts University in Boston at the request of employees in both places. Rondeau assigned Joie Gelband to the Middlebury drive, and Marie Manna returned from a leave of absence to take charge at Tufts. A third effort, at a large medical center operated by the University of Massachusetts in Worcester, Massachusetts, was led by Elisabeth Szanto, who had joined Rondeau's team as a Harvard student in 1987. Started in late 1989, the University of Massachusetts drive was only beginning to near the election stage in 1997. Szanto and her staff had to contend with a cynicism about organized labor dating from 1986 when four unions unsuccessfully waged a bitter, interunion battle at the medical center.

The long, patient, slow effort was the hallmark of a Rondeau campaign that always had drawn criticism from other unionists, and it did again in the 1990s. Scouting reports said that she had an excellent hitting percentage, the best in any league, but it took her too long to get to the plate. By the mid-1990s, as once-mountainous union membership continued to slide out to sea, national union leaders were desperately searching for organizers and organizing techniques that would shore up the hill faster than it could crumble beneath them. Some organizers experimented with the "blitz" method, inundating workers with leaflets and home calls in a brief burst of effort over a couple of weeks. Others sought out "hot spots" of labor unrest and tried to exploit the anger. All the while, union leaders and political allies on Capitol Hill were proclaiming the "right" of workers to organize, as if knowledge of being legally "right" will spur massive self-organization around the country.

Rondeau remembered, years ago, being lectured to by a union leader who thought he knew a shortcut. "He told me, 'All you need to do is find the progressives in the work force, and they will organize the workers for you.' His idea was that progressive ideas would organize workers. But the shortcut doesn't work. Ideas alone will not organize people. Ideas presented in trusting relationships will organize workers. That means one-on-one organizing. The only way to speed it up is to do more of it with more organizers."

In 1991, at the request of Gerry McEntee, Rondeau and several of her staff helped AFSCME organizers in campaigns at two state-related schools, the Universities of Minnesota and Illinois. Using HUCTW's one-on-one organizing techniques and emphasizing participation instead of specific bread-and-butter issues, the union won elections covering clerical workers at both schools. The Minnesota unit had about 3,200 employees and Illinois 2,400. These were important victories, though winning an election in a state university system is easier than at a private university like Harvard. Public sector employers, being under the control of legislative bodies, do not want to offend prounion politicians by mounting strong antiunion campaigns.

After these victories, McEntee offered Rondeau a position as assistant director of organizing with an office in Washington. The invitation had its appealing features, but the call to stardom—if that's what it was—had come too late. She had a satisfying life in Cambridge and wanted to stay there. She turned down the Washington job but offered to fill the same role from her Harvard office.

National union presidents are not used to having people reject promotions to Washington, but McEntee accepted her decision. It was either that, he said in a 1992 interview, or lose her to another union. "She's a woman of immense talent," he said. "She's also a woman with a strong will. I'd prefer to have her work for AFSCME than for another union."

Several factors went into Rondeau's decision. She had been caught up in building the union–management relationship at Harvard, finding that she liked this work very much. "I wanted to do real life projects with workers in the workplace, and I didn't think I'd be good at the 'up-here' projects in Washington," she explained (or rationalized). She didn't want to leave her long-time friends at Harvard, the women with whom she'd spent what seemed like a lifetime creating something good.

There was something even more important. By 1991 Rondeau and Jim Braude had decided to have children and to raise them in Cambridge. Rondeau wanted both a career and a family life. Despite the impression given by some women's magazines, she felt that having the best of both rarely happened in real life. Rising to the top in her career would mean working in a large office in the overheated Washington environment, traveling all the time, leaving children in the care of nannies for days at a time. For all the fights she had had with Harvard, she loved the university atmosphere. Cambridge had been her Camelot from the years when she was growing up in Whitinsville. She despised the elitist pretenses that ruled in some Harvard circles, but she cherished the ideal of leading a disciplined life, giving proportionate time to family, friends, culture, work, and a continuing education by one means or another.

She realized that in turning away from Washington she left herself vulnerable. Her ideas were still controversial in organized labor, particularly her belief in participation, or "labor–management cooperation," as it is referred to in scornful tones. Washington for labor professionals is like it is for political professionals. If you are not there, battling in person for your point of view, you tend to lose the battles. She had had a generally good experience in AFSCME, though there were tensions and personality clashes, as in any large organization. During her years in the UAW, Rondeau had acquired a reputation for being too critical. Her honesty was seen as a refusal to acknowledge "those who came before," as unionists refer to labor leaders and organizations of the past, whether they were good or poor, heroic or merely bureaucratic. She did have enemies who pictured her as holed up at Harvard, ignoring the rest of labor.

Jim Healy, who knew his way around the world of labor, had this to say about Rondeau: "The more orthodox union leaders regard her as a maverick. A lot of it is just plain envy, and I think also fear. I think she scares them with her sincere philosophy and capacity to be unorthodox.

And her tenacity. Staying with it as long as she did at Harvard and building it the way she did, is a quality which I think is quite rare."

That Rondeau did not spurn what is so hopefully called "labor solidarity" could be seen in her work with the Coalition of Harvard Unions and the help she and her staff gave to other AFSCME locals in New England. But she recognized that her personality contributed to the isolation she was beginning to feel by the mid-1990s. She did not extend herself, did not reach out to people in Washington. "It's fifty percent my fault," she said. "Culturally I'm apart from them [union insiders in Washington]. Politically there's a kind of skill I recognize that I don't have."

These concerns grew over the years, but they seemed most unimportant in 1991 when she and her husband decided to have children. Rondeau was now forty years old. She had spent most of her childbearing years in an occupation hostile to family life, working ten to twelve hours a day, six or seven days a week. She and Braude decided to adopt a Chinese baby. The arrangements took many months, and in 1992 they traveled to China and brought home eight-month-old Mimi. Two years later, Rondeau again went to China and returned with another infant daughter, Xia, only three months of age.

Life for the women organizers of Harvard now entered a new, family-oriented phase. Children burst into the magic circle with joyous and almost frightening regularity. In late 1992, the Harvard union moved out of the old office on Winthrop St. and took up new quarters on the second floor of an upscale building on Mass Ave. directly across from Harvard Yard. It had bigger, cleaner offices, conference rooms worthy of the name, and, as a sign of changing times, a nursery with bright-colored toys and a crib. Shortly after Rondeau became a mother, Martha Robb and Marie Manna, each of whom already had sons, adopted babies. Bill Jaeger and his wife had a second child. By 1996, Stephanie Tournas, Joie Gelband, Jeanne Lafferty, Tina Casteris, Bob Mendelson, Lynda Reid, Gloria Buffonge, and Laurie Peterson also had children. On any day, two or three infants were crawling around the office, and staff members took turns cuddling and handling them while mother or father went to a meeting or worked the phones. Rondeau was a mother or older sister to them all, children and adults.

By 1997, Rondeau had been organizing workers for twenty years. What meaning had she drawn from this experience? Her answer came, characteristically, in a stream of thoughts.

"Many workplaces," she said, "are isolating and anti-community, not just antiunion. There is distrust among workers and a cynical attitude about the boss. We don't cultivate many values in the workplace, and the ones we do cultivate are bad for the soul. People really do want to live by simple values, and they want to say 'please' and 'thank you' to each other. They want to help when someone is down. The question is, does the labor movement have the right set of values? If we just superimpose a union on the boss's culture, generally speaking we get a sick union. We have to sweep away some of the boss's values first and bring our better values into the workplace. The strong take care of the weak, we're all in this together, and what makes you stronger makes me stronger too."

The term *organized labor* has a very bad meaning for Americans. Over many decades, opponents have succeeded in convincing much of the nation that the neutral *organized labor* is synonymous with the pejorative *Big Labor*, which refers to huge unions of the long ago, led by dictatorial old men in Washington or loan-sharking racketeers in New York or Chicago who have long since died or gone to jail. If it were possible to wipe away the image to conform with the reality of the nineties, people would see something very different. They would see, for example, the office of the Harvard Union of Clerical and Technical Workers in Cambridge.

The essence of the union had not really changed by 1997. Still it was talk-and-meet, meet-and-talk, "a bunch of women and skinny guys with glasses," as Jaeger put it, making a community of workers. But now there were fresh new voices babbling in the nursery. Every time Rondeau walked into the office and heard these sounds, she felt good about the future. She liked very much what her union had turned out to be. Ordinary women could do extraordinary things. They could create something meaningful for themselves by organizing around their own values. If they stuck together, with stamina and persistence they would prevail.

Bill Jaeger, director of HUCTW, speaking at a union rally in May 1994. Behind him is Randall Kromm, the local's first secretary. Credit: Ellen DeGenova

Clerical and building trades workers parading in Harvard Yard at a May 1994 rally marking formation of the Coalition of Harvard unions. HUCTW set up the coalition to help smaller blue-collar unions in their fight against Harvard's use of nonunion maintenance workers. Credit: Ellen DeGenova

HUCTW's singing group, the Pipets, performing at a rally in May 1994. Formed in the Harvard Medical Area in the early 1980s, the group took its name from a laboratory tube used to siphon and transfer fluids. Credit: Ellen DeGenova

EPILOGUE

The story of the women's union at Harvard will continue to unfold, and like all good stories, develop in unforeseen ways. Some chapters contain threads of other tales that continue to unwind in other directions. Many people and organizations came in contact with the Harvard Union of Clerical and Technical Workers, gleaned, and moved on. But one chapter, involving District 65, the union that first supported the efforts of women to organize at Harvard, has come to a jarring conclusion.

For years District 65 had been operating at a deficit. As membership contracted and dues income declined, the union had to borrow large amounts of money to meet expenses. It fell behind on loan payments and eventually defaulted on a second mortgage taken out on the headquarters building in New York. In 1994, District 65 declared bankruptcy. It had become an empty shell by then. David Livingston had resisted consummating the affiliation agreement with the United Auto Workers. But several local leaders within 65, such as Julie Kushner, who headed units of white-collar workers, broke with Livingston and petitioned the UAW for local-union charters. Eventually, the UAW took over all of 65's members and distributed them into different UAW locals. Livingston's dream of establishing a council of all former 65 locals within the UAW did not come about.

At about the same time, District 65's pension and self-insured health care plans also collapsed, causing financial pain to many workers and retirees. The pioneering District 65 Security Plan, which provided lifetime medical benefits to union members, had outstanding debts exceeding $50 million in June 1993. It was dismantled and creditors paid off at the rate of about fifteen cents on the dollar. About fifteen to twenty thousand workers and retirees were covered when it went under. Local union leaders negotiated new plans for many active workers. Most of about eight thousand retirees were eligible for Medicare, but some active and retired workers became liable for unpaid medical bills.

David Livingston retired in 1993. He died on March 18, 1995 at the age of eighty. His long-time associate, Cleveland Robinson, secretary-treasurer of District 65, also died at the age of eighty, on August 23, 1995.

In 1997, 9to5, The National Association of Working Women was headquartered in Milwaukee and still developing a movement of women office workers. It does not organize unions but often mounts joint projects with District 925 of the Service Employees International Union (SEIU). Karen Nussbaum, a co-founder of 9to5 and former head of District 925, later served as director of the Women's Bureau of the Department of Labor. Ellen Cassedy, another 9to5 founder, became a speech writer for the Environmental Protection Agency in the Clinton administration.

In 1995, the SEIU's president, John Sweeney, leading a revolt of union officers within the AFL-CIO, was elected president of the federation. He appointed Nussbaum to head a newly created Women's Department. Named as chief counsel of the AFL-CIO under Sweeney was John Hiatt, son of Dr. Howard H. Hiatt, who, as dean of the Harvard School of Public Health in the 1970s, refused to be involved in an antiunion campaign. Dr. Hiatt still teaches at Harvard Medical School. His daughter, Deborah, lives with her husband and two children in Waban, Massachusetts.

AFSCME President Gerald McEntee assumed even greater importance in the AFL-CIO because of his leading role in the Sweeney revolt. But AFSCME lost two men who were early supporters of the Harvard Union. Ernie Rewolinski, McEntee's chief of staff, voluntarily retired in an internal union dispute. Rob McGarrah, AFSCME's public policy director, transferred to Sweeney's staff in the AFL-CIO as an expert on health issues.

Leslie Sullivan and John Rees live with their two children in Brookline, a suburb of Boston. Dr. Mary Howell directs an adoption agency in the Boston area.

INDEX

AAUP. *See* American Association of
   University Professors
Affirmative Action Plan, at Harvard,
   37–38
AFL-CIO, 58, 60, 71, 111, 269
AFSCME. *See* American Federation
   of State, County and Municipal
   Employees
Albert, Margie, 58–59, 62, 64–65,
   113–115
American Association of University
   Professors (AAUP), 83, 107–108
American Federation of State, County
   and Municipal Employees (AFSCME)
   affiliation with HUCTW, 4–5,
      187–189, 194
   executive staff of, 269
   and Harvard University, 186–187, 196
   and United Auto Workers, 191
Anderson, Mary, 110
Anthony, Susan B., 110, 164

Ballooning, 1, 6, 8–9, 205, 212–215
Barrett, E.W. (Ted)
   and District 65, 140–141, 145, 161
   and Kris Rondeau, 135, 137–138,
      151, 166–167, 171–172, 177–178
Barry, Leonora, 110, 114
Becker, Craig, 210, 214–215, 221

Bell, Derrick, 203
Bieber, Owen, 159, 191
Bok, Derek, *234*
   antiunion campaign of, 216–217
   biography of, 94–95
   decision to recognize union, 223–224
   and Doug Fraser, 158–159
   on ethics of a university, 203
   during first union attempt, 103
   meeting with Rondeau, 222–223
   relationship with HUCTW, 224–231,
      260
   retirement of, 231, 248–249
   during second union attempt,
      123–124
   on unionization, 8–9, 204
Bok, Sissela, 95
Bonavita, Joseph, 188, 209, 211
Boston
   employment opportunities in, 26
   unions in, 56–57
Boston Globe, 47, 132, 160, 216
Boston Labor Guild, 57
Boston University, unionization at,
   105–108
Boston Women's Health Book Collective
   Inc., 33
Braude, James A., *232*
   and Kris Rondeau, 5, 142–146, 170,
      263–264

Braude, James A.—*continued*
    on Rondeau/UAW split, 178
    during third union attempt, 6, 12, 15,
        180, 193–194, 209–210, 221
"Bread and Roses," 60
Brennan, Richard, 184
Brickman, Edie, 43, 72, 74, 90, 93
Briefing Book, 193, 196
Broken Promise (Gross), 139
Bronfenbrenner, Kate, 157
Buffonge, Gloria, *234, 264*

Cambridge, Harvard-UAW in, 161–163
Campbell, Margaret A. *See* Howell, Mary
Canel, Tom, 11–14, *234*
Cantor, Daniel, 102, 192
Captive audience meetings, 101, 193,
    195
Carnesale, Albert, 259
Carpenters Local 40, 247
Cassedy, Ellen, 47, 49–51, 53, 58, 200,
    269
Casteris, Tina, 264
City Women for Action, 48
Civil Rights Act of 1965, 32
Clifford, Nancy, 72
Clifton, Drago, 73, 90
CLUW. *See* Coalition of Labor Union
    Women
Coalition of Harvard Unions, 247, 264,
    267
Coalition of Labor Union Women
    (CLUW), 111–112
Coles, Robert, 226
Collective bargaining, U.S., 226
Columbia University, unionization at,
    108
Committee on the Status of Women
    (CSW), 36–37, 41–42, 54
Communications Workers of America,
    111
Communist Party, and unions, 59
Community, fostering of, in unions,
    153–154
Cornell University, unionization at, 168
Costa, Barbara, 72

Cox, Archibald, 95, 222–223
Crain, Marion, 200
CSW. *See* Committee on the Status of
    Women

David Copperfield (Dickens), 263
DeGenova, Ellen, 10–11
Dershowitz, Alan, 203
Discrimination, in workplace, 52–53
Distributive Workers of America, 59
District 65
    collapse of, 268
    constitution of, 98
    decline of, 118
    and Harvard union attempt, 64,
        71–72, 83, 86, 125
    Harvard's campaign against, 96–103
    history of, 59–62
    merger with United Auto Workers,
        119–120
    in private universities, 108
    sexism in, 115, 117–118
    shortcomings of, 116–118
    white-collar organizing, 113–114
    women in, 141
District 65 Security Plan, 61
    collapse of, 268–269
    decline of, 98–99, 118, 131–132
District 65-UAW, 140
District 1199, 58, 60
Dolan, Kerry, 172, 181, *207*
Dotson, Donald, 160–161
Dunlop, John T., 233—234
    and Derek Bok, 95, 222–223
    on Harvard administration, 250–251
    and Kris Rondeau, 218–220
    negotiations with HUCTW, 224–231
    resignation of, 248–249
Dynarski, Sue, 14

Eaton, Nathaniel, 162
Ebert, Robert E., 34–36
    reaction to union threat, 68–69
Eisner, Eugene, 61, 77

Election day
  1977, 103
  1981, 133–135
  1988, 5–15, 205, 209–211, 232
Elitism
  at Harvard, 93–94, 163, 263
  in women's movement, 42
Ellison, Ralph, 52
Emerson, Ralph Waldo, 162
Equal opportunity employment, 32
Equal Pay Act of 1963, 32
Equal Rights Amendment (ERA), 32, 44,
  119
Erlich, Mark, 247
Estrich, Susan, 203
"Every tub on its own bottom," 67, 81,
  227

Fanning, John H., 91
Farm-to-factory migration, 25
Female temperance movement, 31
The Feminine Mystique (Friedan), 31
Feminism, 30, 57, 165. See also Women's
  movement
Fischer, Karen, 72
Fitzsimmons, Frank, 111
Flynn, Elizabeth Gurley, 110
Foner, Moe, 60–61
Frank, Barney, 184
Fraser, Douglas A., 119, 158–159, 176,
  190, 206, 220
Freeman, Richard, 165, 203, 218
Friedan, Betty, 31, 124–125
Fuchs, Robert S., 84–86, 92, 138–139,
  161, 194, 222

Gage, Phineas P., 65–66
Galatin, Lisa, 147, 149
Gang of Four, 227
Gas shortage, and women workers, 54
Gays, in HUCTW, 247
Gelband, Joanna (Joie), 10, 181–182,
  240, 261, 264
Gender issues, 191–192
Gender Politics (Klein), 32

Gender solidarity, 42
Get Out the Vote, 7, 213, 222
Giamatti, Bart, 217
Gilligan, Carol, 155, 165, 203
Gittes, Betty, 48
Glazer, Nathan, 204
Goldman, Marlene, 57, 72–74, 90
GOTV. See Get Out the Vote
Gould, Stephen Jay, 204
Grievance procedures, in HUCTW,
  239–240
Gross, James A., 139

Harmatz, Joel S., 212, 214–215,
  221–222
Harper & Row, unionization of, 99–100,
  114
Harper, Ellen, 113
Harris, Mary, 110
Harvard Community Health Plan, 68
Harvard Corporation, 67–69
The Harvard Crimson, 10, 64, 80, 82,
  123, 133, 202, 224
Harvard, John, statue of, 8
Harvard Medical Area
  employees in, 40
  layout of, 17
  salaries in, 40
Harvard Medical Area Employee
  Organizing Committee, 57
Harvard Medical Area Women's Group
  (HMAWG), 38, 41, 55
  conflict in, 39
Harvard Medical School
  elitism at, 93–94
  founding of, 76
  history of, 17–18
  layout of, 17
  women in, 34–36
  work conditions in, 88
Harvard School of Public Health, 23,
  26–27
Harvard Trade Union Program, 96, 216
Harvard Union of Clerical and Technical
  Workers (HUCTW), 208, 233
  achievements of, 239–244

Harvard Union of Clerical and Technical Workers (HUCTW)—*continued*
  affiliation with AFSCME, 4–5, 187–189, 194, 208
  atmosphere of, 245–247
  first contract negotiation, 227–231
  founding of, 4, 179–182
  framework of, 237–239
  fund-raising campaigns of, 182
  health insurance battle with Harvard, 256–260
  leadership of, 236–237
  members of, 4
  philosophy of, 197–202
  psychological rewards of, 243
  relations with Rudenstine, 249–256
  on striking, 255
Harvard Union of Clerical and Technical Workers Ladies' Auxiliary, 12, 180
Harvard University
  during first contract negotiation, 227–231
  during first union attempt, 66, 94, 96–101
  hiring practices of, 123
  history of, 3, 68, 162–163, 203
  relations with HUCTW, 239, 248–260
  during second union attempt, 125–126, 130–134
  sex discrimination at, 123
  during third union attempt, 1–15, 191, 193, 205, 212–216
  women workers at, 50, 153
Harvard-Cambridge, 161–162
Harvard-UAW, 161
Health insurance, and unionization, 98–100, 256–260
Healy, James J., 226, 240–241, 251, 254, 257–258, 263–264
Heckman, Paula, 72
HERE. *See* Hotel Employees & Restaurant Employees
Hiatt, Deborah, 54–55, 57–58, 63, 71–72, 269
Hiatt, Howard H., 35–36, 54, 66, 69–70, 269

Hiatt, John, 269
HMAWG. *See* Harvard Medical Area Women's Group
Hollingsworth, Jana, 14
Hotel and Restaurant Employees Union, 111
Hotel Employees & Restaurant Employees (HERE), 136
Hotel Employees & Restaurant Employees Local 34, 137, 160, 183, 188, 217
Hotel Employees & Restaurant Employees Local 35, 136
Howell, Mary, 33–37, 41–42, 54
HUCTW. *See* Harvard Union of Clerical and Technical Workers

In a Different Voice (Gilligan), 165
In Dubious Battle (Steinbeck), 127
Industrial democracy, 199–200
Industrial Revolution, 25
International Workers of the World (Wobblies), 110
Invisible Man (Ellison), 52
"It's Not Anti-Harvard to Be Prounion," 184

Jackson, Jesse, 204–205, 220–221, 233
Jaeger, Bill, *207*, 264, 266
  after union victory, 227, 237, 245, 248, 258–260, 265
  on feminism, 246
  during first contract negotiation, 228, 230–231
  during third union attempt, 13–14, 173–174, 179–182, 210
  on UAW, 185
Jarndyce v. Jarndyce, 86
JC. *See* Joint Council
Jenkins, Howard Jr., 91
Joint Benefits Committee, 258–259
Joint Council (JC), 229, 237, 241–244. *See also* University Joint Council
Jointness, 244
Juravich, Tom, 157

Katz, Debbie, 147
Kautzer, Kathy, 83, 113
Kennedy, John F., 32
Klein, Ethel, 32
Knapp, Christina, 172, 180
Knights of Labor, 110
Knox, Carol, 113
Kovitz, Johanna, 127
Krawczyk, Bernice, 114–115, 132
Kromm, Randall, *234*, 266
Krupat, Kitty, 114–115
Kuechle, David, 8, 192
Kushner, Julie, 108, 114, 268

Labor and the American Community
   (Bok & Dunlop), 95
Labor unions. *See* Union(s)
Lafferty, Jeanne
   after union election, 264
   during first union attempt, 72, 93
   during second union attempt, 128,
      134, 147
   during third union attempt, 7, 12,
      14–15
Lawrence, D.H., 29
Leavitt, Susan, 243
Lesbians, in HUCTW, 247
Levy, Richard, 76–79, 81
Little, Regina, 118, 142
Livingston, David, 60–62, 71, 78,
   113–115, 118–119, 135, 137, 140,
   145, 161, *206*, 268–269
Local Problem Solving Teams (LPST),
   237, 239–240

Macalester College, 54
MAD. *See Medical Area District 65 at
   Harvard*
Madar, Olga, 119
Maher, Brendan, 163
Mahon, Kristin, 72, 74, 93, 128, 147
Mailer, Norman, 29
Manna, Marie, *207*
   after union victory, 224, 227, 242,
      261, 264

biography of, 127–128
conflict with UAW, 167–169, 171–178
and District 65, 141
during second union attempt,
   130–132
during third union attempt, 7, 137,
   147, 164, 179–181, 183, 187, 205,
   209–210
and UAW, 141, 146, 161
on union philosophy, 148, 198–199
Manning, Timothy, 252, 257–258
MAPO. *See* Medical Area Personnel Office
Massachusetts General Hospital, 26
   unionization at, 149–150
Maybury, David, 128, 147
Maybury-Lewis, David, 204
McCreight, Mac, 12, 15, 180
McEntee, Gerald, 187–191, *208*, 216,
   224, 262–263, 269
McGarrah, Robert, 186–188, 269
Meany, George, 71, 111
Mediation/arbitration provision, with
   HUCTW, 240
Medical Area 65, 64, 84–85, 90, 97–98,
   100. *See also* Harvard Union of
   Clerical and Technical Workers
   (HUCTW)
Medical Area District 65 at Harvard
   (MAD), 71, 79, 81, 83, 89–91, 101
Medical Area Personnel Office (MAPO),
   81–82
Medical profession, and women's
   movement, 33–35
Medical schools, sex discrimination in,
   34–35
Medoff, James L., 165
Memorial Hall, on election day 1988, 209
Men
   in Harvard union campaign, 73
   in HUCTW, 246–247
   reactions toward HUCTW, 244–245
Mendelson, Bob, 228, 266
Metcalf, Robert, *207*
   and Purity Caucus, 147–148
   during second union attempt,
      127–129, 134–135

Metcalf, Robert—*continued*
   during third union attempt, 12, 160,
    180
Microinequities, 52–53
Miller, Jean Baker, 155
Millet, Kate, 29
Minorities
   at Harvard, 123
   in workplace, 52–53
Monell, Joel, 254
Moore, Mark H., 254
Morison, Samuel Eliot, 162
Mother Jones, 110
Ms., 32, 58
Mullaney, Kate, 110
Murphy, Betty Southard, 91
Myrdal, Alva, 95
Myrdal, Gunnar, 95

The National Association of Working
   Women. *See* 9to5
National Labor Relations Act (NLRA), 43,
   63, 79–80, 82, 139
National Labor Relations Board (NLRB),
   84
   and Boston University election, 107
   criticisms of, 85–86
   and first Harvard union attempt,
    76–82, 85–86, 89–93, 103–104
   on private colleges and universities,
    66–67
   and second Harvard union attempt,
    126, 137–139
   and third Harvard union attempt, 4,
    10, 13, 157–158, 160–161, 212,
    221–222
National Labor Union, 110
National Organization for Women
   (NOW), 32
National Organization of Legal Services
   Workers, 142
Navin, Thomas R., 19
New England Regional Primate Research
   Center, 103, 121
New Talent Night, 182

9to5, The National Association of Work-
   ing Women, 47–51, 53, 56, 83–84,
   269
9to5 News, 47
*9to5: Women Office Workers Interpret a
   Social Movement,* 49
NLRA. *See* National Labor Relations Act
NLRB. *See* National Labor Relations
   Board
Normand, Carrie, 244
North Adams, Massachusetts, 24
NOW. *See* National Organization for
   Women
Nussbaum, Karen, 47, 49–50, 53, 58,
   83, 200, 269

O'Donnell, Thomas L. P., 77, 79, 86
Office and Professional Employees
   International Union, 58
One-on-one organizing, 129, 154–155,
   157, 262
OPEC, 53–54
Opperman, Mary, 227
Organization, approaches to, 148, 154,
   156
Organized labor. *See* Union(s)
Our Bodies, Ourselves, 33, 37

Participation, 198–202, 253–254
Paternalism, in unions, 166
Paulsen, Cory, *234*
Pendleton, Richard, 73, 93, 123–124,
   128, 199, *207*
Penello, John A., 91
Perkins, Ben, 167–168, 171, 177
Peterson, Laurie, 264
Pipets, 182, *267*
PIs. *See* Principal investigators
Pool, Jeremy, 73–74, 91, 93
Powers, Edward W., 67, 94, 96–98, 101,
   125–126, 131–132, 192–193, 196,
   253–254
Presidential Commission on the Status of
   Women, 32
Principal investigators (PIs), 18, 24

Protective legislation, 31, 48
Purity Caucus, 147–149, 157

Rahke, Barbara, 107, 113, 168, 177, 184
RAs. *See* Research assistant(s)
Rathbun, Jennie, 237, 243
Reagan, Ronald, 86, 122, 129–130, 133
Rees, John, 73, 91, 93, 150, 269
Reid, Lynda, 264
Research assistant(s), at Harvard, 23, 27,
    79, 88
Research Assistant II, 104
Retail, Wholesale and Department Store
    Union (RWDSU), 59
Reuther, Walter, 60
Rewolinski, Ernest, 187–189, 191, *208,*
    209, 211, 269
Robb, Martha, *207,* 264
    during second union attempt, 122,
        127, 134–135, 147
    during third union attempt, 7, 12, 15,
        164, 170, 172, 175–176, 180–181
Robinson, Cleveland, 61, 269
Rocker, Jerry, 137–138
Roman Catholic Archdiocese of Boston,
    57
Rondeau, Joseph, 19, 21
Rondeau, Kristine, *206–208, 232–234*
    and AFSCME, 187–190, 261–265
    and Derek Bok, 222–223, 231
    and District 65, 141, 145–146, 166
    and District 65 Security Plan, 131–132
    and District 65/UAW merger, 119–120
    early life of, 18–21, 25, 45–46, 74–75,
        136
    family life of, 263–264
    during first contract negotiation,
        224–231
    during first union attempt, 91–94,
        99–102
    as Harvard research assistant, 16–18,
        22, 87–89
    and HERE Local 34, 188
    as HUCTW leader, 235–236, 238,
        245–246

    and HUCTW relations with Harvard,
        244, 249, 258, 260
    and Jesse Jackson, 220–221
    and Jim Braude, 143–146, 170,
        263–264
    and John Dunlop, 219–220
    and Leslie Sullivan, 93, 112–113, 151
    on organizing, 128, 147–148,
        152–157, 183–184, 262
    on participation, 197–202, 244, 260
    during second union attempt, 109,
        121–122, 127–130, 133, 135, 153
    and sexism in unions, 117–118
    during third union attempt, 5–8,
        12–15, 141, 145, 147–148,
        164–166, 181, 183, 193–195, 204,
        210–212, 214, 224
    and UAW, 136–138, 141, 146, 159,
        161, 167–169, 171–181, 185
    as union organizer, 105–107, 112–113
    on union philosophy, 156, 198–199,
        201–202, 264–265
    and women's movement, 29–30, 124,
        191–192
Roosevelt, Eleanor, 31
Ropes, Gray, 67, 77, 81, 212
Ross, Nelson G., 77, 79, 86, 212–213,
    215
Rowe, Mary P., 51–53
Rubeski, Vivienne, 102, 227, 244, 249,
    251
Rudenstine, Neil, 248–249, 256, 259
Rush, Bob, 14, 247
RWDSU. *See* Retail, Wholesale and
    Department Store Union

Salary(ies)
    contract negotiation about, 230–231
    at Harvard
        after unionization, 239
        before unionization, 40, 87–88
Salary and wage (S&W) employees,
    38–39, 42. *See also S&W Notes*
Sanders Theater, on election day 1988,
    209, *232*

Schneiderman, Rose, 110
Schubarth, Ross, 73, 89
Scott, Robert, 192–193, 213, 231
Scudder, Emily, 256
The Second Stage (Friedan), 124
Self-representation, 198, 239–240
Seneca Falls Conference of 1848, 31
Service Employees International Union
    (SEIU), 58, 83–84, 269
Service Employees International Union
    Local 925, 84, 269
Sex discrimination
    in District 65, 115
    at Harvard, 37, 123
    in medical schools, 34–35
    in workplace, 52
Sexual harassment, in District 65,
    117–118
Sexual Politics (Millett), 29
Shepard, Thomas, 162
The Shop. *See* Whitin Machine Shop
Silber, John, 107–108
Sisterhood Is Powerful, 30
Skocpol, Theda R., 123
Socialist Workers Party, 73
Solidarity, 42
Spiegelman, Donna, 147, 149
Stadecker, Adriana Nasch, 49
Steinbeck, John, 127
Steiner, Daniel, 43, 67, 70, 77, 86,
    94–95, 101–102, 126, 139, 192, 222
Strikes, 23
    at Boston University, 105–108
    during Industrial Revolution, 25
Students for a Democratic Society (SDS),
    68, 73
Suffrage, 31
Sullivan, Leslie, *206*
    after union career, 269
    and CLUW, 112
    and Committee on the Status of
        Women, 41–42, 44
    and District 65, 71–72, 74, 107, 113,
        115–118
    on District 65 Security Plan, 131–132
    and District 65/UAW merger, 119–120
    early life of, 24–28
    family life of, 150–151
    during first union attempt, 57–58,
        62–64, 76–83, 85, 90, 93–94,
        97–98, 100, 102–104
    as Harvard research assistant, 22–24,
        36–38, 54–55
    resignation of, 180
    role in HMAWG, 38–40
    during second union attempt,
        108–109, 112–113, 127, 130, 135
    and sexism in unions, 115, 118
    during third union attempt, 164, 172
    and UAW, 141, 146, 149–151
    as union organizer, 112–113
    and women's movement, 30, 33
Support Staff Action Committee, 196
Sutton, Anthony, 164, 166, 172,
    175–176, 180, *207*
S&W employees. *See* Salary and wage
    employees
S&W News, 55–56
S&W Notes, 39–41
Sweeney, John, 269
Swenson, Norma, 33, 37
Szanto, Elisabeth, 261

Taft-Hartley Act, 139
Tax Equity Alliance for Massachusetts
    (TEAM), 178
Taylor, Anne E., 8, 192–193, 195–197,
    202, 209–212, 218, 223, 225
Teamsters, 58, 111
Tice, Janet, 72
Torrey, Sue, 72
Tournas, Stephanie, 14, 181, 210, 264
Tribe, Laurence, 204

UAW. *See* United Auto Workers
UE. *See* United Electrical Workers
UJC. *See* University Joint Council
Unfair labor practices, 90
Union(s)
    in 1930s–1950s period, 154
    in 1960s, 89–90

in Boston, 56–57
Communist Party and, 59
decline of, 165–166
eligibility for, 43
philosophy of, 197–202
psychological rewards of, 243
in universities, 108
in Whitinsville, Massachusetts, 18–21
women in, 198, 200–201, 245–246
and women's movement, 49, 100
Union containment, 250
Union Election Fact Book, 131
Union organizer, role of, 128, 236
Union rally, *208*
United Auto Workers (UAW)
    and AFSCME, 191
    conflict with HUCTW, 167–169,
        171–178, 184–185, 191
    merger with District 65, 119–120, 270
    paternalism in, 166
    withdrawal from AFL-CIO, 60
    women officeholders in, 111
    and women's movement, 119–120
    and Yale union attempt, 136–138
United Electrical Workers (UE), 154
United Steelworkers of America, 19–20
University Joint Council (UJC), 248–249,
    252
University Problem Solving Team
    (UPST), 240
UPST. *See* University Problem Solving
    Team

Vetters, Ralph, 14–15, 181–182
Vorse, Mary Heaton, 110

Walesa, Lech, 134, 159–160
Walther, Peter D., 91–92
"We Can't Eat Prestige," 64
What Do Unions Do?
    (Medoff & Freeman), 165
Whitin Machine Shop, 18–19
Whitin, Paul, 19
Whitinsville, Massachusetts, 18–21

*Why Would A Girl Go Into Medicine?
    Medical Education in the U.S.: A Guide
    for Women* (Campbell/Howell),
    34–35
Wilhelm, John, 136–137, 160, 183, 188
Williams, Donene, 11, 195–196, 210,
    228, *234*, 237–238, 245, 258
Windham College, 45–46
Wobblies, 110
Wolfgang, Myra, 111
Women
    in District 65, 141
    stereotypes concerning, 46
    as union organizers, 110–112
    in unions, 153, 166–167, 198,
        200–201, 245–246
        after World War II, 111
    workers. *See* Women workers
Women Employed in Chicago, 48
Women Office Workers in New York, 48
Women Organized For Employment in
    San Francisco, 48
Women workers
    in 1960s, 31–32
    in factories, 29
    gas shortage and, 54
    at Harvard, 27–28, 50
    increase in, 46–47
    migration patterns of, 25–26
    salaries of, 87–88
    and unions, 111, 153, 166–167, 198,
        200–201
    women's movement and, 38–39,
        49–53, 83–84
    during World War II, 25, 31
Women's Bureau of the U.S. Department
    of Labor, 47, 110
Women's movement. *See also* Feminism
    in 1970s, 32–33
    in 1980s, 124–125
    effect on Kris Rondeau, 30
    effect on Leslie Sullivan, 30
    elitism in, 42
    history of, 30–33
    media and, 32–33
    medical profession and, 33–35

Women's movement—*continued*
   role of women workers in, 38–39,
     49–53, 83–84
   and unions, 49, 100
   United Auto Workers and, 119–120
Women's Trade Union League (WTUL),
   110–111
Woodcock, Leonard, 111
Work security, 241–242
Worker(s), women. *See* Women workers
Worker migration, patterns of, 25–26
Worker solidarity, 42
Working mothers, 125

World War II, and women workers, 25,
   31, 111
WTUL. *See* Women's Trade Union League
Wurf, Jerry, 186

Yale University, unions at, 160, 217
Yokich, Stephen, 191
Young, Ned, 172, 175–176, 180
YWCA, Boston, 48

Zeckhauser, Sally, 248–249, 251